Essays on
Critical Conscio

METROPOLITAN COLLEGE
OF NEW YORK LIBRARY
75 Varick Street 12th Fl.
New York, NY 10013

THEMES OF URBAN AND INNER-CITY EDUCATION
Series Editors:
Fred Yeo, Southeast Missouri State University
Barry Kanpol, Indiana University-Purdue University Ft. Wayne

Commitment to Excellence:
  Transforming Teaching and Teacher Education in Inner-City and Urban Settings
    Linda A. Catelli and Ann C. Diver-Stamnes (eds.)

Essays on Urban Education:
  Critical Consciousness, Collaboration and the Self
    Chapman University Social Justice Consortium (eds.)

Teacher Education and Urban Education:
  The Move from the Traditional to the Pragmatic
    Barry Kanpol (ed.)

Charting New Terrains of Chicana(o)/Latina(o) Education
    Carlos Tejeda, Corinne Martínez, and Zeus Leonardo (eds.)

forthcoming

The Politics of Inclusion:
  Preparing Education Majors for Urban Realities
    Barry Kanpol (ed.)

Essays on Urban Education
Critical Consciousness, Collaboration and the Self

Social Justice Consortium
With Suzanne SooHoo

Chapman University

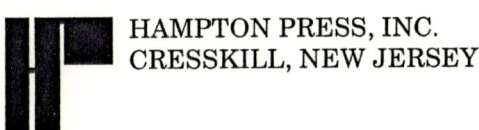

HAMPTON PRESS, INC.
CRESSKILL, NEW JERSEY

Copyright © 2004 by Hampton Press, Inc.

All rights reserved. No part of this publication may be reproduced, stored in a retrieval system, or transmitted in any form or by any means, electronic, mechanical, photocopying, microfilming, recording, or otherwise, without permission of the publisher.

Printed in the United States of America

Library of Congress Cataloging-in-Publication Data

Essays on urban education : critical consciousness, collaboration, and the self / Social Justice Consortium with Suzanne SooHoo.
    p. cm. -- (Themes of urban and inner-city education)
  ISBN 1-57273-435-3 -- ISBN 1-57273-436-1 (pbk.)
  Includes bibliographical references and index.
  1. Education, Urban--United States. 2. Critical pedagogy--United States. I. SooHoo, Suzanne. II. Chapman University. Social Justice Consortium. III. Series.

LC5131.E77 2003
370'.9173'2--dc21

                                                                              2003056625

Hampton Press, Inc.
23 Broadway
Cresskill, NJ 07626

Contents

Preface
   Narrative and the Politics of Urban Possibility:
   From Cynicism to Collaborative Joy   vii
     Barry Kanpol

Introduction: "and so it all began. . ."   1
   Suzanne SooHoo

PART ONE: A PARADIGM SHIFT

1. Thinking About Collaboration, Change, and Aesthetics   7
   Suzanne SooHoo and Tom Wilson

2. Dispelling the Myth of Moral Bankruptcy in American
   Urban Youth   35
   Donald N. Cardinal

3. Exception to the Perception   57
   Dolores Gaunty-Porter

PART TWO: RETHINKING CURRICULUM

4. Community Matters   87
   Tom Wilson

5. The Curriculum of the Self: Critical Self-Knowing
   As Critical Pedagogy   115
   Jeff Sapp

PART THREE; UNIVERSITY FACULTY IN THE SCHOOLS

6. Reworking Urban Educational Leadership Through Naming
   and Narrative Inquiry   137
   Penny S. Bryan

PART FOUR: STUDENT VOICES

7. Crossing Cultural Borders Into the Inner City   163
   Suzanne SooHoo

8. Gatekeepers   183
   Jan Osborn

9. Expect the Unexpected: A Practitioner's View of Urban   193
   Susie Weston

10. Can We Talk . . . About Collaboration?   213
    Chapman University Social Justice Consortium
    Penny Bryan=Don Cardinal=Dolores Gaunty-Porter=
    Jan Osborn=Jeff Sapp=Suzanne SooHoo=Susie
    Weston=Tom Wilson

Author Index   249
Subject Index   253

Preface

Narrative and the Politics of Urban Possibility: From Cynicism to Collaborative Joy

Barry Kanpol
Indiana University-Purdue University Ft. Wayne

I have had the privilege of working in higher education for over 15 years. Admittedly, I have been able to survive the ideological game of publish or perish mentality that pervades the elite walls of social advantage—the individualistic logic and highly competitive ambiance—that permeates the academy. Despite writing from the "critical" tradition, I have clearly fallen prey to a type of Darwinian mentality; a mind-set that could be argued is needed for political survival, but one that in its worst senses contradicts the political and critical traditions out of which I write. Without trying to sound to righteous, I have also known that the nature of our social lives in the academe often replicates those ideological realities in the "real world" that I have clearly written against and that I can't be totally blamed for. Regarding schools and teachers, that means issues of tracking, deskilling, authoritarianism, patriarchy, sexism, racism, and so forth have been pervasive both publicly and, also, personally (Kanpol, 1999). More than admitting to one's particular contradictions, however, I have learned that social action in the academe, from my place of employment, can take on a variety of faces—from teaching about urban realities, to student and faculty rights, and to curricular issues and so forth. But, I have also learned that to "resist" or challenge the individualistic logic and other forms of University constraints that work against creating counterhegemonic blocks is a real concern that faculty must deal with in order to create democratic and perhaps liberating and emancipatory moments of opportunity. When I was at Saint Joseph's University, as in my other places of employment (formerly Chapman University and Penn State University), lip service was often given to creating a community of educators who worked well together in the interests of the outside public. Good and well. No mechanisms were ever put into place that allowed community to flourish, to challenge the individualistic logic I have historically encountered, to create democratic imaginaries, and to reskill faculty in a way that galvanized differences in a common and liberating cause. Although I realize that Utopia doesn't exist, real efforts need to be made to create communities of resistance that allow faculty to flourish as a group, to permit one's individual as well as group voice to emanate from the closet—without feeling that academe will swallow voice within its own institutional and ideological constraints. To achieve such a mission—the gathering of faculty to iron out differences and take on ideological and hegemonic nuances—is no small assignment. In short, to accomplish the above from my position as a faculty member and now as an educational leader (Department Chair) has become a driving force behind a proactive cultural politics of resistance in the educational field in the academe.

I open with the above kinds of confessions because I think it poignant to come to grips with the fact that no collaborative or counterhegemonic project, at least in my mind, can reach its potential without what I have termed elsewhere as confessional moment's (Kanpol, 1998). Those moments can, I argue, draw us together in common dreams and hopes. Those areas of narrative accounts that include confessions, can, I argue, enlighten a group as to where we start and how far can we go.

This book by the Chapman University Social Justice Consortium combines various forms of "confessions" as related to urban education. More than that, however, this volume's subtext, whether conscious or not, is a political statement of a group of caring individuals who use confession as a tool to both challenge and alter, it seems to me, both the perceptions of urban education's stereotype as well as the academe's reward for individualism. These forms of what I have described elsewhere as cultural political resistance (Kanpol, 1989) have an emancipatory tone to them, bordering on a move from a traditional form of critical inquiry to viewing the labor of a collective body as a spiritual place for communal effort to enunciate itself, an area where one's work becomes not only emancipatory, but sacred text, where places groups meet become holy territory, where the intellectual labor that "gets done" gives groups a sense of the possible or, in short, challenges the pervasive academe dogmatic logic of a Darwinian survival of the fittest mentality. Talking back and breaking bread, an image provided in my recent writings, illustrates where emancipatory type work is used to creatively challenge forms of institutional oppression, alienation, and subordination. Using testimony as a theoretical tool, it is also as if bell hooks and Cornel West's (1991) words echo at the heels of this group's united project:

> Testimony is a very hard spirit to convey in a written text . . . it struck me that dialogue was one of the ways where the sense of mutual witness and testimony could be made manifest. I link that sense to regular communion service in the Black Church at Yale where we would often stand in a collective circle and sing, "Let us Break Bread Together on our Knees," and the lines in the song which say, "When I fall on my Knees with My Face to the Rising Sun, Oh Lord Have Mercy on Me." I like the combination of the notion of community which is about sharing an d breaking bread together, of dialogue as well as mercy speaks to the need we have for compassion, acceptance, understanding, and empathy. (p. 1)

The above quote from hooks and West perhaps adequately describes the struggles groups may have in personal and collective testimony. Tied to this struggle is the realization that this form of engagement can be lonely, cynical, or joyful; it can be unified with others. Ultimately, personal testimony is hard as well as committed toil. With that in mind, teacher education has historically using personal testimony as a form of pedagogical reflection and interrogation. Rather, teacher education has been historically wedged in methodological practices that distance teachers and professors from the self.

The above theoretical point has pushed the educational left to seriously and unitedly critique practices that deskill teachers and, resultantly, communities of public school and higher education for various reasons, be they economic and/or cultural. The various harsh critiques haven't carried the educational left too far, however. Lost within these critiques are spaces for collaborative action, a united politics that seriously engages institutional constraints—be they in public and/or private institutions such as Chapman University or in urban school districts. Critique from the left has bordered on cynicism, a hopeless albeit important response to social conditions. Mired in postmodern critique, where deconstruction often for the sake of deconstruction reigns supreme, critique of urban areas from the educational left has rendered on a reductionism of sorts, an essentialism that speaks to anger, angst, disgust, and so on. All this is quite justified, given the "savage inequalities" in our urban areas. Lost within the educational left cynicism, however, is collaborative joy—those possibilities that life affords us to hold hands together and use cynicism in an emancipatory light. Lost in our midst are the kinds of efforts generated by the Chapman University Social Justice Consortium to unite people and unearth the moments of testimony that will allow faculty to collectively and joyfully resist the images in the institution that keep community apart, and what I have also defined elsewhere as negatively competitive (Kanpol, 1999). Lost in our University institution, and from teacher education departments in general, is the collaborative and reflective possibility to collectively work towards both realizing and resisting the cynicism of hopelessness about urban education. It has taken Jonathan Kozol 35 years to realize that we had better get on our prayerful knees and realize that urban renewal in his latest book, *Ordinary Resurrections* (2000), is about finding similarities despite differences, is about inserting the personal into the public, and is about generating a collective effort with what I would describe here as a "critical edge." Put differently, let's never lose sight of the criticality needed to understand institutional constraints, but more importantly, let's use criticality both joyfully and collaboratively to arrive at our collective destination.

It is to the absolute enormous credit of the Chapman University Social Justice Consortium that a group of well-intentioned theorists and practitioners have come together over a period of three years to challenge those dominant images that intrude on emancipatory work—urban reductionistic stereotypes and the realities of immediate institutional constraints such as time and place and support and recognition. Culturally resisting those constraints make this book a compelling read. Moving from narrative to narrative and difference to difference, the unity of this work lies in individual and collective testimony that joyfully travels within the hearts and souls of the writers as well as the institutional confines of our urban schools and in the the hallways of the institutional professors work in.

Upon deep reflection, perhaps the years in higher education and working out of the critical tradition are beginning to pay off in some ways that are not only about individual gain. I have come to learn that collective and collaborative solidarity across differences within a democratic imaginary that pervades time and place can be created. It has taken me 15 years to fully realize that potential. With that in mind, I invite readers to partake in what could be a model for future teacher educators to learn and grown by in their collective and united quest for social justice in their immediate urban and institutional surroundings.

REFERENCES

hooks, b., & West, C. (1991). *Breaking bread.* Boston: South End Press.
Kanpol, B. (1999). *Critical pedagogy: An introduction.* Westport, CT: Bergin & Garvey
Kanpol, B. (198). *Teachers talking back and breaking bread.* Cresskill, NJ: Hampton Press.
Kanpol, B. (1989). Institutional and cultural political resistance: Necessary conditions for the transformative intellectual. *Urban Review, 21*(3), 163–179.

About the Authors

Penny Bryan is an associate professor in the School of Education at Chapman University. She received her doctorate in Educational Leadership from the University of Pennsylvania. Her areas of interest are leadership and literacy that promote democracy, ethics and equity in education, critical theory, and practitioner inquiry.

Don Cardinal has been with Chapman University since 1988 and is Professor and Dean of its School of Education. He received a doctorate in Education from the Claremont Graduate School. He was a teacher in public schools for over a dozen years. His research has been cited in more than 100 professional and media sources worldwide and has received many awards for his teaching and research.

Dolores Gaunty-Porter is a faculty member in the Graduate School of Education at Vanguard University, Costa Mesa, CA. She holds a PhD in Reading from SUNY Albany and a MAE from the University of Southern Mississippi. Her interests include integrating literacy across the curriculum, exploring cross-cultural connections, and developing models of mentoring.

Jan Osborn is both a faculty member in the Chapman University Department of English and Comparative Literature where she teaches rhetoric, advanced rhetoric, and linguistics and in the School of Education's Single Subject Program, where she teaches content area literacy and foundations of education. As a critical pedagogist, she focuses her work on student empowerment through literacy skills.

Jeff Sapp received his doctorate from West Virginia University in 1993. He teachers in both Single Subjects and Masters Programs at Chapman University. His research agenda is focused on queer theory and ending homophobia in public schooling.

Suzanne SooHoo is an associate professor in the School of Education at Chapman University. She received a doctorate from Claremont Graduate School. She has been both a teacher and a school principal. Her lines of inquiry focus on critical multiculturalism, participatory research, and democratic classrooms.

Susie Weston has been an elementary public school teacher since 1989. She completed her undergraduate work at California State University, Fullerton, and is currently a part-time instructor in its teacher credential program. She obtained her Master's in Educational Administration from Chapman University.

Tom Wilson teaches part time at both Chapman University and Pepperdine University. With an enduring interest in democratic/moral education, workplace democracy, and social justice, he directs the Paulo Freire Democratic Project within Chapman University's School of Education.

"and so it all began..."

Suzanne SooHoo

"and so it all began" are the both the first and the last words of this book because, as most of you know who have been involved with collaboration and social justice, there is never an end, only temporary punctuation to life's work. Collaboration is a continuous process (Heron, 1996). Democracy is indigenously incomplete and unfinished. And of course, the joy of being human is our unfinishedness (Freire, 1995).

We invite our readers to take a journey of making sense of urban education as guided by "ever becoming" authors. What is special about these writers is standpoint epistemology; their knowing from lived experience (Lather, 2000). Through this collaborative writing process, these intellectuals learned to trust their own personal and cultural biographies as significant sources of knowledge (Hill Collins, 1991). Personal subjectivity coupled with academic training required courage and vulnerability. In return, we found the "freedom both to be different and to be part of" (Hill Collins, 1991, p. 54) the world of research. The reader will find each author's mark of distinction within his/her chapter as each consciously situated him/herself through descriptions of his/her relationships within urban settings. These accounts responded to the full-bodied, uninhibited sharing we had about the "urbanness" of our lives. We see this approach of starting with ourselves as a democratic obligatory, because "any serious engagement with the world includes a questioning of one's self" (West, 1999, p. 1)

In virtually every one of our meetings, the question "what is urban?" surfaced. Is it a geographical location, groups of people, a set of economic conditions, marginalization, a social construct? The chapters in this book grappled with these issues and problematized the conventional notions of urban as dark, deficient, disadvantaged, and powerless, which facilitated the generation of alternative social perspectives. It was our attempt to reimage the world by renaming it (Freire, 1995).

The first three chapters of the book tease out the social construction of urban. In "Thinking Through Collaboration, Change and Aesthetics," SooHoo and Wilson provide an overview of our approach to this book. They describe how seven faculty members and one student challenged the dominance of individualism and competition in traditional research through their collaborative project. The reader will find results of our self-study of collaboration and our success and failure to cultivate a collectivistic orientation to benefit all faculty and their collectively determined agendas. The chapter is divided into six sections, which include (a) thoughts on our context, (b) thoughts on the word "urban," (c) thoughts on collaboration, (d) thoughts on working against the grain of most academic writing conventions, including situating the self, the voice of practitioner, and book writing as an impetus for cultural change, and (e) thoughts on the imperatives of justice and aesthetics.

In Cardinal's chapter, "Dispelling the Myth of Moral Bankruptcy in American Urban Youth," he sees the urban cup full rather than empty, but chooses to make the water better by describing how one person traveled from antisocial behavior to service to the greater society using the same moral code. A stranger to writing subjectively, he finds "the undiscovered self is an unexpected resource" (Bateson 1989, p. 5) in this collaborative book experience. The lesson here is never to underestimate the academic intelligence of gang members who were pushed out of the system.

Writing from a black, middle-class perspective, Gaunty-Porter tells us in "Exception to the Perception" that "racism does not end with economic and professional ascendancy." Like other black female scholars, she is concerned with the distortion of facts and observations about black women and therefore makes visible the paradox of her white hegemony and her black experiences. The reader finds in her italicized self-reflections what she is thinking when she hears false assumptions about urban as she offers her version of "in the hood."

The next two chapters propose curricular reforms as a way of working with urban schools. Wilson argues in "Community Matters" that previous reform of public schools has been superficial and has done little to significantly transform schools into democratic communities. He recommends that schools give conscious attention to the development of democratic personhood, which when developed in concert with others, will spawn a democratic culture. To operationalize this vision, Wilson describes, in detail, an educational plan that he directed in which students spent a majority of their time within the community using community resources as the curriculum.

In "The Curriculum of the Self: Critical Self-Knowing as Critical Pedagogy," Sapp uses the magic of story as a vehicle of advocacy to fight homophobia. He shares with us that upon his realization of his exclusion from the metanarrative, he embarks upon a literary journal to find his voice. He finds the critical interconnection between the cognitive and the affective; between personal liberation and social change.

The following two chapters portray faculty interactions with urban schools. Bryan uses the moral power of narrative in her chapter, "Knowing the Worlds; Knowing the Words: Defining Urban Educational Leadership" to illuminate how to build leadership capacity in urban schools. Through codification and decodificatiion, humanization, and connection to the community, Bryan asserts, we can begin to imagine the redistribution of power and the transformation of leadership in urban contexts. She completes her chapter with an interesting biographical self-inventory about why social justice matters to her.

SooHoo describes in "Crossing Cultural Borders Into the Inner City" the cultural lessons she has gleaned from a collaborative action research project with elementary school students, a teacher researcher, and a community member. Her work focuses on how cultural identity can inform the research with respect to gaining entry, collecting data, and coparticipation in action. Coming from a stance of decolonization, she offers insights into the concept of researcher as cultural activist.

The following two chapters capture voices from the schools. In Osborn's artful metaphor of the wooden gate in "Gatekeepers," she identifies existing urban school practices that keep students out of school such as tracking, loss of faith in students, and the colonization of English language learners and those practices that she believes keep students in schools such as affirmation, engaged dialogue, and validation. Throughout her chapter, she makes note of the theorists such as Dewey, hooks, and Freire who whisper in her ear and prompt her to examine conditions of disenfranchisement. Straight from the school halls, Osborn calls out to us to move from what isn't to what should be.

Third grade teacher and graduate of our Masters in Education program, Weston-Barajas in "Expect the Unexpected: A Practitioner's View of Urban," offers her daily experiences in an urban school and how these conditions relate to the multiple authors' works in this book. Urban schools are not deficient, but the preparation for teachers in urban schools is. Finding little support from her credential courses or the teachers' lounge, Weston discovers her best resources have come from the relationships she has had with the community.

Chapter 10, "Can We Talk . . . About Collaboration?" was authored by all the contributors to this book. Authorship was designated with equal signs "=" to designate equal authorship (Mullen=Kochan, 2001). This chapter was our way of seizing the dynamic nature of collaboration and was our attempt (now recognized as naïve) to put closure to our work. After hearing the cacophony of our voices, we are confident the reader will discover the value of communal knowledge. It was both an aesthetic and soul-filling experience.

REFERENCES

Bateson, M.C. (1989). *Composing a life*. New York: Plume.
Freire, P. (1995). *Pedagogy of hope: Reliving pedagogy of the oppressed*. New York: Continuum.
Heron, J. (1996). *Co-operative inquiry*. London: Sage Publications.
Hill Collins, P. (1991). Learning from the outsider within. In M. Fonow & J, Cook (Eds.), *Beyond methodology: Feminist scholarship as lived research*. Bloomington: Indiana University Press.
Lather, P. (2000, April). *Educational research and advocacy*. American Educational Research Association. New Orleans, Louisiana.
Mullen, C.= Kochan, F. (2001). Issues of collaborative authorship in higher education. *The Educational Forum, 65*(2), 128-135.
West, C. (1999). *The Cornel West reader*. New York: Basic Civitas Books.

I

A PARADIGM SHIFT

1

Thinking About Collaboration, Change, and Aesthetics

Suzanne SooHoo

Tom Wilson

> *Recent calls to restructure universities have focused on the need for systemic, comprehensive change that models collaboration in research and educational programs and courses.*
> (Mullen=Kochan, 2001, p. 128)

We open our book with a chapter describing a three-year collaborative writing project that resonates with this call for the reacculturation of academe. What follows are our reflections about the process, how we worked against the grain to introduce new ways of knowing, and our appreciation of the aesthetics of working together as academic collaborators.

THOUGHTS ON OUR CONTEXT

We start with Johnson's (1998, p. 9) notion of collaboration that ". . . from an ideological standpoint . . . it is the democratic thing to do." To understand the context of our collaborative and hopefully democratically just and beautiful book project, one must know our history and our modus operandi. Most of the faculty authors were also program coordinators who committed several years ago to working democratically within and among programs. We were determined to cultivate a school culture that was humane and just. Working democratically meant an ongoing political commitment to ending domination in all its forms; it meant a consciousness of maintaining a flat collaborative organization. For example, program coordinators resisted the titles of "program chairs" because of the inferred hierarchy. Nameplates on office doors displayed faculty names only, no titles or program affiliations to divide us. We resisted the traditional trappings of program specific labels and structures that might cause us to be territorial of programs. Along these same lines, faculty members deliberately taught across programs; they taught courses in regular education, special education, credential and master courses, as well as in undergraduate courses with a consciousness to demolish artificial discipline walls.

Another illustration of faculty's commitment to collaboration was our agreement to voluntarily add collaboration to our annual performance reviews as a way of holding ourselves accountable to our vision of democracy. Each year, faculty members reported collaborative initiatives such as team teaching, grant writing, development of joint credential programs, and so forth, to the Faculty Review Committee. The School of Education, one of five schools at our university, made this adjustment in its evaluation reports for our own accountability and as a demonstration to others of a faculty bent on rethinking the culture of academe.

Several years ago, the University administration initiated a pilot program of merit pay. Faculty members were given financial incentives to improve their performance. Individual faculty members received different financial awards depending on quantified improvements in teaching and scholarship. The faculty in the School of Education protested. We believed that merit pay wrongfully promoted competition and social stratification among us. Merit pay, we argued, would destroy our embryonic efforts toward collaboration. Those School of Education faculty members receiving merit bonuses reasoned that to benefit personally from this system would put our collaborative community in jeopardy. Consequently, we made a bold move.

We pooled our merit awards, homogenizing our monetary differences to form a healthy resource fund that was ours to manage. We collaborated about how to spend this money. We asked ourselves, "What could we do to resist the capitalist intent of this money and replace it with something that more appropriately matched our worldview? What could we do that was humane and just?" Our decision was to award student scholarships and loans to individuals in need. Ultimately, the final commitment of our funds was directed to supplementing an endowment that financed a life-sized, bronze bust of the great international educator, Paulo Freire. The bust's creation was coupled with the University awarding him an honorary doctoral degree. The bust, currently embraced by a ring of colorful flowers, stands magnificently in a quad on the campus as a tribute to him. As far as we know, it is the only one in North America, if not the entire world.

Other markers of our commitment to a democratic, socially just culture include a number of artifacts such as program posters, ads, and syllabi espousing social justice, faculty search teams that zero in on the candidates' philosophies about social justice through oral interviews and written prompts, students' exit portfolios, which require evidence of competencies as social justice educators, and two School of Education collectives: the Center for Equity and Social Justice and the Paulo Freire Democracy Project, whose vocation are to bring to bear a synthesis of progressive/critical and ethical/democratic practices upon both formal and informal educational contexts.

THOUGHTS ON THE WORD "URBAN"

According to the *Oxford Universal Dictionary* (Onions, 1955, p. 2322), there are two senses of meaning for word "urban." The first pertains to place or location. In 1619, it meant "pertaining to, characteristic of, situated or occurring in a city or town," and by 1841 this understanding had not changed appreciably: "constituting, forming, or including a city, town, or burg." The second sense is more normative. In 1651, the word was defined as " exercising authority, control, etc., in or over a city or town" and in 1837, as "residing, dwelling, or having property in a city or town." The quotations used in the *Oxford* with appropriate dates to illustrate this sense are "All Magistrates are either Urban or forren, viz. of Town or Countrey 1651" and "The vehemence of urban democracy 1849" (Onions, 1955, p. 2322). In current usage, it is rare to find "urban" as a marker of space. Rather, it has been replaced by the more value-laden notion involving elements of control and vehemence, with the latter characterized by "great force and violence, of physical action or agents" (Onions, 1955, p. 2339).

Media, literature, and popular discourse, depict "urban" as synonymous with "ghetto" (a word derived from the Italian *borghetto* for the section of the city in which Jews were restricted). Another synonym, "inner city," adds to the collection of images, which portray despair, ennui, and Gotham-like darkness. Immigrants, dysfunctional families, economically depressed and racially separated neighborhoods and schools, a holding space for people no longer of use to the larger economy—all of these equal "urban" (Hamilton, 1991; Howard, 1999; Kozol, 1991, 1994)—a place, a social condition, a social construction one wouldn't want to be stranded in.

Yet, this sense of despair, of darkness, is merely a social construction (Ayers & Ford, 1966). And as such, who built this mental construction of urban, the hegemonic boogeyman? Was the intention to keep outsiders out or insiders in these physical and conceptual spaces? Who benefits when people feel trapped in a condition of perceived hopelessness, immobilized by self-adjusted disempowerment? Can fish critique their own glass walls? Can urban dwellers interrogate their own "psychic prisons" (Morgan, 1997)? These conceptual penitentiaries hegemonize us to believe in the dark rendition of "urban" and thus we all become wards of this ideological court.

Stereotypes of urban, so ingrained in our social consciousness, warrant multiple perspectives, diverse deconstruction. What then might a counterhegemonic perspective of urban look like? From our understandings of and work within inner-city schools, we, the authors in this book, attempt to critically examine urban educational contexts by (a) intersecting our own sociocultural positions with our mental models of urban, (b) accessing multiple urban voices in order to broaden our own perspectives, (c) designing new liberatory educational environments through the language of possibility and practice (Giroux, 1988; Kanpol, 1994), and (d) holding ourselves accountable in the way we work together to address these issues in public education.

THOUGHTS ON COLLABORATION

Schools are political sites; they are part of the reproduction of knowledge and power. They are capable of both limiting and enabling possible change. Whereas some say public schools often represent an integration of society's most crippling diseases—"indifference, injustice, and inequity" (Maeroff, 1994), others see them as sites of hope and promise (Kanpol, forthcoming; Kozol, 1995). Because school reform has largely ignored the social construction of power and privilege in its transformative efforts (Kretovics & Nussel, 1994), it becomes incumbent for education faculties to target the political and ideological nature of schooling in order to resist a metanarrative of cultural deficiency. This book illustrates a strategy in which a group of university faculty members attempts to realize this social responsibility by beginning with a critical self-assessment of its own knowledge base and an experiment in collegial collaboration as a way to respond to this call for action.

This collected effort takes the form of a collaborative book of critical essays on urban education. The purpose of the essays was to focus and to disrupt common misconceptions held by educators about urban schools. Some three years ago, interested faculty members brought their scholarship, epistemology, and vulnerabilities to the table. How would this project enhance or fracture our professional relationships, our school's mission, our academic reputations, our individual frames of knowing, and our understandings of collaboration? How much might we gain or lose in our work within urban contexts as a result of sharing our knowledge and working through our differences? How might we move our scholarly work from self-interest to collective interest?

Typically, one can uncover a balkanization of education programs in schools of education. Regular education is separate from special education, bilingual education is separate from education administration, and so forth. We encourage teachers to collaborate with school personnel yet seldom apply this principle to our own university-based lives. On the one hand, we grumble about professional isolation. On the other hand, we do everything we can to preserve our individual independence and privacy. Most of us in academe conduct our research and scholarship singly, independent of colleagues (Goodlad, 1990). Individualism is the norm, yet we hunger for our individual action to be united with a collective movement for social justice.

This book project was promoted as an opportunity for faculty to write a book together. "Together" was the operative word. What did that mean? Did it mean building a community around a central topic of interest? What were the individual risks? What were the benefits? How could we build community while preserving individual autonomy? Would this new community threaten other existing communities? How did it enhance the overall mission of a School of Education? What forms of support did we need to sustain our activity? We asked ourselves three years ago, could it be done?

The literature is replete with research on the benefits of collaboration within higher education, less is known about the inherent problems (Austin, 1992). We wish to identify those landmines for other faculties who may decide to initiate a collaborative book project. Throughout our (the faculty authors) efforts, we have been deeply conscious of our self-imposed charge to work together, that is, to collaborate. Thus, as we proceeded, the word itself was always present, obvious when spoken but when not, still always in the air. Although we have produced this book, did we actually collaborate? Did our paean to collaborative action, our espoused theory, match our actual behavior, our theory in use of which Chris Argyris (1990) has written so much? To answer this question it seems necessary to give first some definition to the word "collaboration" itself and then match it with our own understandings of how we operated.

Turning again to Onions and the *Oxford* (1955, p. 340), we are informed that "collaborate" comes from the Latin *collaborate* (*com*, together + *laborare*, to labor); thus, to labor together, to cooperate, especially in literary, artistic, or scientific work. *Webster's Third New International's* (Gove et al., 1967, p. 443) definition is essentially the same, wherein to collaborate is "to work together, especially with one or a limited number of others in a project involving composition or research to be jointly accredited." Such a move is a serious commitment to "co-labor" (Murphy & Dudley-Marling, 1999) through the halls of the unknown and the unfamiliar as well as infused with vulnerability, new insecurities, and new competencies (Pounder, 1998).

There is also a negative, pejorative sense of collaboration, which means to cooperate usually willingly with an enemy or an opposed group rather than struggling or resisting. Thus, those in Europe who aided the occupying Nazis during World War II came to be known as collaborators.

Now clearly, we view our cooperation as falling into the former category rather than the latter. Because we did not perceive ourselves under any direct attack, there was no enemy to which we could give allegiance, although we—at least some of us—did feel we were struggling against often unstated norms of academic writing convention, of which more will be said.

Minutes from our meetings reflect discussions about social and professional discomfort with collaborative writing. Some of us found it difficult to put our ideas or opinions out for public purview. We feared negative judgment by our peers. Initially suffering these questions of inadequacies alone, we soon found safety among our group members. Those of us comfortable with the writing process offered their services as peer editors. Acting as a second set of eyes, they helped several of us see the holes in our writing and find voice to our inner thoughts.

Pounder (1998) claims the most common conflict in collaboration is the imbalance of inputs and influence, ranging from too much control over the group's action to too little input by individuals for group activities. Any member of the group can be guilty of dominating a group's discourse and thus strangling the voices of diversity. Likewise, any group member may be guilty of nonparticipation, which subsequently restrains group progress. Collaboration could not be a spectator sport! We found ourselves both supportive and impatient with our group's journey; conflicted by the labor-intense opportunity to creatively engage in a communal act of scholarship and a desire to "get it done!" Expecting to synchronize everyone's writing was our first misconception of the book project. It was also a matter of perception. When any of us was overwhelmed with other faculty responsibilities, we saw the book process as moving too fast. We wanted the world to slow down so we could be deeply reflective about our writing. We needed more time to complete our work. When we were more in control of our lives, the book projects seem to move too slowly. Of course, all of us never felt the same way at the same time, which cast a syncopated (up and down beat) rather than a synchronized cadence to our work.

Not only were our personal writing metronomes adjusted by collaboration, but collaboration also entailed making our positions public as we problematized both our topic—urban education—and our process—collaboration. Sometimes this would mean opposing a colleague's position publicly. Faculty members heretofore could protest anonymously. For example, at one meeting we discovered multiple forms of collaboration. The case in point was, how should we, as faculty, interact with the student author outside of our group meetings. One faculty member met with the student about her chapter and provided immediate feedback. By making himself readily available to the student, he perceived he had initiated a collaborative relationship with her. However, a fellow faculty member offered a different definition of collaboration. "Collaboration is when the group consults with its members about its intentions and expectations and *then* makes a group decision on how to move forward. The action is defined by the group."

Were these two definitions of collaboration on a collision course? Both faculty members were sincere in their efforts to work collaboratively. Both faculty members, one by moving toward the student and the other by seeking group consensus, had the student's best interest in mind. The opportunity to talk this through illuminated the distinction between the role of "we as individuals" and "we as a group."

Faculty authors also had different views on the modes of inquiry. The process of how to study a question was seen differently by different group members. For example, at an early point in our project, some of us decided to consult with local urban teachers about the significance of our study. A field trip was arranged to visit a public urban school with which the credential program had had a long relationship. At the school faculty meeting, we asked, "Be honest. What should we know about urban education that we don't know?" Rich dialogue unmasked several blind spots, but one theme painfully emerged from a long list of critiques. Our cultural ignorance, they reported, unintentionally assaulted a rich, Hispanic, cultural/linguistic knowledge. Urban teachers told us that students from our programs had misconceptions about the school and the community. Our university students described their students as "at risk" and "less than"; terms that the kids do not use to refer to themselves, they reminded us.

Upon return, we debriefed the merits of our venture. Whereas some of the attending faculty found the trip a meaningful ethnographic experience with our public school partners, others felt the trip was unnecessary in order to participate in the book project. They were interested in contributing a book chapter but not in the joint inquiry of "urban." The brief respite from the fundamental nature of the academy and the norm of private and individual scholarship (Tye, 2000) was not enough to mobilize individuals to form a group.

It was not until the group asked itself, "How do we know what we know about urban education?" that a serious interest in each other's chapter came about. As we publicly shared our individual credibility on the topic "urban education," we recognized the need to conduct honest self-assessments. It was at this juncture that the faculty authors arrived at their first group consensus, a merging coherence that what we were attempting, beyond the thrust for authentic collaboration, in many respects was running against the conventional grain of much of academic writing.

CHANGE MEANS WORKING AGAINST THE GRAIN

Situating the Self

Drawing from Paulo Freire's (1998, p. 12) notion that ". . . learning begins with taking the self as the first object of knowledge," our first antigrain decision was to place a special emphasis on using the self as a source of knowledge rather than traditionally referencing from sacred texts. Using the authority of standpoint epistemology (Hill Collins, 1991; Lather, 2000), in which the claims of knowledge come from the lived experiences of social positionings, each author excavated and made public his/her "personal knowing." We described how our own social locations influenced the development of our frames of understanding. Then, in a communal potlatch, we anted our urbanesque experiences into the collective intellectual pool. Thus, the contextualized lives of teacher educator, researcher, and practitioner were used as frames of reference. This infrastructure brought a new light to the dark forces of urban and facilitated the "deghettoization" of urban education for each of us.

The pragmatics of implementing this vision was not easy. Lost somewhere in formal schooling and higher education's socialization, some of us were unfamiliar with using ourselves as points of reference. We were uncomfortable with using a subjective frame. It became necessary to reincarnate the self by reinstating the "I" in our writing, thus acknowledging our subjectivity as legitimate voices (hooks, 1999). As researchers, we had been taught that one could only know the truth from afar. The subjective self was the enemy most to be feared (Palmer, 1998).

In the academy, objectivity is an expression of neutrality (hooks, 1999) and the hallmark of academic writing. This form of writing dominates academe and effectively excludes other forms of scholarly writing. Faculty authors disrupted the status quo by deliberately inserting themselves into their chapters for the purpose of integrating their subjective selves within their academic frame of reasoning. Additionally, well aware that public school reform largely ignored the social construction of knowledge as a topic to problematize in urban education, we discovered that our new-found writing style was teacher-friendly and more accessible to practitioners. We recognized the need to appeal to a larger audience. Our book is an attempt to bridge the gap between the academy and education's public sector. And finally, we are further affirmed in our use of a subjective frame of reference by Kanpol (forthcoming), who argues that personal narrative in assorted forms is critical for a counterhegemonic agenda.

The Voice of the Practitioner

We recognized the possibility that other educators could criticize us for writing a book about urban education from our privileged "outsider" status—academics sheltered behind ivory tower walls. Writing from this perspective could compromise our credibility in that we cannot write with authority or speak for those "others," those "insiders" who live and work in the inner city (Howard, 1999; Smith, 1999). The best we can do is to interrogate ourselves as we work beside them and bring our "outsider" perspective to bear upon their issues and inquiries. This often recurring and uncomfortable realization lead to a number of discussions that resulted in our asking a former Masters of Education student to join in our endeavors. The inclusion of Susie Barras-Weston, as a critical friend marked an exciting moment in our collective experience. Asking her to read and critique our chapters meant making public our pimples and warts. Weston provided us with the valuable perspective of an urban classroom teacher. She brought to our attention dimensions we may have overlooked. Our relationship with her is like the zoom lens of a camera. She starts with her classroom and zooms out to gain a wider perspective. We in academe typically start with a wide-angle lens and then zoom in (Borko, 1998). Weston's classroom-focused eyes helped us see dimensions of urban education that may not be seeable from our academic perspectives or our social location. She forced us often to confront that rock of reality of urban education when we academics began to drift off into the comfortable world of generalized abstractions, as we often are wont to do, given that we university teachers don't routinely ask students how to improve our programs (Sarason, 1990). We see this collaboration as another opportunity to dismantle traditional power relationships between students and teachers as well as a means to counter the outsider-insider, the "one foot in, one foot out" dilemma of which Freire has spoken.

Book Writing and Cultural Change

Very early in our deliberations we asked ourselves how might our collaboration contribute to positive cultural change within the School of Education? This concern was driven by our initial attempts to include as many faculty in the project as possible. To accomplish this, a call went out to all 47 full-time faculty from the Orange and Academic Centers campuses combined. From this potential pool of writers, 12 of the 18 faculty members (67%) from the Orange campus and 7 of the 29 (24%) from the Academic Centers indicated an interest in participating. Desire was demonstrated by attending a number of exploratory meetings. Then the dropout commenced. Remaining faculty—a final group of 7, all from the Orange Campus, puzzled by this turn of events, began to search for reasons. Although anecdotes filled the air, there was little concrete information available. As a result, we decided to use a modified form of Transactional Evaluation (TAE)

(Rippey, 1973; Wilson & Regosin, 1981) to gain greater clarity about the dropout rate.

TAE was selected not only to provide understanding of the above, but also as a possibility by which deeper issues in the culture of the School of Education (SOE) might be addressed. The function of TAE is to find issues of conflict within a system and use such discoveries as a means to bring about system change. Thus, the struggle to write a collaborative book becomes a process beyond itself; it becomes a metaphor by which the culture of the School of Education can be interrogated.

One of the characteristics of TAE is that all parties affected by a system or subsystem and who have a stake in its proceedings are involved in the evaluation from its conception. Rather than the final seven School of Education faculty members designing a questionnaire for submission to all faculty, a request went out for all faculty members, including the seven, to submit items that they felt were critical to understand the book writing project. From these submissions, the final seven constructed a questionnaire using the most representative and divergent statements, with original wording of the statements kept intact as much as possible (see Appendix for the questionnaire). The introduction to the questionnaire laid out its specific intent while at the same time it called attention to the larger purpose of cultural change:

> This brief questionnaire is designed to gather information about a 2 1/2 year ongoing SOE collaborative writing project. Beyond the specific content of the book, we faculty authors have been concerned about the question of collaboration among ourselves as well as the book's place in the larger SOE culture. The anonymous responses you provide will assist greatly in this task. While the specific intent of the questionnaire is to gather data to inform the content of the book's opening chapter, a more general goal is to provide valid information, which serves as a basis by which we all can improve our collaborative practice.

It needs to be recognized again that the intent of the TAE process is not to attain statistical precision but to identify points of tension in the system. Statistical tests may be useful to provide a standard to determine at what point disagreement is "program significant." Such points may or may not match with levels of statistical confidence. The critical issue is to derive some level of meaning that is acceptable to participants.

The instrument was then distributed to all faculty. Of 47 forms distributed, 24 were returned for an overall 51% return rate. Eleven (61%) of the Orange faculty and 14 (48%) of the Academic Center faculty returned usable forms. The questionnaire first presented five statements to ascertain the percentage of faculty's degree of participation in the project according to either the Orange or Academic Center (AC) campus locations. Table 1.1 offers this information.

Because the intent of the TAE instrument is to locate areas of agreement and disagreement, some standard of agreement is required. Recognizing that any standard is ultimately arbitrary, we authors wished to establish one high enough to give us a degree of confidence that indeed, there was agreement. We therefore settled upon "around 80%" as a "good enough" criterion. This means that on any one of the 35 questions, about 80% of the responses had to be a combination of either Strongly Agree/Agree (SA/A) or Disagree/Strongly Disagree (D/SD) to count as educationally significant. For example, from Statement 1, "I am aware that a number of SOE faculty members have been writing a collaborative book," 15 (88%) faculty—8 from Orange, 7 from the Centers—selected SA and 2 (12%)—1 from Orange, 1 from a Center—chose D. Thus, we are confident that there was a general awareness across the campuses of the project, at least from those who chose to rate the first statement. There is also the issue of agreement to disagree. Item 18 reads, " The

Table 1.1. Percentage and Number of Faculty's Degree of Participation by Campus

Statement	Orange (number, %)	AC (number, %)
1. I am unaware of the faculty-writing project.	2 (15)	8 (80)
2. I was initially interested in the project but chose not to participate.	3 (23)	2 (20)*
3. I began to write for the project but did not continue.	2 (15)	0
4. I submitted an initial chapter but later withdrew.	1 (8)	0
5. I have submitted a final chapter.	5 (40)**	0

*One respondent altered the statement to read "I was initially interested in the project, but was not allowed to participate. Submitted a chapter proposal too late."
** Two of the seven faculty authors did not respond to the questionnaire.

SOE book was simply a way for me to get an item on my annual report." Of the 10, 8 (80%) either indicated D or SD. From this finding, we can make somewhat problematic the often-heard belief that SOE faculties tend to be instrumentally driven in their publication efforts. It should be noted here that not all statements were numerically rated by all respondents and often Not Applicable (NA) was the most predominate. This is illustrated by Statement 14 that reads, "My perceptions of SOE (School of Education) support impacted my decision to discontinue with the project." Within the SA/A-D/SD continuum, 5 (83%) selected D/SD, and 1 (17%) chose Agree. However, of the total of 19 respondents who answered this statement, 13 (68%) checked Not Applicable. This result may mean that the perception of SOE support either was not a factor for discontinuing or that the statement was not applicable to those who continued with the project. The data itself cannot provide an answer.

Therefore, regardless of the numbers and percentages from the survey summary, it needs to be recalled that such tabulations become mere points, rough problematics for further analysis by all those who responded. Findings from Statement 21, "I had some fear about the entire process," or from number 24, "There are forces that obstruct collaboration in SOE," cannot nor should not be subjected to a final analysis by we who originated the TAE process. To do so seems to us to be a serious breach of the collaborative spirit, which we had hoped we had engendered.

However, this position should at the same time not make us completely mute until all can come together to examine the findings. Thus, we offer a few tentative conclusions in the spirit of inquiry in which ". . . data and ideas have to have their worth tested experimentally: that in themselves they are tentative and provisional" (Dewey, 1916, p. 189). And this testing needs to be a public and open activity (Argyris, 1990, p. 105). These conclusions come from both the numerical summaries and respondents' comments of those who returned the survey. It does not speak for the entire SOE faculty.

Conclusion 1. The book collaboration project was well known.
Conclusion 2. At least at the level of rhetoric, collaboration is seen as desirable.
Conclusion 3. There is recognition that there are forces within the SOE as well as in postsecondary education that obstruct collaboration. At the same time, there are perceived forces that facilitate collaboration: collaboration could be improved.
Conclusion 4. Although some faculty, primarily from the Academic Centers, lamented the lack of administra-

tive support, time constraints, and the lack of an intellectual atmosphere as factors negatively impacting scholarship efforts, they did not contribute to either continuing or discontinuing with the project.

Conclusion 5. The use of personal narrative is perceived as not being embraced.

Conclusion 6. The degree of fear within the entire process has high variance among the faculty.

Conclusion 7. If the opportunity arose to write another SOE book, faculty would consider contributing, particularly if administrative support were forthcoming.

As the function of the TAE process is "to pinpoint areas of open conflict as areas of mutual agreement within groups and among groups" (Talmadge, 1975) and thereby critically examine the SOE organizational culture, it is necessary to construct a process that moves us in praxis from (and with) reflection to action. Not to do so freezes reflection dichotomized from action, " . . . into idle chatter, into 'verbalism', into an alienated and alienating 'blah'" (Freire, 2000, p. 87). Although critically aware of this obligation, at this writing we have not gone beyond the collection of the TAE information, which thereby remains at the level of initial reflection.

What we have done is to broaden our reflection to consider the implications of our efforts from an organizational justice and aesthetic/beauty perspective. If we believe that our collaborative writing experience has merit beyond the production of the book itself to effect positively the School of Education's cultural life—which we do—then our obligation is to lay out some grounds upon which action might accrue.

THOUGHTS ON THE IMPERATIVES OF JUSTICE AND BEAUTY

We return to the survey. Its final two statements concerned the issue of regret. The reason for this inclusion was to determine the degree to which respondents believed the book writing process was fair. This move then served as a starting point to examine the issue of organizational justice and eventually the often-neglected importance of organizational aesthetics and beauty

As it is hopefully clear at this juncture, a critical element within our labors was the conscious attention paid to the manner in which we worked together. As an organizational system, albeit a small one, we clearly had an objective to complete the book. Yet, there is more to this that needs to be taken into account when examining the quality of our collaborative attempts. Keeley (1988, p. 5) writes that ". . . one can define organizations as systems for something besides collective goal attainment." But what is this something to be? Keeley then offers a powerful example as he describes a goal-directed system from the late 1930s into the mid 1940s characterized by ". . . some of the most advanced, participative and humanistic organization and management theories . . . (that) . . . discouraged 'group think' . . . opened lines of communication, and built a climate supportive of contingency approaches to decision making" (p. 6).

Yet this system, in the end, caused untold suffering and pain, for it was used by Adolph Hitler's Minister for Armaments and War Production under the directorship of Albert Speer. Those who did the work were millions of forced laborers, concentration camp inmates, and prisoners of war who suffered starvation, beatings, and death. After laying out the above description in further detail, Keeley concluded "that organizational goals and their attainment are not, in the final analysis, our most important private concerns" (p. 8).

Accepting Keeley's analysis as we do, what, in a retrospective sense have been, or at least ought to have been our private concerns in terms of working together? Two such concerns then become the aforementioned justice and aesthetics. Beyond the book as product, the book, to what degree can our small social system's efforts be considered as just and beautiful.[1]

For justice, we again turn to Keeley (1978). He posits a socially just organizational life informed by John Rawl's (1971) principle of justice as fairness. Because individuals in any organization, even our relatively small faculty authors group, might have various and sundry " . . . desires for certain 'primary goods' . . . resulting from mutual cooperation in an organized system of activity, then how can fairness of the organization be gauged, what can be considered as a primary good?" (Keeley, 1978, p. 283). Keeley argues that satisfaction in participation is the only common denominator that reflects diverse interests of organizational participants. In our case, faculty authors might have different motives and reasonably disagree about the worth and significance about our end goal, yet the good of satisfaction in the process is one in which all could agree. And this meaning of satisfaction is not to be framed in utilitarianism's classic dictum of

---

[1]This does not mean in any sense separating the end—the subject matter, completion of the book—from the means by which it came about. With Dewey (1916) we reject any dualism that separates means from ends and we accept congruence, the ". . . essential unity of method and subject matter. . ." (p. 323).

"the greatest good for the greatest number" in which, to paraphrase Keeley, aggregate satisfaction can be promoted by increasing individual A's satisfaction at B's expense as long as average satisfaction is increased. Thus, rather than the maximization of satisfaction, Keeley, from Rawls, adapts a principle of minimization stated as "... *regret over the actual consequences of interaction* ... that minimizes the regret of the most regretful participants" (Keeley, 1978, p. 286).

The issue then became one of determining regret within our work. As mentioned previously, this was accomplished by having the seven faculty authors respond either Yes or No to the statement, "I wish I had not become involved with the book writing project" (adapted from Keeley, 1978, p. 287). This procedure has only one point of reference, that of yes or no to regret. Keeley (1978, p. 287) explains:

> Above this regret-point individuals may experience satisfactions, indifference, or even mild dissatisfaction with system outcomes. Below the regret point system outcome points are such that individuals would not voluntarily choose to continue cooperation, though they may actually continue active participation or toleration of aversive organizational consequences due to a lack of subjective viable alternatives.

All seven of the faculty authors checked "No" to the statement of regret. From this we conclude that, in general, Keeley's criterion of social justice has been met and that our ethical process in and itself has contributed to our goal. We do agree with Keeley's summary:

> Finally, the social-justice model—specifically, the minimization-of-regret principle—manages to balance participant interests in an ethical, yet pragmatic, fashion. It may seem perverse to focus on regretful organizational participants rather than on those, possibly more in number, who enjoy the outcomes of collective activity. But the point is that generally aversive system consequences ought not, and in the long run, probably will not, be tolerated by some participants so that positive consequences can be produced for others. Systems that minimize the aversive consequences of interaction are, therefore, claimed to be more just as well as stable in the long run. (Keeley, 1978, p. 290)

It needs to be made clear that this finding pertains only to the faculty authors, all of whom are from the Chapman Orange Campus. To the statement, "I regret not participating in the book writing project" on the TAE form, 6 of 11 (55%) respondents (2 from the Orange campus and 4 from the Academic Centers) indicated either strong agreement or agreement. This seems to imply that the inclusion of more faculty members in future, similar endeavors have positive potential.

Now, what of the aesthetic dimension. Seemingly insurmountable challenges faced us as we moved to create this community of writers. Faculty authors painstakingly carved a space and staked ground for our right to meet, like a candle that stubbornly holds back the darkness. We stubbornly resisted administration's erasure of our meetings, which we viewed as insensitive. From our perspective, it was attempting to hold our intellectual minds hostage in exchange for yet one more administrative duty. Whereas scholarship was part of the school's public dialogue, it was not honored in practice. There was no infrastructure to support this dimension of our work. Although publications were expected, scholarship was expected to be completed individually and privately, as if a manuscript got produced through immaculate conception. Yet in spite of these barriers, faculty members found time to write. They held a deeper understanding of what it means to be an academic; they persevered for intrinsic reasons, for the aesthetics of scholarship.

To further an aesthetic understanding of our work, we turn primarily to John Dewey for whom the aesthetic was grounded in the developmental nature of experience. For him, ". . . it is in the enjoyment of the immediacy of an integration and harmonization of meanings in the 'consummatory phase' of experience that . . . the fruition of the readaptation of the individual of the individual with the environment is realized" (*The Internet*, 2001). By consummatory aesthetic experience, Dewey meant one in which there was "immediate enjoyed intrinsic meaning" (Westbrook, 1991, p. 385), ". . . the immediate appreciation of things—things directly possessed, enjoyed, and suffered in and of themselves" (Westbrook, 1991, p. 330). Such appreciation was essentially noncognitive in that its qualities could not be directly known but must speak for themselves.

And this speaking occurs in the commonplace experiences of everyday life. Aesthetic enjoyment is not, therefore, the exclusive purview of a select few nor restricted to the fine arts and their consumers.

> Whenever there is a coalescence into an immediately enjoyed qualitative unity of meanings and values drawn from previous experience and present circumstances, life takes on an aesthetic quality—what Dewey called having "an experience." Nor is the creative work of the artist, in its broad parameters, unique. The process of intelligent use of materials and the imaginative development of possible solutions to problems issuing in a reconstruc-

tion of experience that affords immediate satisfaction, the process found in the creative work of artists is also found in all intelligent and creative activity. (*The Internet*, 2001)

For us then, the act of creating this book has indeed been an experience of consummatory, aesthetic, and artistic form characterized by such qualities as frustration, various degrees of anguish, satisfaction, enjoyment, and occasionally downright elation. As well, there has been an enlarging sense of community in which we have become more conscious of our individual development and our relationships with each other. Westbrook (1991, p. 416), while referring to democracy, writes that Dewey brings together the self, the community, and the artistic:

> [D]emocracy was the social ideal not only because it nurtures individual growth but because it envisioned a growing community that would itself be a complex, organic work of art, harmonizing the development of each individual with the maintenance of a social state in which the activities of one will contribute to the good of all the others.

We do believe that our efforts can be characterized in a similar manner. We consistently interrogated ourselves by holding the word democracy to the mirror to see what it reflected. Although we are sure that the image given by the mirror at times was distorted, the mirror itself was never cracked. What we viewed were our democratic private concerns of ethics/justice and the aesthetic, not as separate entities, but as intrinsically and developmentally bound. Westbrook (1991, p. 416), drawing once more upon Dewey, captures this sentiment for us:

> [T]he moral self is the growing self and it was in the quality of becoming that virtue resides. The good person was one "most concerned to find openings for the newly forming or growing self; since no matter how 'good' he has been, he becomes 'bad' (even though acting upon a relatively high plane of attainment) as soon as he fails to respond to the demand for growth." A bad self was mired in mere subsistence while the "growing, enlarged, liberated self, on the other hand, goes forth to met new demands and occasions and readapts and remakes itself in the process." A bad self was a hopelessly divided self or a static and isolated whole. But the good self was constantly refashioning itself into a more complex, internally differentiated yet harmonious unity into a work of art.

Based upon these perspectives, we have come to a fuller understanding of the necessity to view our work not only for its completion but also for its just ethical and aesthetic dimensions. The process by which an endeavor is carried out is a critical and salient evaluation criterion of effectiveness as much as is the achievement of the final goal. Although hardly tight or "objective" (can questions of ethics and beauty ever be so?), we do feel and believe that we have met the test. We have given birth to the book—a longer gestation period than any of us imagined—and at the same time we have had a fine, often contentious, usually critical, more than occasionally humorous but always committed time. Our dream, our "pedagogy of hope" (Freire, 1995), is now to struggle with ways by which our ethical and aesthetic consummatory experience can further infuse our work both within the School of Education and the urban educational contexts in which we find ourselves.

FINAL THOUGHTS

A paradigm of social justice was the fabric from which our chapters were cut. Our moral imperative was to work on ourselves rather than work on others. We wanted to get our own house in order or we would have little to offer urban houses. To recommend collaboration to public school faculties and not engage in systematic collaboration among ourselves would be a serious contradiction. Could we hold ourselves accountable for what we actively promoted in our courses; collaborative critical inquiry?

Throughout our efforts, we have been deeply conscious of our self-imposed charge to collaborate. Thus, as we proceeded the word itself was always present, obvious when spoken but when not, still always in the air. Although we have produced this book, did we actually collaborate? Did our paean to collaborative action, our espoused theory, match our actual behavior, our theory in use? (Argyris, 1990).

All things considered, we believe we have. To the best of our comprehension of the word, our collaboration was real; we believe we have had a strong degree of congruence between our rhetoric and our practice. At the same time it needs to be said that although we recognize the critical necessity of collaboration in university as well as public education settings, urban or otherwise, collaboration must not stand alone. It needs to be always considered in light of ultimate ends, which for us is the beauty of social justice. We need never to forget that the aforementioned Nazis labored together quite well in committing atrocities—the ultimate ugliness—almost beyond representation and our ability to understand.

The test that lies in front of us is the degree that collaborative critical inquiry is sustained by us beyond the scope of this project. Will our experience together influence the way we do business? How will our work inform the work of urban educators? Will they see our work as useful and practical?

> Becoming informed about one's own and others' practices, connecting practices with theory, and developing trusting relationships with colleagues are all examples of powerful actions. These are not "getting ready" or warm-ups, or first steps—these are themselves practical achievements that promote excellent learning opportunities and social justice for students. (Dukes & Lipton, 1999, p. 351)

We have added to Oakes' and Lipton's sentiment of the just, the aesthetic, for the processes of connection, of shared information, and of trust among us all done in true collaboration speaks loudly: We did have both a just and beautiful time.

For many of us, writing this book was an act of courage and risk taking as we struggle to make a difference in urban education and our academic selves. The following chapters are about our multiple pathways of moving from the "outside" toward our inner-city partners. Our intentions are to illuminate the multilayered structures that underlie the formations of darkly constructed conceptions of urban schools. Our pedagogy of hope is that the following collection of essays will bear out the truth of our assertions, that they will liberate both those from the inside and those on the outside of urban schools from the misconception that urban is "a place you wouldn't want to get stranded in." Based on what we have learned, our challenge now becomes one of constructing, in a collaboration of justice and beauty, a cultural, problem posing action plan which, again turning to Freire (1998), demands praxis where reflection and action are directed at the structures of SOE to be transformed.

REFERENCES

Argyris, C. (1990). *Overcoming organizational defenses: Facilitating organizational learning.* Boston: Allyn and Bacon.

Austin, A. (1992). *Faculty collaboration: Enhancing the quality of scholarship and teaching.* ERIC Document #ED347958.

Ayers, W., & Ford, P. (Eds) (1996). *City kids, city teachers.* New York: The New Press.

Borko, H. (1998, April). *Conversations about social change: Bringing together policy and classroom researchers*. Paper presented at the American Educational Research Association conference, New Orleans, LA.
Dewey, J. (1916). *Democracy and education*. New York: The Free Press.
Freire, P. (1995). *Pedagogy of hope*. New York: Continuum.
Freire, P. (1998). *Pedagogy of freedom: Ethics, democracy, and civic courage*. Lanham, MD: Rowman & Littlefield.
Freire, P. (2000). *Pedagogy of the oppressed*. New York: Continuum.
Giroux, H. (1988). *Teachers as intellectuals*. Granby, MA: Bergin & Garvey.
Goodlad, J. (1990). *Places where teachers are taught*. San Francisco: Jossey-Bass.
Gove, P. et al. (1967). *Webster's third new international dictionary of the English language*: Unabridged. Springfield, MA: G. & C. Merriam.
Hamilton, C. (1991). *Apartheid in an American city: The case of the black community in Los Angeles*. Van Nuys, CA: Labor Community Strategy Center.
Hill Collins, P. (1991). Learning from the outsider within. In M. Fonow & J. Cook (Eds.), *Beyond methodology. Feminist scholarship as lived research*. Bloomington: Indiana University Press.
hooks, b. (1999). *Remembered rapture*. New York: Holt.
Howard, G. (1999). *We can't teach what we don't know*. New York: Teachers College Press.
Johnson, B. (1998). Organizing for collaboration: A reconsideration of some basic organizing principles. In D. Pounder (Ed.), *Restructuring schools for collaboration*. Albany: SUNY Press.
Kanpol, B. (1994). *Critical pedagogy*. Westport, CT: Bergin & Garvey.
Kanpol, B. (forthcoming). *Cynical reason and joyful possibilities: Critical narrative based leadership in teacher education*.
Keeley, M. (1978). A social justice approach to organizational evaluation. *Administrative Science Quarterly, 23*(2), 272-292.
Keeley, M. (1988). *A social-contract theory of organizations*. Notre Dame, IN: University of Notre Dame Press.
Kozol, J. (1994). The new untouchables. In J. Kretovics & E. Nussel (Eds.), *Transforming urban education*. Boston: Allyn and Bacon.
Kozol, J. (1991) *Savage inequalities*. New York: Crown.
Kozol, J. (1995). *Amazing grace*. New York: Crown.
Kretovics, J., & Nussel, E. (Eds.). (1994). *Transforming urban education*. Boston, MA: Allyn and Bacon.
Lather, P. (2000, April). *Educational research and advocacy*. Paper presented at the American Educational Research Association conference, New Orleans, LA.
Maeroff, G. (1994). Withered hopes, stillborn dreams: The dismal panorama of urban schools. In J. Kretovics & E. Nussel (Eds.), *Transforming urban education*. Boston, MA: Allyn and Bacon.
Morgan, G. (1997). *Images of organization* (2nd ed.). Thousand Oakes, CA: Sage.
Murphy, S., & Dudley-Marling, C. (1999). Lumbering over labor. *Language Arts, 77*(2), 103.

Mullen, C.= Kochan, F. (2001). Issues of collaborative authorship in higher education. *The Educational Forum, 65*(2), 128-135.
Oakes, J., & Lipton, M. (1999). *Teaching to change the world.* Boston: McGraw-Hill College.
Onion, C. T. (Ed.). (1955). *The Oxford universal dictionary* (3rd ed.). New York: Random House.
Palmer, P. (1998). *The courage to teach.* San Francisco: Jossey-Bass.
Pounder, D. (1998). *Restructuring schools for collaboration.* Albany: SUNY Press.
Rawls, J. (1971). *A theory of justice.* Cambridge, MA: Harvard University Press.
Rippey, R. (1973). What is transactional evaluation? In R. Rippey (Ed.), *Studies in transactional evaluation* (pp. 3–7). Berkeley, CA: McCutchen.
Sarason, S. (1990). *The predictable failure of educational reform.* San Francisco: Jossey-Bass.
Smith, L. (1999). *Decolonizing methodologies: Research and indigenous peoples.* London: Zed Books.
Talmadge, H. (1975). Evaluation of local/community programs: A transactional evaluation approach. *Journal of Research and Development in Education, 8,* 32–41.
The Internet Encyclopedia of Philosophy—John Dewey. www.utm.edu/research/iep/d/dewey.
Tye, B. (2000). *Hard truths: Uncovering the deep structure of schooling.* New York: Teachers College Press.
Westbrook, R. (1991). *John Dewey and American democracy.* Ithaca, NY: Cornell University Press.
Wilson, T., & Regosin, R. (1981). Transactional evaluation and program change. In B. Eckstein & W. Looss (Eds.), *Zeitschrift für Hochschuldidaktik, 5*(1), 136–149.

APPENDIX

Transactional Evaluation
Questionnaire

Dear Colleague

This brief questionnaire is designed to gather information about a 2 1/2 year ongoing SOE faculty collaborative book writing project. Beyond the specific content of the book, its faculty authors have been concerned about the question of collaboration among themselves as well as the book's place in the larger SOE culture. The anonymous responses you provide will assist greatly in this task. While the specific intent of this questionnaire is to gather data which will help inform the content of the book's closing chapter, a more general goal is to provide valid information which serves as a basis by which we all can improve our collaborative practice.

A. Please check either 1 or 2 as your primary work site:

   1. Orange Campus

   2. Academic Center Campus

B. Please check either 1, 2, 3, 4, or 5 from the below:

   1. I am unaware of the faculty book writing project.

   2. I was initially interested in the project, but chose not to participate.

   3. I began to write for the project, but did not continue.

   4. I submitted an initial chapter, but later withdrew.

   5. I have submitted a final chapter.

C. Please rate the below statements either 1, 2, 3, 4, or N as follows:

1 = Strong Agreement, 2 = Agreement, 3 = Disagreement, 4 = Strong Disagreement, N = Not Applicable to Me. Place the appropriate number in the space after each statement

   1. I am aware that a number of SOE have been writing a collaborative book.

Comments:

   2. I know the theme of the book being written collaboratively.

Comments.

   3. I know the names of the faculty who are writing the book.

Comments:

    4. The process of writing the book has affected/altered my perceptions of scholarly/creative activity as a "collaborative" pursuit.

Comments:

    5. The process and/or product from this experience inform our/my thinking and decision making.

Comments:

    6. I believe that productive lines of inquiry flow from this project.

Comments:

    7. I began to write a chapter, then decided not to.

Comments:

    8. I think the book group was an asset to the SOE democratic process.

Comments:

(NOTE: Due to error, there was no number 9 on the questionnaire.)

    10. As I began or completed writing a chapter, the book writing process added to my scholarship as I expected.

Comments:

    11. The development of this collaborative scholarship could have been different in ways that would have better served our ideals, our function, and the individual scholarship of the faculty.

Comments:

    12. The idea of a collaborative project was more intriguing than the particular topic or urban education.

THINKING THROUGH COLLABORATION

Comments:

13. This project is an effort valued by SOE.

Comments:

14. My perception of SOE support impacted my decision to continue with the project.

Comments:

15. My perception of SOE support impacted my decision to discontinue with the project.

Comments:

16. There are particular issues which collaboration pose for me.

Comments:

17. I enjoy the writing process and putting words and ideas to paper.

Comments:

18. I feel that the writing was demonstrative of who I am.

Comments:

19. The SOE book was simply a way for me to get an item on my annual report.

Comments:
20. The academy isn't often embracing of the use of personal narrative in what they consider "academic writing."

Comments:

21. It was difficult for me to place myself personally in my chapter.

Comments:

22. I had some fears about the entire process.

Comments:

23. I was fearful of allowing colleagues to read my initial drafts.

Comments:

24. There are forces which obstruct collaboration in higher education.

Comments:

25. There are forces which obstruct collaboration in SOE.

Comments:

26. There are conditions which facilitate collaboration in higher education.

Comments:

27. There are conditions which facilitate collaboration in SOE.

Comments:

28. I think faculty members need to collaborate.

Comments:

29. There are some ways faculty members could collaborate together professionally which they do not now.

Comments:

30. If there was another opportunity to write an SOE book, I would consider contributing a chapter.

Comments:

31. I would need support from administration in order to fulfill a writing commitment.

Comments:

32. I would need support from fellow authors in order to fulfill a writing commitment.

Comments;

33. I would need support from nonparticipating colleagues in order to fulfill a writing commitment.

Comments:

34. It is meaningful when administration is absent in the process.

Comments:

35. I regret not participating in the book writing project.

Comments

36. I regret participating in the book writing project.

Comments:

D. Please make any other comments not made above.

2

Dispelling the Myth of Moral Bankruptcy in American Urban Youth

Donald N. Cardinal
Center for Educational and Social Equality

Do you know the answer to this riddle? What is the diffrence between being a university professor and being a drug abusing, frequently arrested, easily violent, high school kid living in urban America? Here are some hints. Each lived in the same home, had the same dad and mom, experienced the same things in life. Each had the same education and went to the same school and each received the same grades. Each went to the same church every Sunday during childhood. Do you have the answer yet? How can one set of life circumstances turn out two such different people? Give up? The answer is, they are the same person. Did you get it right? If not, maybe you "unityped" the professor, or worse, maybe you unityped the high school kid!

Unityping is the false assumption that because a person can be regarded as embodying or conforming to a set image, that that person will always be so regarded. To unitype, one makes two spurious assumptions. In the case above, one must assume that the two character types are stereotypical and thus possess some oversimplified conception of each character (stereotype). Second, one must assume that the stereotypical characters are *not* capable of change. That is to say that if the two characters described above were first stereotyped and then denied the capability of becoming (or having been) someone else, then they were, in fact, unityped. Unityping then becomes a double-whammy for the character—she is not seen as all that she is, only as her stereotype, and she is viewed as incapable of changing over time. The evils of stereotype are well known. But the peril of unityping is much worse in that it assumes a permanence of the stereotyped character.

The question in front of us is this: If a child behaves in a manner that appears to be similar to one whom we assume either chooses to be antisocial or who may be victimized into such a social role, does this necessarily mean that his values differ significantly from those of yours or mine—let's say from an average university professor, for example? Could the fundamental moral tenets (morality, loyalty, collegiality, family, etc.) drawn on to make decisions of social interaction by the urban youth be very similar to the fundamental moral tenets drawn on to make decisions of social interaction by the university professor? I will argue here, yes. The moral tenets of decision making can be very similar, but the manifestation of those moral tenets into human behavior can be vastly different based on the social rules inherent to a certain environment. This is not to say that all urban children who engage in antisocial behavior live by the same values, but, of course, neither do all university professors. Thus, my argument is this: A child in urban America who behaves in a manner that is judged to be unfit, can be operating under the same set of moral values as is the university professor who is viewed quite differently, and invested in quite differently, by society.

If this is true for any portion of American youth,[1] then we must ask how do we as educators create an educational environment where the urban child is revered for his values and shown how to transition his *behavior* into a more socially accepted norm without devaluing the fundamental intent of his past actions. (Show the student how to get everything he was getting before—belonging, respect,

---

[1]There is no assumption on my part that all people (including all youth) who live in urban America engage in antisocial behavior. Yet, one can not ignore the overall impact that gang or gang-like behavior has on today's urban youth and the barriers that these behaviors create for their education and thus their future. On the other hand, I do not completely suppose that all professors are free from moral bankruptcy.

action, expertise, and so forth—but maintain the benefit of the larger social acceptance). For example, an urban youth is physically attacked and defends his honor by later retaliating and beating up his opponent. The university professor, on the other hand, is attacked in a journal by another author who suggests her data are questionably reported. In defense (retaliation) the university professor writes a scathing retort to be published in the following journal issue. Both the urban youth and the professor were attacked in a deep and hurtful way. Both felt their pride and their reputation was in jeopardy. Both possessed the value that self-pride and personal reputation were worth defending. Each person's peer group learned that this person is not to be fooled with. Again, the difference between the urban youth and the university professor was not that one had good (acceptable) values and the other did not. The difference was simply, but meaningfully, in the manifested behavior of their shared values. Thus, as educators, our time may be better spent assuming that the urban youth who engages in antisocial behavior is not morally bankrupt, but rather, that he needs to learn how to manifest his values into behavior consistent with the rules of "our" streets (the streets of the larger society). First acknowledging, and even celebrating, the commitment he has to his values, we could then demonstrate how one can manifest these revered values into behaviors that yield the elusive desired benefits in the "streets" of the greater society. Adapting the axiom of least dangerous assumption developed by Anne Donnellan in 1984, we could say that the least dangerous assumption in reacting to urban youth is to assume that their actions are a result of a socially accepted (even admired) value. If we err in that assumption, we only find ourselves reverting to the existing social reaction to such a youth. If we assume that the youth who engages in a socially unacceptable act is doing so from a place of moral bankruptcy, then we cause great harm both to the youth and to society. The least dangerous assumption, then, becomes one of assuming moral character and disjoining the behavior of the youth from the assumption of a deviance from socially acceptable values. Implementing the least dangerous assumption axiom forces society to focus on the education of urban youth rather than on hopelessness and punishment.

At this point I must momentarily discuss a personality type that easily fits in the category of an urban youth who engages in antisocial behavior, but who *does not* fit in any other way into the scheme I am attempting to build regarding shared values.[2] This is not to say

---

[2] A second exception to my thesis should also be noted. It revolves around drug addiction. The thesis that an urban youth who engages in antisocial

that this specific character type will never have shared values with the greater society, but, as I see it, that is highly unlikely. Call it unityping on my part, even stereotyping, but it is my current belief that there are some people who, for whatever reasons, have extremely little or no social conscience. I am talking about a person who will kill someone and feel no apparent remorse and have no sleepless nights—she is not connected to other people in any meaningful way. I fear this character is more prevalent today than ever before—maybe as a social consequence of so many babies born to parents addicted to drugs where the baby receives little or no bonding whatsoever. However, how this character exists or why this character type is proliferating, if that is so, is beyond my expertise. The only point I make here is that this person *does* exist and that my experience strongly suggests that she operates outside of any recognizable set of moral tenets with which I am familiar. Thus, when I speak of "urban youth who engage in antisocial behavior," and for the purpose of this thesis, I will exclude this character from that description. Although I do not have an assessment instrument to differentiate these character types (thank God), I have found that a response to the question "Why did you do what you did?" yields divergent results from the two character types. The character I wish to exclude from this thesis would characteristically respond to why they hurt someone, for example, by saying "I didn't like him" rather than "They did me wrong." The former response troubles me much more deeply than the latter.

---

behavior may possess the same moral tenets as does a university professor is completely reliant on the assumption of the lack of *addiction* to drugs. This is an extremely complicated topic and this chapter is not the forum for a detailed conversation about drug addiction. I am not sure there is even a way for a person who has never abused drugs to understand the radical chasms between drug use, drug abuse, and drug addiction. Each magnifies its predecessor by a thousandfold. I think that those who "use" drugs probably fit into the thesis I have laid out. Even some, maybe even most, who "abuse" drugs also fit into the thesis of moral singularity. But rest assured, for those humans who are addicted to drugs, no thesis will hold and definitely no thesis of morality.

    Unlike the first exception to my thesis I outline here, the drug addict may very well have a conscience, but the conscience is no match for the addiction. The addict may care about you, and hurting you may be against her moral tenets, but if you stand between the addict and her drugs, and hurting you is the only way for the addict to get to the drugs, she will hurt you—absolutely and unconditionally. All sense of morality is temporarily erased for as long as the particular state exists—sometimes this is for the rest of addicts' lives.

This chapter will focus on the fact that we should create an educational environment with the assumption that for many urban children, it is not the morality of the children that needs to be revised, but rather, it is the behavioral manifestation of their intact moral tenets within the social contest. Possibly then, our pedagogy may need to emphasize the "rules of social interaction" within the greater society instead of expecting urban youth to conform to these new standards as if they had a void of social culture waiting to be filled. That which is needed could very well not be learning how to behave in a certain manner, but rather, to learn an alternative interpretation of the manifestation of intact moral tenets. More on this later.

To accomplish this goal I will share with the reader my personal experiences in being cultured during my developmental years within an urban environment and contrast my core morality held at that time with the tenets I currently hold as a university professor. I will argue that there are great similarities behind the core values responsible for my actions in my childhood through young adult years—label them antisocial—and my actions as a university professor, which are viewed by most as highly moral and socially beneficial.

Based on a less complex argument, and as a secondary purpose to this chapter, the reader may find my life analysis useful simply as gaining greater knowledge of the urban community and culture in hopes to better understand the process of one man's travels from antisocial behavior toward service to the greater society. According to a 1997 study, experienced teachers, student teachers, and university teacher educators, unanimously ranked "Knowledge of Community and Culture" as the most important themes for being a successful teacher (Ilmer, Snyder, Erbaugh, & Kurtz, 1997). If knowledge of the community and culture in which one teaches is in fact critical to being a good teacher, then this small glimpse into such a life may very well promote "better teaching." If we as teacher educators are responsible for creating learning experiences for our teacher candidates that will prepare them to have knowledge of the community and culture in which they will be working, then doesn't it become a mandate upon us to understand our collective subjectivity about our urban community and then to learn from others about these communities? With this mandate as a moral guide, I will delve into my background to uncover how my upbringing influences my participation in urban education as a teacher educator. Additionally, I will attempt to maintain the theme of a singularity of morality and a duality of behavior between urban youth who engage in antisocial behavior and those members of the greater society who are perceived to behave in a manner beneficial to that society.

I Have Reservations

I have deep concerns about what you will think of my early experiences and how you will evaluate me because of them. After all, if the reader is guilty of even some unityping, then you will believe that my early behaviors are still part of my current repertoire. The reader may "know" this to be untrue or highly unlikely, but unityping (as does stereotyping) runs deep within us all. But I have kept most of these thoughts and experiences silenced within me for too many years. I am willing to take on this risk based on the encouragement of colleagues professing the value that my experiences and subjectivity may offer about the inner city. If my colleagues (some of whom are associated with this book) are right, then they, and maybe even other readers, will benefit from what I know to be my reality of inner city consciousness. Even at that, I will be unable to confess my darkest moments, because those can only be shared with those who have been there. It is simply impossible for me to create the context for understanding given the limitations of the written word, absent of experience. Entangled in that same logic, I will refrain from presenting my thoughts in a theoretical framework. These words are my truth. Whether they are consistent or inconsistent with current theoretical thought will have to be another paper and another time. I invite the reader to "experience" what you read here while continually reconciling it with your own subjectivity.

In order for the reader to "understand" what I will share, it may be beneficial for me to first discuss who I am now. I do not speak for the School of Education, but I am a member of the School of Education and thus a part of its collective perspective of urban life. My subjectivity of inner-city realities then becomes part of the faculty subjectivity.

PERSONAL BACKGROUND

My parents were both first generation American citizens. Their parents were from a very modest background in southern Italy, never receiving any formal education and unable to read or write in either English or Italian. My grandparents signed their names most of their lives with an "X." I remember how proud my mother was when she talked about the day her mother learned to sign her name, which occurred about a year before my grandmother died at age 84. My mother quit school in the 5th grade and my father completed 8th grade—they were viewed as being educated. I was never read to as a child—never. My school work was never discussed in my home—although I remember a year when my family hired a tutor to help me. My sister was an A student and one year my senior. My grades were C and below—I was consistently a C student with the occasional exception of a B in math or business classes or a D in classes requiring verbal/written performance. I don't think I ever received an A grade from elementary through high school. Education was highly valued in my family, but as I eventually discovered, "education" had an elusive meaning for them. Going to school meant being educated. "Reading the classics" was not in my family's consciousness. I didn't read an entire book until the 11th grade (about Warren Spahn—a great baseball pitcher) and that was the *only* book I read until college. (I always feel diminished in some way when educated people assume everyone has read the classics.) In high school I attended several remedial classes along with other "gangster-types." In fact, my first memory of thinking of myself as a teacher (in a very abstract way of course) came from one of those remedial classes where the instructor allowed me to help others in the class, because I was the only one the students would allow to speak to them about academic issues.

I did not have success in school of any kind except for making friends and winning the beard-growing contest when I was 16 years old. (I won the contest in the "most artistic" category. I had a good friend who was a barber. The night before the contest I visited him for my beard shaping. He was very much under the influence of barbiturates—he answered the door by falling to his knees, laughed, and said, in a very slurred voice, "Hi Don, have a seat, I'll get my straight-edge razor!" He did, and I won.) Drugs and hooligan-type behavior became my equalizer. I remember when, to apply for my first teaching credential, I had to obtain my high school records only to find out that my verbal IQ score was 96 (average is 100). Although slightly stunned, I remembered having two strong emotions. First, I was so glad I had not seen this score earlier in my life, because my confidence was already low. Second, I thought how nonpredictive these scores were for me and thus probably for others. IQ never carried much weight for me after that. After all, I had an honors GPA in college and finished my Bachelors degree in three-and-one-half years—taking as many as 23 credits per semester to finish while working full time. I suppose that experience also added to my "anyone can succeed" view of life and fed my belief that all children can learn, regardless of their diagnosis or tracking.

Part of me believes that my passion to liberate oppressed people comes from being oppressed in my preteen and teenage years. Yet, cognitively and in retrospect, I realize that my oppression was more the close observation of oppression rather than the lived experience of it. In other words, I was "with" those who were genuinely oppressed by society, but I was not really "of" that group. I believe educators who wish to make a difference in urban schools must first recognize and acknowledge their privileged status and the differences between themselves and their students—regardless of how similar they want to believe they are. Only then can they focus on their similarities.

The difference between the others in my group and me was that I came from a family of relative affluence—a family where education was stressed, albeit naively so (my mother has yet to understand why I didn't stop going to college after my Associate degree)—and the others did not. Whereas my dreams of affluence and success came from the model my father had shown me (and as I later understood, the role my mother played in the family), theirs did not. Their dream for a life of affluence came mainly from the "con" (vernacular oration designed to persuade the listener) or in making the big "score" (obtaining big money on contraband) from illegal activity. Actually, I don't think most of them even had these dreams—what they had then was all many of them thought they would ever have. They had little to lose! Through some sort of osmotic process, I, at times, believed I had nothing to lose. At least I was much more like the others than I was like the "straight" (people who did not take drugs) people I knew then.

I suppose, as compared to the average person in America, and certainly when compared to the average academic, I have seen and experienced things that would force many to view my life then as belonging to the "urban underclass." Interestingly, I actually lived two lives. One was with the group of friends from the "wrong side of the tracks," a group of friends I was raised with until I was 11 years old when my family moved to the proverbial other side of the tracks—the affluent side. Both were clearly geographically suburban, but that is where their comparison stopped. It is the former group of friends that occupied a significant portion of my adolescent life and served to provide me with the rich experiences I draw on today and that I will discuss in greater detail here. Until recently, I have characterized these early years as my "druggy" period. That is, these years (say, from age 14 until my 19th birthday) were occupied by the search for, and consumption of, drugs.

GEOGRAPHY AND ITS RULES

I lived close to Los Angeles where the urban life extends many miles outward—solid humanity of 10 million souls stretching tens of miles from the city's center. Ten miles in one direction you will find some of the most affluent areas in the country. Ten miles in another direction and you will find urban life at its worst. A place where your street smarts were far more important than your school smarts, so much so that even small cultural mistakes could easily result in serious bodily injury, death, or incarceration (i.e., looking at someone for more than a quick glimpse, "sleeping with" a neighbor's significant other without permission, or crossing the wrong street at the wrong time).

The rules were omnipresent, and there were more of them than in any environment I have been in since (including state and federal bureaucracy). The rules were not only plentiful, but the consequences for breaking, or even bending, them were harsh. Some rules were easy to figure out, like not stealing someone else's drugs. This happened often, however, and was the reason for many of the beatings and shootings that occurred. This was also a curiosity to me.

The harshest penalties were given for breaking rules that are also rules, though modified, of the greater society, like not stealing. A more subtle one was eye gaze. Looking at someone who you did not know well for more than a portion of a second was considered a challenge to that person. Once done, you had only two choices—cower or fight! If you cowered, you would be forever relegated to this lesser status, making you easy prey for others who wished to hold a higher place in the pecking order.

Fighting, even when you lost, was at least respectable. Fighting in schools is wrong, not because fighting is wrong, but because fighting is not one of the socially agreed upon solutions for conflict resolution within the school setting. When we expel someone for fighting in school, we seem to be punishing the behavior of fighting instead of punishing the behavior of breaking the agreed upon rules of our local society.

We establish rules of what not to do, but fail to make clear the rules of what one should do. In contrast, the rules of how to behave in a gang or other urban social group are made very clear. It has also been very perplexing to me that our schools have chosen to guide youth on how not to be, yet fail to provide equal guidance on how one should be.

There is only a narrow chance for escaping the rules of urban America. One may be able to create a smaller, more controllable, environment in the home or within a few blocks of home, but the rules of behavior are omnipresent—break them and you pay the consequences. I remind the reader that my comments are not aimed at the urban family—my experience there is limited. I am speaking of the groups of teenagers and young adults who spend more time with their peer families than they do their natural families (why this occurs is beyond my commentary, yet extremely worthy of inquiry). I was frequently amazed at how so many people could simply pass out (drug related) and wake up the next day and apparently not be apprehensive about how they were going to explain this to their parents. Instead, they'd be ready to start the whole thing over again. This type of "partying" varied from that of the suburban group. The urban party seemed to be life, not just detachment from it as with the suburban party.

The other comparison was the degree of violence. Whereas partying with the suburban crowd may have resulted in the violent destruction of the rival high school's concrete bear mascot (hypothetically, speaking, of course), in contrast, the urban violence resulting from the partying was often directed at a member of, or related to, the "party." For example, someone would feel the drugs they paid for had been "cut" (reduced in strength to obtain a greater profit for the seller). This may lead to the hunting down of the seller by the buyers, often resulting in a beating or killing.

I remember one time during a party when the group decided to seek retribution from a perceived wrongdoer. About eight people loaded into two cars. My body was halfway in one of the cars when I thought we may be gone all night—the perceived wrongdoers were about 100 miles away. I remember thinking that I could not be gone all night. Knowing this would be too hard to explain to my mother, I begged off, under great protest from the remaining members. (I was a physically large teenager and was viewed as being valuable in a confrontation.) The group came back later the next day. Something horrible had happened. Four of the seven members who went were arrested the next day on four counts of mayhem (the offense of willfully maiming or crippling a person). All four went to jail and did serious jail time.

Why did I almost go with them? There was a perceived injustice. At the time, righting the injustice seemed equally as admirable and right as fighting for social justice is for me today. The common moral tenet, to right an injustice, felt identical to, for example, advocating for a person with a severe disability to be educated with the general population. The feelings behind both situations (and I can "feel" them both at this moment) are nearly identical. I reasoned that someone with greater power is forcefully exerting their power over someone with lesser power without their consent.

I remember another time when a good friend's girlfriend was physically abused by a rival gang (we did not use the term gang, but I think it is the best descriptor of the social grouping of the time, 1969). The perpetrators had been constantly harassing this friend, which led to more and more violent encounters. The abuse was the latest in this progressive string of retaliations. The gang members lived only about eight miles away, but in urban neighborhoods this is an extremely great distance—sometimes crossing several neighborhoods in which we did not belong, which opened us to violence by neighboring groups.

The plan was to retaliate for this perceived wrongdoing. Remember now, I was completely motivated by the fact that a wrong had been done—a lone woman was physically violated by several larger and stronger men. I organized over 100 people to travel with us across several neighborhoods to the home of the "wrongdoers." By the time we left that house, the front porch was completely collapsed, windows were broken, and the front door was hanging on its hinges. The rival group was never heard from again.

In my mind, and in the minds of my "colleagues," we had done the right thing. We had protected a friend and righted a wrong. There was no question that that is how it felt. The feeling is extremely similar to the feeling I get now when I, for example, win a victory over an insensitive school administration wanting conformity over liberation. The difference is not one of values or morals, but rather in the manifestation of those values and morals based on my social context. With a jury of my "peers" I was innocent of any wrongdoing. In fact, I was judged by my peers as being value-centered. Of course, this verdict could only have come from those peers who were members of the same urban culture.

Members of the greater society focus far too much on the behavior of youth rather than centering on the reasons why they do what they do. Behaviors have consequences, but personal reform must start with the belief that "I" am worth reforming. If I am consistently unityped by those of the greater society, then I will behave accordingly. If, along with the consequences of my actions, the moral underpinnings of my actions are acknowledged, I am then provided an acceptable foundation on which to build my reform.

For me, there was always hope for the good life (although, I must admit, I never really thought much about it, but probably assumed it). Consequently, I was never really "of" the urban group, just "with" the group. My very closest urban friends knew this and would remind me of my "outsider" status frequently, calling me "rich boy," for example, when I bought a used car. My "sin," and the reason I could never be completely part of the group, was that I was "white" and they were black. It was not that I could afford a car. To them, anyone white was not a real part of the neighborhood and thus always an outsider. So, again, I found myself with the group but not of the group. I have curly black hair, some color to my skin, and possessed an appropriate attitude for the streets. I often felt that this allowed me some degree of membership by the inner-city group. But, by their measure, it was certainly a marginal benefit.

I learned the rules however, and periodically stepped into, then out again, of the urban culture. I knew when I was "in" because of the joy of hopelessness I felt. By this I mean a feeling of belonging to a group where the enemy is everyone except the very few you fully trust (sometimes called a gang). This made life very clear. The thought was that "The Man" (the establishment, the police, and anyone who looked down on you) had power and a need to use it. The Man was the evil King and we were the "peasant-people" fighting to be left alone, to live our lives the way we thought best.

Every opportunity to exert our own power was maximized. The very act of taking drugs was a clear message to everyone; we will "party" in the midst of The Man's oppressive acts. Even right and wrong got redefined. Instead of using The Man's right and wrong as moral guides, as did mainstream America, we used them as a map to discover the plan of oppression. This map clearly outlined the ways in which The Man would exert its power over its people. For example, school itself was thought of as a place designed to hide people from the real world and to replace street truths with blind conformity. School, I thought then, was an obstacle to learning and doing—a place that consumed important time, better spent living within the rules of the street. School was not real life, I thought, it was simply The Man trying to replace what really was with what it thought it should be. I already knew what I needed to know to survive in the streets; everything else was "their" rules to live in their controlled world. It all seemed so obvious. The Man wanted you under its control, living by its rules. I, and nearly everyone I knew, resisted The Man's attempts at indoctrination. Interestingly, the more the rules were imposed, the greater the resistance. And the more we resisted, the more we felt victorious. We lived by our rules, and, in my logic then, it was the admirable thing to do.

What was right within the group was measured by its members. We decided on what was right and wrong in the neighborhood. Power going to those who were strong in will and physical strength was right, because they produced their own power. To be given power because of what your family did (wealth, for example) was wrong, because it was not about you. Paradoxically, those in power in the streets could, and did, "adopt" people who were not powerful, protecting them with a cloak of transferred power, which, in effect, gave them power.

I would be taken by a sense of calm, belonging, and meaningfulness, which was a euphoric belief that I finally understood the rules; the main rule being that there is nothing else for me beyond the immediate, that I was not created to do something special with my life, and that my strength came from the group, not from within me. This euphoric sense of relief came from the unknowns of the social rules. It never lasted long, however, because the reality of purpose beyond this reality was hard to block—although being lost in the pseudo-protected world of a drug-induced safe house could last for days, even weeks at times. Thus my realization (although not until two-and-a-half decades later), was that I lived a life with oppression but never of oppression. I think (I know), that most of the others in the group lived their lives in their joy of helplessness.

The "with/of" distinction has been difficult for me—so much so, that I only recently have made this distinction about this time of my life. When I was "with" the group, all human life around me screamed oppression. So I felt oppressed when I was "there." For example, security would immediately be called if I entered a shopping mall and I would be followed. I would be stopped by the police anytime I dared to go into "white" neighborhoods (remember, I am white). School officials seemed to be afraid to mention to me that I was under the influence of drugs (although it was very obvious). No one thought I might be smarter than my grades dictated. Schools oppress children by making unityping decisions about them. That some children are not worth as much energy as others or that the amount of energy is simply too great—how sad a statement about our culture. It is as if one who demonstrates poor academic behavior (and even engages in antisocial behavior) will, in fact, be destined to a life of subaverage functioning. I often wonder how many great minds get ignored because of what their character "appears" to be when viewed through a unityping lens. I can think of only one high school teacher who saw me differently and I think of him often. He looked beyond the gangster and saw a teacher (his prognosis, not mine at the time).

HIDING MY SUBJECTIVITY

I remember a colleague, just a few years ago, had appeared incredulous about the fact that an inner-city child in Los Angeles, who was about 14 years old, had never been to the beach. How could this possibly be true, because the ocean was only a dozen miles away? I remember distinctly thinking, "Does he (the professor) really not know the answer to that question?" I remember the colleague told the story to anyone who would listen within the School of Education, each member of the audience being more surprised than the former. I felt very much the outsider then, because I knew many young people who had never seen the ocean. I was afraid that if I revealed my knowledge the academic community would discover I was a fraudulent professor—the one who shouldn't really be there.

Only recently, well after my 40th birthday, had I begun to think that my early experiences could ever be shared in a professional arena. Until that time, only my closest friends knew of my background. Those who did know, only knew the surface facts of those early years.

As an adult, I have voice. So, why have I been so unwilling to discuss this time period of my life, even though I thought it may help some become better educators? Maybe my "gang" of today (my school, my university) offers me the support I needed to self-disclose. Maybe gaining tenure and becoming full professor offered me the security I needed. Maybe the world of academe has changed just enough that, as a profession, it has come to celebrate the lived experiences that make us who we are, instead of pretending we were just born to be who we are.

I remember university colleagues, across several different colleges, contemplating the possible reasons for gang activity in inner-city schools. I secretly knew why, but never spoke up on the topic. I had no one to quote; no studies to cite; no familiarity with the literature. I knew it because inner-city "gang" life was real to me.

BACK TO THE NEIGHBORHOOD

To survive in a neighborhood, you must know the rules of the neighborhood. You must know whom you can turn your back on and whom you cannot. You need to know how far you can travel on foot and how far in a car. All this varies depending on strategic configurations like the time of the day, the day of the week, who is in the car with you, who owes money to whom, and how many drugs you are carrying. Given one configuration, you could be extremely cool, driving two blocks from your house. That same configuration, ten blocks from your house, would most likely get you busted (arrested) or even killed. The closer you were to "yours," (your streets, your friends, your rules), the safer you were. The more you strayed from neighborhood and friends (aka gang members), the less control you had over your destiny.

Why Are There Gangs?

Because gangs make rules—sometimes terrible rules—but rules that are clear, much clearer than the unwritten social rules of general society, rules that are, for the most part, based on family values, friendship, and survival. Maslow was not too far off-base here. For example, don't ever snitch (tell) on a hommie (friend in the neighborhood). Beating the crap out of someone, even killing him or her, is better than snitching on them (of course not as measured by the hommie, but certainly as measured by the "gang").

Another rule: don't go into another neighborhood without being invited or unless you are adequately accompanied by "yours"—for any reason. This rule applies even if there is no gang. For example, your brother needs to go to the hospital that is three miles away in another neighborhood. You have three choices. Don't go, go with yours, or ride in the ambulance. Never just put your brother in the car and drive there. This rule explains why the 14-year-old had never been to the beach. It was not in his neighborhood and he's too young to get his gangster friends to come with him. Even if he did, then you have The Man (the police) to deal with. Five minutes out of your neighborhood, they have pulled you over; asking questions, searching you, and probably arresting you. You left your safety zone. The rules changed.

I knew exactly what streets I had to stay within to avoid arrest. I could be weaving from side to side in my own neighborhood, but the police basically left me alone. The key was to stay on streets where there were no police or the police would most likely just honk their horn, but not arrest you. One "game" I remember playing was finding a way to go long distances without ever going on a main street. Friends would share these routes with one another—and mapping good routes would win you prestige. Avoiding The Man was both a game and a necessity. It allowed one to extend the neighborhood a little farther, like using underground tunnels through The Mans territory.

How "Then" Influences "Now"

Entering the cave. I took my first drugs at about 14 years old and my first serious drugs at about 16 (an "older" child by toady's standards). My father died the day after my 17th birthday—things got very bad from there. I began to get loaded daily. My senior year in high school is a blur—it was like living in a cave—a cave I would not escape for several years. Everyone knew I was loaded (under the influence of drugs); at least every student knew and I suspect most school professionals knew too. I would fall in the hallway and frequently fall asleep during classes. Fighting, destruction of property, consumption of drugs, and other illegal activity was a serious part of my personal repertoire.

Once I graduated, things got even worse. I went further and further into the drug cave where few people lived. For the next two years, nothing was out of bounds; any drug in any quantity. If you wonder why there are heroin addicts, just try the "stuff" (actually, don't). Your question will be answered within five minutes. This will also be the best "high" you will ever get in your life. I never met a person who could stop at only once, and I never met a person who ever even tried!

My best friend overdosed and died at the age of 34. He was a smart, fun, and moral man, according to the neighborhood rules. Nearly all of my good friends from that time of my life are dead. What a waste. Sometimes I think that my life is their lives, reincarnated into mine. They are given a second chance at life. Sometimes, I feel I have "made it" for them.

After high school, came college. I was still using drugs regularly. I hardly remember taking the courses at my community college in the first year.[3] After one semester, I had a 1.68 GPA and was put on scholastic probation. The next semester was even worse and I was asked to leave. I was very lost. I spent my 17th and 18th birthdays in jail for being "drunk" in public, although I never really drank alcohol. By my 19th birthday, I had 26 moving traffic violations, owned 14 cars and crashed several of them. Life kept repeating itself. On my 19th birthday, I again found myself in jail. This time was different, however. Instead of a friend or older brother (he was 16 years my senior) coming to pick me up, it was my mother and other family members. She had no idea of any of my previous doings. This was her introduction to her son having anything to do with drugs.[4]

I stopped taking drugs on September 6th, the day after my 19th birthday and the third anniversary of my father's death. (Birthdays have a double meaning for me.) It took me six months to begin to think even somewhat clearly. It was like living in a cloud, a

---

[3] I promised my father I would go to college and be the first Cardinal to ever go to college. I suppose I was there because that had been the plan all along—a sort of plan within chaos!

[4] Some of my friends now say they cannot believe this, that my mom did not know all of this was going on. She never knew how to drive. She was always home. I left home to live on my own when I was 17. She just didn't know.

cave. Simple thoughts were unclear and it required great energy to focus. Casual conversations with people were also very difficult. They expected answers for the things that required a storehouse of lived experiences I did not possess, or at least could not remember. I was trying to make a transition from the rules of the street to the rules of the greater community.[5] Frequently people assumed I knew the rules, but I simply did not.[6]

Confrontation was easier than everyday talk. For example, being assertive as a consumer was much easier than having a cup of coffee with someone I did not know well. It is easy to see why some people stop taking drugs and then start again (as I did several times). It can be analogized to being on a bad vacation and just wanting to go home. The vacation (being straight) was promised to be a grand event. But, instead, it was filled with demands I simply was not equipped to meet. I really wanted to go home where everything made sense. It was tough in the neighborhood, but everything was so very clear.

I had to stop seeing all of my old "friends," to avoid getting back into the drug life, with the exception of two good straight friends who stayed with me during the difficult times. I honestly don't think my transition would have been successful if it were not for them.

Getting out of the drug culture was not easy. Craving drugs was the least of the issues, although consuming. Friends would call and come by frequently, ready to party. They were relentless. I was forced to move in order not see them anymore. This is probably the most difficult thing I have ever done in my life. Sometime I think that my loyalty to friends today and my ability to forgive them for their imperfections is a result of my lack of self-forgiveness for abandoning these old friends.

I stopped taking drugs the day after my 19th birthday. I have kidney stones and when I refuse to take drugs for them until the very last minute, sometimes after days of severe pain, people think I am trying to be macho. No, I just choose to feel all of life. Even the worse pain being straight (not under the influence) is better than no pain loaded (well, almost).

---

[5]When speaking to at-risk youth today I always assume they may not know the rules of the greater community, so I state the rules clearly and respectfully—also stating the range of possible acceptable behaviors that most likely would result in their desired outcome.

[6]I think it is important for the reader who works with children to understand that drugs have a way of claiming a person's personality even when they are not under the influence of drugs—even when they have stopped taking drugs.

Acclimating to the forest. I am a university professor in the area of teacher education who focuses on the education and liberation of people with the most challenging disabilities in our society. Consistent with my thesis, I believe I am currently the same person I was in terms of my core values. The transformation was not so much a metamorphosis as it was an acclimation to a new environment. In contrast to the process of metamorphosis, I was *not* first a caterpillar and then a butterfly. Rather, I was always a butterfly, first living in a cave, then, once released, living in a beautiful forest.

In this forest there was more to see and do than I ever knew existed, but with new and much more confusing rules for survival. At first, the light from the sun was blinding and I wanted to go back into the cave, but I knew if I went back I might never come out again. I quickly noticed that there were still enemies in this new environment; they simply did not declare themselves as such—as I was used to. And, as peculiar as it may sound, I missed most the people around me in the cave who would have literally died for me. These people were plentiful in the cave, but extremely rare in the forest.

The environment had changed radically and I fought desperately to figure out the new rules. I then began to discover that each rule I had known in the cave had a congruous rule in the forest. This realization took about two years, but then all the new corresponding rules began to fall into place. The formula was set. All that had to be done was to replace one addiction with another, one behavior from column A (the cave) with one from column B (the forest)—see Table 2.1. I simply traded the reputation of being someone who could take more drugs than anyone else for someone who worked harder and produced more than anyone else around me. I traded the loyalty covenant I had with others in the cave for loyalty to employers and friends, always being the one who went the extra mile. I traded the clear rules of the streets for the clear and absolute rules of behaviorism.[7] I traded righting wrongs through violence for righting wrongs through social activism. Everything had a correlative in my acclimation. I did not "become" someone else, I began to trade behaviors, behaviors that stemmed from the same values.

The best (and in some ways, maybe worst) trade I made was coping with fear. In the cave, fear is dealt with by either avoiding conflict (doing nothing) and thus assuming a lower position in the pecking order or power within the group, or fighting to establish a

---

[7]Behaviorism offers great security to us cave dwellers. It has its defined limits, contaminates are known and manageable, and all things can be measured and understood within their definition.

Table 2.1. Matrix of Moral Singularity and Behavioral Dualism.

The Value	The Behavior in the Cave	The Behavior in the Forest
Taking pride in where you live and play	Fighting a turf battle	Pride in the school
Righting wrongs	Physical retaliation; shooting a rival gang member, for example	Writing letters of protest, civil disobedience
Proving your capabilities	Taking more drugs than others; making a big score	Taking on a school-wide project
Commitment	Taking a beating from other gang members	Seeing a task to its completion

greater power—nothing in between. I had always chosen the latter—not everyone did.

In the forest, there is even more fear. I was very surprised at the amount of fear in the average person in the forest. Even those I thought who were in power in the forest seemed to have great fear. They seemed to fear almost any display of their own courage, as if they would lose what they had worked so hard to gain.

I soon noticed that in the forest, people were rarely forced to prove their courage; this was not so in the cave, where courage was tested daily. As I became a teacher, I saw this conflict occur regularly in the schools. Teachers would observe a student being "courageous," as defined by the rules of the cave (neighborhood), but they interpret this behavior as the student not understanding the rules of the forest. Instead, the teacher could have chosen to deal with such situations by showing the "courageous" student how to be courageous within the school environment and rule structure.

We do a great disservice to a student when we fully associate one's behaviors with one's values. When we fail to differentiate between the two, we ask the student to abandon a value; a value that I maintain should have been fed, not starved. Instead, it is the behavior that needed changing, not the value.

As a university professor, I hear this statement from my colleagues frequently: "I can't believe you said that!," referring to a direct statement to an administrator, for example. Although I do not say it out loud, I think: "I can't believe you did not!" Those that know me today may think I speak from the protections of tenure. However, those who knew me before tenure know that speaking up against injustice, for me, has little to do with tenure. If something is wrong, it is wrong, and not acting on the wrong is a lack of courage, not political savvy. It is hard to ignore the fact that sometimes we take our most courageous youth and "train" them to see that their courage is wrong rather than focusing on the "wrong" behavior and teaching alternative ways of behaving courageously.

FINAL THOUGHTS

We must rethink the connection between our supposition that youth who behave in an antisocial manner need value adjustment. Troubled youth need *not* be viewed as morally bankrupt and only "we" can make deposits into their account of morality. The urban streets can teach values consistent with values of the greater society. But the urban streets tend to teach behaviors that are frequently incompatible with success in the greater society. This chapter argues that youth in the urban setting who engage in antisocial behavior do not need a values adjustment; rather, they need to be shown alternative ways of behaving that are consistent with both their values and the rules of the greater social structure. To the degree that we are successful with this task, we will be successful with allowing our school system to have an authentic impact on the acclimation of our urban youth from the way of the streets to the way of the greater society. Best of all, we gain a courageous cadre for a society so in need of courage.

My attempt at developing this scheme has not been reliant on scientific "fact." I am not sure we will ever have a body of knowledge adequate to "prove" that urban youth who demonstrate antisocial behavior meaningfully share common moral tenets with the greater society. But I must hope that the examples I have provided and the story I have told allow the reader to connect, in some way, with a portion of urban youth.

I hope you do not unitype children as their character—a gangster, for example—and fail to invest yourself in their lives on the assumption that they have limited potential. Remember the least dangerous assumption—if we are wrong, then the harm we do to them and to our society is horrific and probably irreversible. However, if we assume competence and moral character of all individuals and find ourselves to be wrong, we can lose nothing.

REFERENCES

Donnellan, A. M. (1984). The criterion of the least dangerous assumption. *Behavioral Disorders, 9*(2), 141-50.
Ilmer, S., Snyder, J., Erbaugh, S., & Kurtz (1997). Urban educators' perceptions of successful teaching. *Journal of Teacher Education, 48,* 379–383.
Maslow, A. H. (1998) Toward a psychology of being. NY: Jossey-Bass.

3

Exception to the Perception

Dolores Gaunty-Porter

Culturally and linguistically deprived, at-risk, gang infested areas, poverty, violence, aging buildings, welfare, drugs, inadequate resources, and a shortage of licensed teachers: What do these words and phrases have in common? Media reports typically use these words and phrases to catalogue the urban communities of America. Generally, these conjure up negative images about people and lead to strong prejudices or stereotypes. For one to embrace media accounts about life in the urban community, one has to determine the accuracy of accounts. There are, however, untold exceptions to these perceptions of life in the urban communities of America.

Media reports about urban communities are generally presented through print and films. In 1981 a *Los Angeles Times* headline read, "Marauders From Inner City Prey on L.A.'s Suburbs." When presented with headlines of this type, the outcome of a *Washington Post* poll of whites makes sense (McQueen, 1989). The question was this: Was it common sense or prejudice for whites to avoid black neighborhoods because of crime? Three-quarters responded that it was common sense. Broadly defined, "whites" refers to Americans who are of European descent and derive their cultural identification from European ethnic groups. The tendency in America is to think of people in terms of race as the way to confer identity externally. Thus, race is a social construct without biological validity, yet it is real and powerful enough to alter the fundamental shape of our lives (Alcoff, 1996; Ayto, 1990).

News reports are a type of text, according to Teun A. van Dijk (1998), in the article "New(s) Racism." In his systematic review of media in general and news in particular, the author suggests that racial and ethnic inequality is perpetuated through the structures of news discourse. Van Dijk (1998) further examines the many forms of the term "new racism." He concludes that racism is expressed, enacted, and confirmed through text and talk, such as everyday conversations, board meetings, job interviews, policies, laws, parliamentary debates, political propaganda, textbooks, scholarly articles, movies, TV programs, and news reports in the press. These expressions are subtle and, therefore, can be overlooked as normal or natural, even as discussion about urban communities seems to marginalize and exclude people in that community. Van Dijk (1998) outlines the way language is manipulated in the media to thereby leave negative images or negative perceptions. Often, media accounts about discrimination lack information about who discriminated against whom.

Sometimes the media discussion about immigration includes military metaphors, such as threat or invasion. This type of language perpetuates negative images about certain people. Behavior demonstrated by whites and blacks is reported quite differently. For example, when blacks protest working conditions, it's termed "dragging their feet," while working. The perception of this behavior is that it reflects inferiority. But when white union workers behave similarly it is termed "a slowdown."

In 1994 the *USA Today*/CNN Gallup Poll (Sharp & Puente, 1994) indicated that 66% of African Americans were upset at least once a week by the way news organizations cover issues about blacks, and 39% of Latinos were upset by the way their issues were covered. In the media, stereotypes and negative images of ethnic groups reign almost totally. Those in positions of power can justify, legitimize, and gain support of actions they take. When the media depicts a people as savage or inherently inferior, it reflects a mind-set of colonization. This suggests that there is a constant "us" versus "them" at work throughout media.

Television portrayal of race strongly dictates how audiences formulate their perceptions about various groups. From the beginning of television in 1939, blacks have been portrayed as custodians, maids, servants, clowns, or buffoons. The *Amos 'n Andy* show, which began airing on television around 1964, and *Good Times*, which aired during the 1970s, are two sitcoms that perpetuated the negative perceptions of black people. These two programs included lots of "canned" laughter about events in which black Americans were portrayed as happy-go-lucky people, without any thoughts about political, social, and economic issues in society.

A few years later the Cosby show began airing on television, depicting a different type of black, the black middle-class family. This program was an exception to the former type of program about African Americans. In the Cosby show, there was a careful attempt to break stereotypes. There was an absence of silly antics, such as people throwing food at each other. Topics on the Cosby show reflected the social issues common to all Americans, such as drug use, sibling rivalry, teenage lifestyles in conflict with adult lifestyles, and struggles with parental authority (Blair, 1988). Currently, there are few media images of black people with Cosby-like content or programs that depict lives of middle-class blacks.

For one to totally embrace the negative media accounts about life in the urban communities means to question if anything good can possibly emanate from the urban communities. Is it possible to suggest that auspicious experiences and enduring dreams of people living and working in urban communities can discredit the overwhelming number of negative reports presented through the media?

"*Don't assume.*" This statement is particularly important for teachers who have limited experiences with urban communities. Before making broad assumptions about families living in urban communities, it is important to examine the aims, claims, values, and beliefs of the people about their schools and their community. It is time to hear the voices of people who live outside of the cultural, economic, and educational lack that is outlined in media. It is time to hear people recount that slice of life in urban communities that is wholesome and healthy. The following discussion contributes information toward dispelling some of the myths associated with life in urban communities. It is particularly important for teachers working in urban schools to examine the possibility that they may entertain myths relevant to the lives of the students in their classes.

Many teachers do have ideological biases that lead them to believe that students in urban communities, particularly students of color (students of non-European decent), are unwilling and or unable to experience academic success. Some authors (Carter & Chatfield,

1986; Means & Knapp, 1991) suggest that too often, people fail to consider that there is a connection between academic failure and teaching methods or tools. Perhaps, when the myths about urban communities are dispelled, we can focus attention on dedicated teachers in urban schools. These are people who teach to the best of their knowledge, skills, and abilities, show students respect, command respect in return, and thereby observe credible student outcomes.

Layers of bureaucracy influence schools in urban communities. Schools in an urban community are generally organized around a large centralized bureaucracy that may be slow to respond to the needs of the schools. Often, these large, unwieldy urban school districts are too encumbered to take the extra steps necessary to successfully address the needs of the students. These problems are further compounded through the appalling lack of resources, facilities, supplies, and instructional materials.

Equal funding may not be adequate funding. Some schools in urban communities need extra funding to be elevated to even an acceptable baseline. In *Savage Inequalities*, Jonathan Kozol (1991) presents a detailed description of financial inequities common in many urban communities. To make matters worse, the least experienced teachers are the ones left to try and address the issues in these "needy" urban schools. Thus, some of the negative comments about urban schools reflect these concerns.

Differences in socioeconomic status influence the stratification of students within schools, through grouping procedures and curriculum differentiations (Brantlinger, 1993; Oakes, 1985). In the less than desirable conditions of some schools, students often respond with high absenteeism, low grades, violence, seeming apathy, and other behavior that leads to low academic success for many students in urban schools. Ogbu (1991, 1994) argues that the academic underachievement of many African Americans rests in the fact that they understand social inequities; they develop a black cultural frame of reference that suggests that hard work is not rewarded equally throughout American society. In other words, a common thought among some African Americans is that white Americans will always devise ways to limit the economic, social, and political participation of African Americans.

Schools are complex organizations, and no single reform strategy can be specified as the most effective for raising academic achievement. However, parental involvement in schools is one area of educational reform that is intended to raise achievements of students in urban communities. Research suggests that there is a high correlation between successful student academic growth and parent involvement with school issues (Flaxman & Inger, 1991). Also, the parents' educational achievement and attainment actually influence students' success. The values, attitudes, and expectations held by parents with respect to literacy have a lasting effect on a child's attitude about literacy practices (Baker, Serpell, & Sonnenschein, 1995; DeBaryshe, 1995; Speigel, 1994). Nevertheless, many parents are being excluded from life inside schools.

Who are these diverse students in urban schools? In the past, the racial hierarchy was dictated by a black-white dichotomy with an unquestionable dominance of white people. According to the 1990 United States Bureau of the Census there has been a significant increase in the numbers of people from various racial groups living in the United States. Between 1980 and 1990, the Asian/Pacific Islander population increased 34% and the Latino population increased by 29%. The rate of population growth for African Americans was 9.5% and for whites 3%. Mexico was the largest source of legal immigration and accounts for over one-fourth of the 22.6 million immigrants in this country (Rumbaut, 1997). In 1994, about 72% of the total school enrollment in America was in 25 of the largest school districts (United States Statistics, 1997).

The shift in numbers of various racial groups includes a shift in the classification of some groups of people. For example, some people who in the past were considered inferior—Jews and Italians—have become white and are thus, considered more respected (Alba & Nee, 1997).

Racial and ethnic relations are complicated. The term "race" commonly refers to distinctions drawn from physical appearance, whereas the term "ethnicity" commonly refers to distinctions based on national origin, language, religion, food, and other cultural markers (Stone, 1985). Too often, the perception in America has been that the discussion about race is considered something in which only people of color engage, or something to consider only in discussions about African Americans, Asian Americans, Latin Americans, or Native Americans. For some people, the Dr. Martin Luther King, Jr. holiday, Black History Month, and Hispanic Heritage Month serve as a reminder that race pertains to people of color. The broad patterns of human biological variations and "race" are distinct. Humans vary in a myriad of ways: skin color, body structure, and genetics. Hence, race is a societal construct and reflects prejudices based on the perception of superficial differences. The patterns of racial and ethnic group relations in the schools are based on the ways that members of a given racial or ethnic group have been included or excluded within American society. Toward understanding these patterns of racial and ethnic group relations in America, it is important to remember the discrimination faced by many groups of people: attacks on Southern

European immigrants, conquests of the Indians and Mexican Americans, relocations of Japanese citizens during World War II, experiences of Cuban and Vietnamese refugees and other recent immigrants, and sufferings of slavery that black Americans endured (McLemore & Romo, 1998).

Some of the immigrants were refugees from countries torn apart by war. Other immigrants arrived as middle-class persons from countries with political, economic, and social stability structures intact. Some people arrived in this country with nothing, others with skills and affluence (Brand, 1987).

John Ogbu (1987, 1992, 1998), a noted educational anthropologist, proposed that there are many forces at work in society and schools that account for students' response to education. He focused his research on the attitudes of two groups of immigrants in the United States; he terms these groups voluntary or involuntary. For example, African Americans began their history in this country as a people brought in against their will, as slaves; thus, involuntary nonimmigrants brought to the United States through slavery, conquest, or colonization. Generally, this led the involuntary group of people to distrust the dominant group, whites. Ogbu refers to the voluntary group of people as those who have emigrated to another country by choice, normally with the idea of having greater economic and political opportunities.

Ogbu suggests that voluntary immigrants often view themselves as better off in the United States, and they consider that they have a homeland to which they can return. According to Ogbu, involuntary nonimmigrants do not have a homeland to compare with the situation in the United States, nor do they consider that they have a place to which they can return. Therefore, the involuntary nonimmigrants view discriminatory situations as permanent. The result can be a sense of hopelessness.

According to Critical Race Theory, storytelling is a way to "analyze the myths, presuppositions, and received wisdoms, that make up the common culture, about race, and that invariably render [B]lacks and other minorities one-down" (Delgado, 1995, p. xiv).

Note: In this chapter, the italicized text unveils the story of my life as it relates to assumptions about the experiences of people who live and work in urban communities. The storytelling format is a natural way to query myths and assumptions about the life of people living in urban America.

SAYS WHO?

I am a middle-class black female and normally refer to myself as an African American. Personally, I use the term black to include all people with African ancestry. However, I use the term African American to address people with African ancestries, but who have lived almost exclusively the American experience. I use the term black very cautiously. It seems that in the United States, the middle class rarely includes blacks. Seymour Martin Lipset (1996), a political scientist, used "invisible man" to describe middle class blacks. This was a reference to Ralph Ellison's 1982 classic Invisible Man. *A noted pollster, Stanley Greenberg (1995), quoted whites in focus groups: Not being black was what constituted being middle class; not living with blacks was what made a neighborhood a decent place to live (p. 39). The term neighborhood connects to the phrase "the hood." This is a phrase that some African American people use in reference to middle- to lower-middle-class communities of predominantly African-American people.*

I write my story from the urban American perspective, after living and working in several urban communities throughout the United States and in Mexico City. My experiences in urban communities are distinctly different from media depictions. Too often, the dominant society portrays urban communities as poverty-ridden, crime-infested locations with run-down, dilapidated buildings, inhabited by uneducated, unmotivated people. This does not relay my story, nor the untold story of many others living and working in urban communities. There are exceptions to the all-too-often negative media accounts of life in the urban community.

My school experiences included private and public school attendance in several urban communities of the United States and in Mexico City. My teaching experiences in urban communities ranged from preschool through adult-level programs, where I served as a teacher and/or administrator in regular, bilingual (Spanish and English), and ESL (English as a Second Language) Programs. Although many comments in this chapter reflect my childhood and adult experiences in the United States as an African-American female in an Anglo-dominated society, I have heard many other people of color recount similar events. My story is consistent with the life of most of the people I grew up with—family and friends, and other African Americans I have met even as an adult.

I was born on the Southside of Chicago, into an African-American middle-class family. The oldest of eight children in the household, I had three sisters and four brothers. Three other siblings, two sisters and one brother, were older and had established their own residences. I recall that during my early years, the racial make-up of people living on the Southside of Chicago was predominantly black middle-class.

During most of my early years, our family lived in one of several family-owned apartment buildings, in a middle-class community. We lived on the first floor, my grandparents lived on the second floor, and my aunt and uncle lived on the third floor. The neighborhood consisted of clean, neatly organized apartments and homes, with well-manicured lawns. In this quiet urban neighborhood, children played safely and peacefully in their own backyards.

The University of Chicago was about 15 minutes east, and the Loop (downtown Chicago) was approximately twenty-five minutes north. The University of Chicago was at that time, and still is, located in the mist of this urban middle-class community. My mother was a graduate of the University of Chicago with a B.A. in French. During my childhood, I recall that although the population around my residence was predominantly black, the population around the University of Chicago was predominantly white.

The media reports and comments from adults in my life shaped my perceptions about elitism as it connected to the Southside and Westside of Chicago. In my mind, the "haves" lived on the Southside and the "have-nots" lived on the Westside. This was perpetuated through negative media reports that referenced the Westside as a dangerous community. (Interestingly, my first teaching experience in the United States was in a public school on the Westside of Chicago. That particular school, although I know this was not true for all schools on the Westside, was indeed a place where I had to be cautious. Teachers were told not to walk alone to their cars, and not to remain in the school building too much time after school was dismissed, for fear of some type of crime.)

As a youngster, political conversations were a normal occurrence in my household. The fact that an African-American judge lived next door to us no doubt inspired lots of discussions about political issues. Ongoing interactions with the judge contributed to efforts my family made to strengthen their political and economic base on the Southside of Chicago. My parents and grandparents were property and business owners in this urban community. They owned hotels, garages, and restaurants during a period of time in Chicago history when many people of color experienced difficulty registering in white-owned hotels and eating in white-owned restaurants. This concerned my family. Through these businesses they established extensive business contacts with Jewish people. Those contacts blossomed into friendships, which meant spending time in each other's homes. Spending time included socially oriented business meetings with lots of food, laughter, and discussion on and off business topics. As a youngster, I understood that in my family, generally, "children should be seen and not heard." Therefore, although children might be present during adult conversations, children did not necessarily interact with adults.

My first schooling was in an all black middle-class private school. I attended this school from kindergarten through second grade. In third grade I began my public school journey, the first of several public schools that I would eventually attend. This public school was not the local school near my residence; however, this school was near the University of Chicago, about 15 minutes east of my residence. The location of this school was and still is in the urban community, but the population near the University of Chicago included a large percentage of Jewish people. This was significant to me, as I remember how empty this urban school was on Jewish holidays. Students in this urban public school near the University of Chicago walked home for lunch and I, with my sisters and brothers, walked to our "second home," an apartment near the school. In order for me to attend this public school, approximately 15 minutes from my residence, my parents made arrangements for a taxi to take my sisters and brothers and me to our "second home" in the mornings and pick us up after school Monday through Friday. This was the arrangement for me during the time I was in third, fourth, and fifth grade.

Initially my parents rented this apartment, our "second home," and hired a friend to "live" in the apartment, prepare our lunch, and provide before- and after-school supervision. This was the arrangement until my girlfriend's parents, friends of my family, purchased the building and moved in. Then my friend's family became the place for our morning drops and afternoon pick-ups by the taxi, as well as the place we ate lunch. I understood that my parents made these special arrangements in order for my sisters and brothers and me to attend, according to my parents, a "good school." My parents' perception of a "good school" was a concept that I would have an opportunity to ponder on many occasions, as I journeyed through several schools.

When I was in sixth grade I changed schools. This occurred because school officials at the public school near the University of Chicago notified my parents that we could no longer use the address of the rented apartment, our "second home," for the purpose of attending the school. Therefore, during sixth grade I attended the school around the corner from my residence.

This was now my third school experience, and I was now in a predominantly black public school, just around the corner from my residence. What an eye-opener. Soon after I arrived at this school, the *administrators suggested that I was "smart" and they wanted to double-promote me, which meant I would skip a grade. My mother in her wisdom refused. Rightfully, she determined that I did not need to skip a grade. Even at that time, as a youngster, I knew my mother was correct. The issue was that at this new public school (around the corner from my residence), a lot of the subject matter included concepts I had already studied at the public school just 15 minutes east of my residence, near the University of Chicago. Therefore, to the students and teachers I appeared advanced.*

I tried to formulate my concept of a "good school," a phrase my parents used often. I was very aware of the differences I had experienced at the two schools, namely teacher expectations of students. It seemed to me that teachers in the school near the University of Chicago offered challenging, thought-provoking assignments, whereas the teachers in the school near my house offered routine, game-like assignments. In other words, I felt that the teachers in this school around the corner from my residence simply allowed students to play games. Therefore, I did not believe that I was learning anything. At least, that was my perception.

Past 79th Street

Racist beliefs and feelings of people in America were not dismantled when the legal aspects of discrimination were dismantled. Literature regarding the mobility of various ethnic groups suggest that although middle-class blacks have experienced unprecedented social mobility, many continue to face racial discrimination in the housing market that constrains their residential mobility (Clark, 1996; Massey & Denten, 1987). Thus, moving has had significance in my family.

My parents decided that we should move from the family-owned apartment building on the Southside of Chicago to a house past "79th Street." The reason was because they were concerned about the apparent lack of "good education" my brothers and sisters and I were receiving from the public school around the corner from my residence. The new residence was still on the Southside of Chicago, but located further south, further away from downtown. The significance of this move was that according to popular concepts of urban, what we generally understand through the media, this new location was not considered urban simply because there were very, very, few people of color, and the community was less populated. There were very few apartment buildings; most of the residences were single-family dwellings. For us to move past 79th Street was indeed notable. It was documented that Chicago was racist, blacks and whites generally lived in separate communities, and black people did not live past 79th Street. I grew up with the understanding that there were some sections of Chicago where whites lived that could be dangerous for black people to even walk or drive through.

    I was now on my way to a different school, my fourth school, because my parents wanted my brothers and sisters and me to attend a "good school." My parents were insistent about finding "a good school." Therefore, it seemed important for us to leave the public school around the corner from our residence. Again I pondered what my parents meant by a "good school?" Was it a good school if it was private? I wondered about this, because my first schooling, kindergarten through second grade was in a private, all black middle-class school. My second school experience had been in the public school near the University of Chicago, a predominantly white community. Following that, my third school experience had been in the public school around the corner from my residence, a predominantly black community. And now on my school journey I was on to the fourth school.

    I was now in seventh grade. The new school, public, was near my soon-to-become new residence, which was located past 79th Street. The student population at the new school was predominantly white and the teachers were all white. I understood later that my parents were looking for a house to purchase in the area, and decided to enroll my brothers and sisters in me in a school in the area where they expected to purchase a house. Again, my parents hired a taxi to transport my brothers and sisters and me to this new public school. Subsequently, however, the address of the new house actually meant that I had to attend a different school for eighth grade, which would then become my fifth school experience. All these moves were made in search of a "good school." Nonetheless, I completed seventh grade at the same school, even after we had moved. For a brief period of time I enjoyed our new home and I enjoyed being able to play outside with some of my classmates, who all lived just north of 79th Street. I understood that for eighth grade I would have to attend school south of 79th Street, as that was the designated school for my now new home address just past 79th Street.

    Leaving the family-owned apartment building to move past 79th Street meant that I was leaving the comfortable quiet community where I had amassed so many warm memories. I was leaving the security of my extended family—grandparents, and uncle and aunt who lived in the same building. The community past 79th Street was possibly dangerous for my family, and certainly tense, given the social, political, and economic strain between blacks and whites at that time.

The Polish family who sold my parents the house past 79th Street explained that they were concerned the neighbors might be upset, if they learned that the incoming family was black. Therefore, the Polish family requested that all meetings with my parents at the house should take place after dark. And that is how my parents completed the purchase of this house. In later years my parents told me that we were the first black family to purchase a home past 79th Street. For years, we remained one of very few black families in this predominantly white community, which was considered urban given the proximity to people of color, and density in population. In other words, the new house was still in the city of Chicago.

In eighth grade I began attending the public school designated according to our now new address. This was now my fifth school experience. At that time, there were only about ten black students in the entire elementary school, and half were my brothers and sisters. I remember that almost daily students threw rocks at me, and yelled "nigga" or glared at me and pointed fingers. I eventually became the first black student to graduate from that local elementary school, just a few blocks from my new home.

After I graduated from eighth grade, I began what I considered a positive ninth grade experience in local public school high school designated per my address. No one yelled derogatory names or hurled rocks at me. The student population in this local public high school was predominantly white. There were a few students of color. I recall that the environment was pleasant and peaceful. To my surprise, during ninth grade my parents began saying that the schools in California were better. However, the groundwork for the move to California was laid through previous vacations we had spent in Los Angeles, California, visiting family. Again, this decision to move the family from Chicago to Los Angeles was inspired by my parent's persistence in looking for "better schools for the kids."

We left Chicago and made the 2,000-plus miles move to our new home in an urban community of California, and I enrolled in the local public school assigned to me according to my address. The school was Los Angeles High School. It was by now the most ethnically diverse school that I had attended. It appeared to me that the numbers were evenly divided among white, African-American, Asian, and Latino students. The Westside location of my home in Los Angeles, a middle to upper-middle-class community was in the "heart of Los Angeles" as defined by the media. It was about 20 minutes east of Beverly Hills, which at that time and presently was considered a wealthy upper-middle class community.

Generally, the Los Angeles High School students assumed that because I was from Chicago, I was "into the latest everything." I was uncomfortable with the assumptions students made about me, being "hip" and expecting me to know all the latest dances and how to date. I was not experienced in any of these areas. I made some feeble attempts to dispel these assumptions and present the "real" me. I tried to change those perceptions of me by explaining that I just did not know the latest dances, and I did not have the answers to those questions so important to teens about dancing and about dating. However, it seemed that the students just didn't hear me and did not want to believe that I was an exception to their perception about a teenager from Chicago.

The students had certain suppositions about people from Chicago, which led them to pressure me for information that I could not supply. When people determine that their image of a given situation is correct, it can be difficult to even suggest that the image is misconstrued. During those initial days at Los Angeles High School, I remember feeling perplexed about comments from my peers and the adults, when they learned that my parents moved our ten-member (two parents and eight children) family from Chicago to Los Angeles. The range of comments from people represented two extremes, which suggested that they thought we were either rich or we were poor: "Didn't that cost a lot of money, and with so many of you? Boy, you live in a big house? How can you afford to buy t-h-a-t (a reference to an item of my clothing, which sometimes was something I'd brought from Chicago)?"

Nevertheless, when questioned, I did not offer any comments or explanations. I did not respond to questions about how and why we moved from Chicago to Los Angeles. As a high school freshman, I seldom voiced my questions or concerns about anything. I believe it was because I didn't want to look silly. Perhaps this feeling was related to the common teenage sense of insecurity, or perhaps my life experiences up to that point resulted in this thought. At any rate, I determined it was more interesting and certainly safer to listen and observe versus talk. I kept my thoughts to myself and marveled at the conjectures many people made about people and circumstances around me.

In retrospect, I believe that at that time, although I generally felt comfortable in my self-imposed position of silence, that silence was an expression of my sense of voicelessness, to me a sense of powerlessness, and at the same time, a sense of being empowered. The sense of powerlessness was through my decision not to express my thoughts for fear of being misunderstood. On the other hand, the sense of being empowered resulted from the advice my parents gave me when I complained about being misunderstood, and the seemingly senseless behavior of people that puzzled me at times. My parents said, "Ignore ignorant behavior."

I questioned why many white students in Chicago shouted racial epithets at me, and I wondered why some people in Los Angeles seemed so curious about our move from Chicago. Repeatedly my parents recommended, "Ignore ignorant people." They were persistent about trying to help me embrace this idea about the questions I had relevant to peoples' behavior. Interestingly, throughout this period in my life of questioning in silence, I felt a sense of being empowered as I maintained this thought: "Ignore ignorant people." Although I decided to remain silent through many of the uncomfortable aforementioned situations, I never felt angry. It was as though I held a secret weapon. For this I credit my parents. They never focused on the negative behaviors of people, but rather modeled for me how to criticize a person's actions and not dismiss or negate the person.

AFTER SCHOOL HOURS IN THE HOOD

To my parents out-of-school activities were just as important as the in-school experiences. My parents believed it was important that their children "have opportunities that they didn't have growing up." For years, two ladies came to assist my mother with household chores such as cooking, cleaning, washing, and ironing. This freed my mother's time so she could make sure that my brothers and sisters and I completed homework assignments on time, arrived at all our after-school appointments, and that we practiced our musical instruments, which were piano and violin.

When I was ten years old my parents enrolled me in typing and shorthand classes that were held after school at a private secretarial school. It was expected that typing and shorthand skills would help me excel in school. Before I reached my teen years I was enrolled in other classes: voice (where I learned the proper way to breathe as I learned to sing in several languages), art (through the Art Institute in downtown Chicago), sewing, drama, and dance. I sang in the church choir, and for a period of time I played the piano for Sunday school. Also, we regularly visited many, many cultural events around Chicago at locations such as the Field Museum, the Natural Museum of Science and Industry, and the Goodman Theater. For me, life outside of school was interesting and rewarding. Activities after school kept us busy, but I enjoyed spending time with family and friends.

My parents were very involved in all aspects of my schooling. My mother attended most of the parent and teacher conferences. Almost every evening my mother read to my brothers and sisters and me before we went to bed. Before marriage my mother had been a librarian. She loved to read and wanted to pass that love on to her children. She cherished books and therefore bought us many.

In my household, education was emphasized, and therefore it was unquestioned that I would attend college. My parents constantly encouraged me to set goals and work them through. The focus in my family was in taking care of the business at hand, which meant, "take care of your studies." The persistence of my parents about finding a "good school for the kids," meant that I attended private and public elementary schools in Chicago, public high schools in Chicago and Los Angeles, and college in Mexico City, La Universidad de Las Americas (University of The Americas), where I earned my B.A. I earned my M.Ed from the University of Southern Mississippi, and my Ph.D from the State University of New York at Albany (SUNY). All of these schools were in urban communities.

I was a very disinterested, disconnected student from the time I entered kindergarten until I student taught, which was during my last semester of the undergraduate teacher education program at La Universidad de Las Americas in Mexico City. I wonder to what extent my attitude stemmed from a subconscious response to the way media marginalized people of color. Perhaps, if I had known any black educators, I might have been more excited about my school experiences. I did not know what I wanted to study in college, although I was certain I would attend and graduate. My mother suggested that I go into teaching. She said, "You could always get a job." What she did not tell me (she could not have known, or did she?) is that I would thoroughly enjoy teaching, and that teaching was my niche.

As an undergraduate student at La Universidad de Las Americas in Mexico City working on my B.A., I student taught in densely populated, very cosmopolitan, very urban, Mexico City. It was during that time I realized how much I absolutely loved teaching. After graduating with my Bachelor of Arts in Education I became an elementary school teacher in Mexico City. After school hours (my teaching assignment) in Mexico City, I completed training in the Berlitz method of English learning and taught classes to adults through that method. Subsequently, I established my own tutoring services and offered private lesson to people who wanted to learn English.

The media would lead us to believe that Americans live in one of two types of communities; an affluent middle-class and higher community like the suburbs, or an impoverished inner city, or ghetto, which are terms often associated with an urban community. My childhood and adult experiences in urban communities defy media accounts of economic and social lack. These accounts often leave the public with the idea that residents living in urban communities are deficient in environmental and personal resources.

DOES WHITE MAKE IT RIGHT?

This is the question a colleague asked as I shared some of my educational experiences with the authors of this book. In other words, what was the connection between my parents' constant, persistent efforts to keep me in "good schools," and the fact that student population in most schools I attended was predominantly white. In American society, white is normally associated with privilege, or what's "right." As a youngster I heard "If you're white you're right, if you're yellow you're mellow, if you're brown stick around, but if you're black get back." I can't help but wonder to what extent this influenced my sense of disconnectedness with school.

It is my opinion that media influences are relentless and clear, and they shape our views about beauty and success. Through the media Americans learn to define beauty and success through the constant barrage of images that suggest what is "right." To people of color the underrepresentation or misrepresentation of people of color in the media is glaring. Anglo-European values, beliefs, and achievements are the markers that define advantaged people in American society. Non-Anglo European people with values, beliefs, and achievements outside the Anglo-European markers are all too often labeled "the disadvantaged." In other words, difference is questioned, seen as less than; thus, difference is something in need of repair or correction (Banks & Banks, 1995; Hixson, 1991; Zeichner, 1992). I have had reason to reflect on the idea of privilege as it relates to my life.

People have questioned me about my life and suggested I was privileged. No doubt, my parents made my life comfortable through the thoughtful and caring living arrangements they provided and the principles they spoke into my life. However, I question the definition of a privileged life. The truth is that America is a race-based society, where by-and-large, people of color do not have a voice in what counts. In other words, in many sectors of our society, people of color do not have a strong voice in the social, political, and economic fabric of our society. The reality is that privilege is connected to skin color, and it is connected to how people decide to relate to each other. Therefore, privilege is strongly associated with the idea that the group in power decides how, when, and where to allow those with less power to offer their "voice," to be heard. With that in mind, the concept of a privileged person is one who has a respected voice in society about issues that impact important arenas in our society.

The race-based structure of our society "forced" my parents to make adjustments in my environment to ensure that I had broad experiences. This was particularly true about the types of schools I attended, and the many after-school events. My parents recognized the unequal structure of schools, so they carefully selected private and public schools I could attend. "Less rigorous" is the term that best describes my parents' description of the instructional program of schools with a large population of students of color. Through the years, I often heard the adult members of my family discussing the virtue of a school that offered students challenging, worthwhile instruction versus schools that just let students play games.

My parents always discussed college with the certainty that all their children would earn at least a bachelor degree. From the time I enrolled in kindergarten, I expressed total boredom with school. Therefore, when I said I wanted to attend college in Mexico City, my parents thought this was definitely a way to perhaps ensure that I would graduate from college. This is an example of my parents' efforts to offer me broad experience whereby I could experience personal and professional growth. And of course they thought I would receive a "good education" in the school in Mexico City.

The student population at La Universidad de Las Americas of course included Mexican Nationals, but also included a large percentage of white students, with many from the United States and Europe. Does this experience qualify me as privileged? Is the term "privilege" associated with the fact that I attended schools with a predominantly white student population? Do those who have not had the same experiences think that I am privileged simply because I earned the bachelor's degree from a university outside of the United States? Is it because I am an African American that sometimes, when people hear about my experiences in various educational settings, the comments suggest a sense of wonderment, as evidenced by questions like: "How did you get to Mexico? Didn't it cost a lot of money to go to school in Mexico? Was your father in the service?" (At that point, I remind the person that there was no American military presence in Mexico).

On occasion, other black people remind me that my schooling denied me the opportunity to learn about my culture or heritage because I attended schools dominated by whites and schools outside of the country. I cannot refute that fact. Throughout my school experiences, information in the textbooks about black people was limited or the information reflected a setting that was unfamiliar to me. In essence, not much information about blacks was included in textbooks, or the scant references to black people were about people living in Africa, which was foreign to me as a black person born and raised in the United States. Generally, throughout elementary and high school the textbook and film images of African people and their customs included only people dressed in loinclothes with spears in hand.

From elementary school through graduate school, for me black influences on the American society were inconsequential. That is to say, I was virtually unaware of noted accomplishments of black people anywhere in the world. As an adult, I began to question my seeming lack of historical presence as a person of African ancestry, as an African-American female. Thus, I started to "uncover" the truths about my African-American heritage. I was indeed proud, and yes, a little sad. As an adult, I was surprised to learn that the homeland of Africa, a portion of my ancestry, was and still is a rich continent where many highly respected scientific and mathematical concepts originated.

I did not study black history in school, and when I consider why not it is disturbing. "Calculated misrepresentation" is a phrase that best describes the reason why information in history books about black people was absent or twisted. To me the message was then, and in many segments of the American society it is still true today, that black people are not valued. In fact, in some locations of this country the educational system is structured in a way to clearly ensure academic failure of blacks and other people of color. Two significant effects on blacks are the result of societal treatment. First, for many black people, a sense of disdain is inherent in discussions about ancestry and physical features. Second, blacks in America are often socialized into their community with these gripping types of statements: "You've got to work harder; and you've got to pay strict attention to your appearance, or they [white folk] will look for ways to keep you down."

When I talk to young blacks, then I am aware of the impact these words have had on my life. I notice that in my efforts to develop the awareness in young blacks relative to the effects on their lives of the social, political, and economic dominance of white America, I have consciously passed on an interesting idea. It is that ingrained in our society are the subtle (and sometimes not too subtle) barriers (the White social, political, and economic structures) erected to keep people of color from their dreams.

I am not sure why my family did not make sure I learned about the history of African Americans. Did they somehow, unknowingly of course, participate in the plan to keep African Americans ignorant of their rich heritage? I attended schools in the urban community with a predominance of white students but attended churches with an all black membership. However, issues relevant to blacks seemed to be on the peripheral of my life. I heard news accounts about Elijah Muhammed and Martin Luther King, Jr. and understood that these men were passionate about social and political issues relevant to *people in the black community.* I heard about organizations such as CORE (Congress of Racial Equality) and The Black Panthers, but I never attended any meetings and I read very little of their literature. In retrospect, I believe the media had convinced me that these organizations had a radical agenda and the leaders engaged in subversive behavior. That type of behavior was definitely unattractive to me, a middle-class African American with a Christian upbringing. If I had participated in events with these organizations and/or others that provided information about my people, I might have embraced my schooling experiences with more "heart." I can only wonder about what might have been.

Clearly, racism does not end with economic and professional ascendancy. As an adult, racist encounters strike a nerve that will not allow me to be lulled to sleep. I look for opportunities to voice my concerns about racist, discriminatory practices toward people of color and African Americans in particular.

Perhaps there is an assumption that I have lived a life of ease and have not had to overcome critical obstacles. Although on occasion some people have assumed that my school experiences classify me as privileged; nevertheless, subtle discriminatory practices were (and still are) the order of the day in my world. I question whether people who are really privileged actually have to think that everything they do must be better, or that they have to work harder in order to experience the same opportunities as others in the society. For many in the black community, the reality is that they do question whether equal efforts result in equal opportunities. For many black people social justice is synonymous with the struggle—and the struggle is ongoing—to find personal fulfillment in a world that consistently excludes you.

Fortunately, through the direction and guidance of my family I have positive childhood memories about living in urban communities—Chicago, Los Angeles, and Mexico City. Interestingly, I remember sensing compassion for any individual who demonstrated negative behavior or tried to create difficult circumstances for me. Respect was emphasized in my home. My parents explained to me that you must first respect yourself, and only then can you respect others. Inherent in respect is the idea that difference does not mean that something is wrong and needs to be corrected. That thought still rings true today for me.

DISPEL ASSUMPTIONS ABOUT URBAN: VIABLE PRESERVICE AND INSERVICE PROGRAMS

The hallmark of democracy is supposed to be the respect for diversity (Hillard, 1991/1992). Multicultural education is a place to begin dialogue about respect. Multicultural education originated in the 1960s as an outgrowth of the civil rights movement (Sobol, 1990), and has developed its own momentum, due to the increasingly diverse student population. The focus on multicultural education marks the nation's efforts to adjust the inequities of our society. The focus of multicultural education is "to create equal educational opportunities for students from diverse racial, ethnic, social class, and cultural groups so that they can function effectively in a pluralistic democracy society"; this is schooling for "equity, justice, and cultural democracy" (Banks & Banks, 1995). Multicultural education encompasses a theory about the content of education, the teaching and learning process, and the very purpose of education. It is a work in progress.

Teacher education programs are under great pressure today to show that they are preparing students to work with diverse student populations (NCATE, 1995). Bennett (1995a) estimated that by the year 2000, over 30% of our school-age population would be children of color. Teacher education programs are responsible for preparing teachers who promote meaningful, engaging, learning experiences for all students, regardless of race, cultural and linguistic background, ethnic heritage, or gender. Virtually all university programs include a required course on diversity. Too often the curriculum is presented through a homogeneous funnel, from the white perspective (Fine, 1991; Tierney, 1992). In these cases, the non-white people are perceived as "at risk" or lacking what is needed to be successful in this society.

Gay (1986) and Zeichner (1992) indicate that most teacher preparation programs present multicultural topics in a piecemeal format. According to Zeichner (1992), the piecemeal format generally includes two approaches to preparing teachers for diverse student populations. One is to integrate issues of diversity throughout course work and field experiences, and the other represents an add-on to regular teacher education programs. These multicultural topics are generally organized around acknowledging and/or celebrating differences, and the process often discourages questioning. I suggest that this process allows false assumptions about people to continue to flourish.

Is it possible that multicultural studies actually provide a platform to guise racism in a politically correct format? This idea is particularly interesting given the current trend in education, which is to include a focus on social justice. A platform of social justice encourages questioning of the status quo. For teachers in urban American classrooms, the questioning process should include discussion about their understanding of culture and how society casts their culture, and the connections between culture, ethnicity, gender, and sexual orientation.

People can be victims of their experiences. Too often people make generalizations about other people, ideas, and events on the basis of their personal constructions of reality (past experiences). Generally, the idea of questioning differences threads multicultural programs. However, some people fail to regard new visions of reality (new experiences) that conflict with their own meaning making. The organization of multicultural education programs can challenge those generalizations. On the other hand, Bennett (1995b) suggested that to study or to dwell on differences could perpetuate prejudice and foster racism. For this reason some people might suggest we should discourage programs in multicultural education and state, "We're all the same. I don't see color." Most recently, the division in America was evident through the highly publicized Rodney King and O.J. Simpson trials during the 1990s.

There are specific learning outcomes for students in teacher education programs that should prepare them to work with diverse student populations. Some outcomes include developing an understanding about other cultures, embracing multiple perspectives, demonstrating appreciation for individuals from different cultural or ethnic groups, and understanding the concepts about power and marginalization as they relate to people of color and people living in urban communities. The scope of multicultural studies is so extensive that it is important for students in teacher education programs to ask questions, search for new ideas, and act as self-directed learners in their studies and throughout their lives. All teachers, but particularly those who are, or will be, working in urban communities, need to develop clear perspectives about historical and present-day issues relevant to urban communities, and possible assumptions about people who live in those communities. There are exceptions to the perceptions. Furthermore, teachers need to define their collective and individual responsibility toward making a difference where they can influence, be that within their family or in the community.

Currently, as assistant professor in the School of Education Chapman University teacher preparation program, my major responsibility includes teaching and research in literacy development. A significant number of the enrollees in the teacher preparation program are recently hired elementary school teachers in the process of earning their teaching credentials. Based on the idea that all instruction flows from relationships, I encourage the credential candidates in my class to examine the assumptions they may have regarding teaching and learning in a classroom with a diverse student population, particularly when the school is located in an urban community. Teacher assumptions influence the curriculum, and it is expected that a strong instructional curriculum should reflect the diversity in the classroom.

To any situation in life we bring the total of all our experiences. I firmly believe that my varied living and teaching experiences in urban communities have helped me formulate ideas about the connections between teaching and learning in a diverse student population. The goal of teaching is to help people learn. Learning is the process of making sense of the world. Coming up with clear learning outcomes can be difficult and sometimes more challenging in the urban schools. Nevertheless, I encourage students in the education program to grasp the idea that good teaching hinges on authentic relationships, wherein teachers let students know they are valued for who they are and what they bring to interactions. Students filter subject matter through the perceived relationship they have with the teacher. Personalized schooling begins when dedicated teachers take a proactive stand in a child's life to accomplish the following:

> Combine content knowledge and subject-specific pedagogical knowledge with an understanding of the dynamics of diversity, the realities of societal oppression, and the impact of a myriad of contextual factors on student achievement will increase opportunity for improved educational outcomes for all students. (Hixson, 1991)

Many multicultural programs outline what to do to people instead of emphasizing respectful interactions among all peoples. It is important to encourage teachers to explore assumptions they have about people from diverse backgrounds. Stereotypes in our culture are widely known and can influence our behavior beyond the limits of what some people might want to admit. Repression of stereotyped thoughts can lead to thoughts that rebound in greater force. For that reason, sometimes people with very strong prejudices rebel against involvement in multicultural programs, as it threatens their way of being.

A discussion about multicultural education has to include a discussion about the underpinnings of education: the aims, claims, values, and beliefs. An important question to consider is this: What would happen if schools actually graduated large numbers of skilled people of color (people of non-European descent) who expected to obtain top positions in society as decision makers? This does not happen, and too often people of color blame themselves and not the system. I believe that the teacher preparation program we need actually threatens the elite.

The power base in the social, political, and economic arenas of America would be shaken if large numbers of skilled people, particularly people in the urban communities who were traditionally unheard, actually graduated and became productive, viable participants in society. The teacher education program we need is one in which the core belief of every teacher is this: Every child is reachable and therefore teachable. However, it takes courage for people in power to admit they feel threatened and not become hostile when laws are passed in an effort to correct inequities. Also, it takes courage for people to admit that the essence of multicultural education in its current state, a cursory review of various cultures, or a celebration of heroes and holidays, is a polite way to maintain the status quo. Multicultural education can provide an academic focus on black people and other people of color, particularly people from oppressed groups.

Absent from most multicultural programs is a discussion about "whiteness" and the privileged nature of being white in America. For some people it is difficult to examine the ideology of whiteness without infusing blame and/or shame about the ways that privilege dominates the masses. Perhaps this is how false assumptions about urban communities are maintained.

I began this chapter with a discussion about the position of power that media has through developing and helping to maintain stereotypes and prejudices. The media helps to shape public opinion by selecting issues, setting the agenda, and framing the issues and thought procedures. Now that overtly hostile racial attitudes are socially undesirable, racial prejudice has gone underground. Nevertheless, as a nation we tolerate media depictions that denigrate various ethnic groups. Stereotypes and prejudices about a people are based on assumptions. These assumptions result when there is a lack of accurate information.

In preservice and inservice programs for teachers, it is important to include discussions about media influences on discriminatory assumptions about people, particularly about the lives of people in urban communities. This type of discussion can draw attention to the deep roots of discrimination. It's time for the media to present a more accurate description of life in urban communities. There are segments of urban life that the media do not illuminate. Many people in urban communities are educated and live happy, peaceful, productive lives as middle-class citizens. However, I suppose that this type of information doesn't sell and produce the dollars. For example, discussion about people in urban communities who are an exception to the poverty and squalor generally associated with urban communities would disturb the public's perception about those communities.

Students are identified through ethnicity and race, and they in turn define themselves through ethnicity and race. Therefore, teachers need to understand how these concepts influence students' school performance. Institutional racism (intentional and unintentional) perpetuates negative images of particular groups and seeks to retain them in an inferior status. Perhaps, as we continue to dialogue, walls of assumptions will crumble faster. This is a hopeful thought.

AFTER THE STRUGGLE

Well, there it is. I've said it. The process of writing this chapter has been a long, arduous task. I am indeed grateful to my colleagues, the other authors in *this* book. Through their encouragement I ventured into the uncomfortable place of self-disclosure to people I can't see, those who will read what I've written. When face-to-face with anyone, I generally don't shy away from an opportunity to share about any portion of my life. However, it feels risky to present this written account about portions of my life. I can't read the faces of the readers, so I can't determine if the reader really understands what I'm trying to convey through this chapter. The black experience is legitimate. My life has been my life, and in a word, BEAUTIFUL!

I'm aware that SOME of my African-American "brothers and sisters" may question why I want to say anything "to those white people. You know they don't care, and they'll only use your information against you." SOME of my white "brothers and sisters" may respond with that all too common comment of "My, you are really unique." Does that statement suggest that I am an anomaly? Not in my opinion, not at all. I don't feel like an exception. Finally, I must admit that I can't imagine possible responses to this chapter from any of my other "brothers and sisters." As I ponder these thoughts, with a peaceful heart, I can only say, "There, I said it."

REFERENCES

Alba, R. D., & Nee, V. (1997). Rethinking assimilation theory for a new era of immigration. *International Migration Review, 16*(1), 45-77.

Alcoff, L. M. (1996). Philosophy and racial identity. *Radical Philosophy, 75,* 5-14.

Ayto, J. (1990). *Dictionary of word origins.* New York: Arcade Publishing.

Banks, J. A., & Banks, C. A. M. (1995). Introduction. In J. A. Banks & C.A.M. Banks (Eds.), *Handbook of research on multicultural education.* New York: Macmillan.

Baker, L., Serpell, R., & Sonnenschein, S. (1995). Opportunities for literacy learning in the homes of urban preschoolers. In L. M. Morrow (Ed.), *Family literacy: Connections in schools and communities.* Newark, DE: International Reading Association.

Bennett, C. (1995a). *Comprehensive multicultural education: Theory and practice* (3rd ed.). Boston: Allyn & Bacon.

Bennett, C. (1995b). Preparing teachers for cultural diversity and national standards of academic excellence. *Journal of Teacher Education, 46,* 259-265.

Blair, C. J. (1988). Writing about the Cosby Show. *English Journal, 61.*

Brand, D. (1987, August 31). The new whiz kids. *Time,* 130, pp. 42-51.

Brantlinger, E. A. (1993). *The politics of social class in secondary school.* New York: Teachers College Press.

Carter, T. P., & Chatfield, M. L. (1986). Effective bilingual schools: Implications for policy and practice. *American Journal of Education, 95*(1), 200-232.

DeBaryshe, B. D. (1995). Joint picture-book reading correlates of early oral language skill. *Journal of Applied Developmental Psychology, 16*(1), 1-20.

Delgado, R. (Ed.). (1995). *Critical race theory: The cutting edge.* Philadelphia: Temple University Press.

Ellison, R. (1982). *Invisible man* (30th ed.). New York:Random House.

Fine, M. (1991). *Framing dropouts: Notes on the politics of an urban public high school.* Albany: State University of New York Press.

Flaxman, E., & Inger, M. (1991, September). Parents and schooling in the 1990s. *The ERIC Review, 1*(3), 2-6.

Gay, G. (1986). Multicultural teacher education. In J. A. Bands and J. Lynch (Eds.), *A multicultural education in Western societies* (pp. 154–177). London: Holt, Rinehart, and Winston.

Greenberg, S. B. (1995). *Middle class dreams: The politics and power of the new American majority.* New York: Times Books.

Hilliard, Asa G. (December 1991/January 1992). Why we must pluralize the curriculum. *Educational Leadership, 4*(49), 12–16.

Hixson, J. (1991). *Multicultural issues in teacher education: Meeting the challenge of student diversity.* Paper presented at the annual meeting of the American Educational Research Association, Chicago, IL.

Kozol, J. (1991). *Savage inequalities; Children in America's schools.* New York: Crown.
Lipset, S. M. (1996). *American exceptionalism.* New York: W.W. Norton.
Massey, D. S., & Denton, N. A. (1997). Trends in residential segregation of Black, Hispanics, and Asians: 1970-1980. *American Sociological Review, 52,* 802-825.
McLemore, S.D., & Romo, H.D. (1998). *Racial and ethnic relations in America* (5th ed.). Boston: Allyn and Bacon.
McQueen, M. (1989, February 23). People with the least to fear from crime drive the crime issue. *Washington Post,* p. A1.
Means, B., & Knapp, M. S. (1991). *Teaching advanced skills to educationally disadvantaged students.* Washington, DC: U. S. Department of Education.
National Council for Accreditation of Teacher Education (NCATE). (1995). *Standards, procedures, and policies for the accreditation of professional education units.* Washington, DC: Author.
Oakes, J. (1985). *Keeping track: How schools structure inequality.* New Haven, CT: Yale University Press.
Obgu, J. U. (1987). Variability in minority school performance: A problem in search of an explanation. *Anthropology and Education Quarterly, 18*(4), 312-334.
Ogbu, J. U. (1991). Immigrant and involuntary minorities in comparative perspective. In J. Ogbu & M. Gibson (Eds.), *Minority status and schooling: A comparative study of immigrant and involuntary minorities* (pp. 3-33). New York: Garland.
Ogbu, J. U. (1992). Understanding cultural diversity and learning. *Educational Researcher, 21*(8), 5-14.
Ogbu. J. U. (1994). Racial stratification and education in the United States. Why inequalities persist. *Teachers College Record, 96*(2), 264-298.
Ogbu, J. U. (1998). Voluntary and involuntary minorities: A cultural-ecological theory of school performance with some implications for education. *Anthropology and Education Quarterly, 2*(2), 155-158.
Rumbaut, R. G. (1997). Ties that bind: Immigration and immigrant families in the United States. In A. Booth, A. Crouter, & N. Landale (Eds.), *Immigration and the family: Research and policy on U.S. immigrants* (pp. 3-46). Mahwah, NJ: Erlbaum.
Sharpe, D., & Puente, M. (1994, July 26). Minorities consider the media unfair. *USA Today,* p. 1A.
Sobol, T. (1990). Understanding diversity. *Educational Leadership, 48*(3), 27-30.
Spiegel, D. L. (1994). A portrait of parents of successful readers. In *Fostering the love of reading: The affective domain in reading education.* Newark, DE: International Reading Association.
Stone, J. (1985). *Racial conflict in contemporary society.* Cambridge, MA: Harvard University Press.
Tiernery, W. (1992). *Official encouragement, institutional encouragement: Minorities in academe—the Native American experience.* Norwood, NJ: Ablex.

U. S. Department of Education National Center for Education Statistics. Digest of Education Statistics 1997, NCES 98-015, by Thomas D. Snyder. Production Manager, Charlene M. Hoffman Program Analyst, Claire M. Geddes. Washington DC.

van Dijk, T. A. (1998). *New(s) racism: A discourse analytical approach.* http://www.hum.uva.nl/teun/racpress.htm

Zeichner, K. M. (1992). *Educating teachers for cultural diversity.* East Lansing, MI: National Center for Research on Teacher Learning.

II

RETHINKING CURRICULUM

4

Community Matters

Tom Wilson

> *To establish a new framework, we need to begin with a frank acknowledgment of the basixc humanness and Americanness of each of us. And we must acknowledge that as a people—E Pluribus Unum—we are on a slippery slope toward economic strife, social turmoil, and cultural chaos.*
> Cornel West (1993, p. 4)

As a white male just entering my 70th decade and in spite of some 45 years of varied experiences in educational institutions as public school teacher, administrator, and university professor, I ask myself what can I possibly contribute to a discussion dealing with urban education that hasn't already been said in one form or another? However, after starting this chapter a number of times, rejecting a variety of drafts, and chewing on the issue as the proverbial dog on a bone, and rejecting a charge of false modesty, I think the best I can do is offer some suggestions that might stimulate further dialogue. In doing this, I need to declare up front that my offering does not come from a base of extensive experience in those schools conventionally characterized rightly or not as urban, (although I have worked in a few that might qualify) but rather from years of struggling with the problem of determining the constituent elements—the "whats"—of a good, moral, and critical democratic education which deconstructs or "deghettos" the mind regardless of setting and then collaboratively designing programs—the "hows"—to actualize these "whats."

I need to add that such struggle draws from a variety of influences. As I have been often reminded, none of us stands alone, but rather we find ourselves perched on a great number of shoulders, some perhaps broader than others, but all necessary to give our beliefs stability. Thus, I find myself looking down upon and simultaneously drawing sustenance from a rather eclectic group, some well known requiring little or no elaboration, others less known, yet all with something to say to me about urban education. Rather arbitrarily, I have divided these influences into three groups. The first consists of "theorists," the second of "practitioners," and the third, "significant others." I do recognize a problem here in that it may make artificial categories. With Dewey, I believe that theory and practice are reciprocal in nature and that theory must have practical consequences and that practice must be grounded in theory. As I have heard it, "We need both plumbers and philosophers, for if not, neither our pipes or ideas will hold water." My division, therefore, is a matter of mere convenience rather than any attempt to create precise distinctions.

In free association and thus in no particular order, the theorists Karl Marx, John Dewey, Paulo Freire, Nel Noddings, Larry Kohlberg, Christian Bay, Abraham Maslow, Angus Campbell, Henry Giroux, Milton Rokeach, Kurt Lewin, Matt Miles, Jack Gibb, Chris Argyris, Elizabeth Léonie Simpson, Carole Pateman, Carol Gilligan, bell hooks, Peter Park, Martin Luther King, Seymour Sarason, Jane Roland Martin, Amy Goodmann, Fritz Perls, Maxine Greene, Michael Apple, Ted Sizer, John Goodlad, Cornel West, Eric Fromm, James Baldwin, John Rawls, Jürgen Habermas, Noam Chomsky, Jacques Derrida, and Myles Horton come immediately to mind. Of these, John Dewey and Paulo Freire arise as the most influential. For Dewey, it comes from my discovery after discovery that most every "great" idea I think I have had, alas Dewey already had it. For Paulo, it comes not only from the virtues of intellect, his humility, his love, his compassion, but also from his courage to place them in concrete action. These two close companions of mine, Dewey vicariously through his writing and that of others about him, Paulo directly through his writing and personal friendship, in combination with my other teachers listed above, continually provide ideas that require, if not force, my constant attention, reflection, testing, and critique. In fact, they are merciless, they rarely leave me alone.

The second collection of influences come from the practitioners—as if, erroneously, they lacked theory—those individuals who daily must meet or have met the contingencies and dilemmas of daily school and community life in urban or poor rural settings, and with a few exceptions, do not carry national or international attention: Debra Meier formerly of Central Park East; Bob McCarthy former Headmaster, Brookline High School, Brookline, MA:, Judy Baca, Social and Public Art Resource Center, Venice, CA; Doris Alvarez, Former Principal, Hoover High School, San Diego, CA; Alex Yussem, Superintendent, Garvey School District, Rosemead, CA; Judy Magsaysay, Principal, and the teachers, Pio Pico Elementary School, Santa Ana, CA; the Rethinking Schools group, La Escuela Fratney Elementary School, Milwalkee, WI; Bill Terrazes and the Students for Cultural and Linguistic Democracy, Channel Island High School, Oxnard, CA; George Wood, Institute for Democratic Education, Ohio University, former Principal, Federal Hocking High School, Stewart, OH, and currently Director, Wildwood Secondary School, Los Angeles, CA; Suzanne SooHoo, School of Education, Chapman University; Neil Schmidt, Superintendent, Santa Monica-Malibu Unified Schools, CA; and the faculty and students of O'Farrell Community Intermediate School, San Diego, CA.

The third group, the "significant others," consists of a plethora of unnamed professional colleagues and thousands of students with whom I have had the privilege of knowing and working with from preschool through graduate education. Their influence, both subtle and direct, has been priceless. These critical democratic and ethical educators, those who in Paulo's terms, "dare to teach," those who have "the courage to teach" (Palmer, 1998), in conjunction with many, many students, steadily serve to disabuse me of my moments of disquiet about the state of education and thereby continually place before me the requirement that to be fully human I must assume ". . . the right and the duty to opt, to decide, to struggle, to be political" (Freire, 1998, p. 53).

Now having said all of the above to make it as explicit as possible for the reader my own orientation, I want to turn to the specifics of my suggestions, which flow from the rich and eclectic stream of ideas and actions of my three groups of influence.

It should not be news to any one that for its entire history the adequacy and effectiveness of American public eduction has been under attack from both the left and the right. During the past 20 years or so, these assaults, primarily coming from the right, have hurled barrage after rhetorical barrage aimed at the schools' failings academically (rarely stated as even "intellectually"), thus putting our nation "at risk" by producing students incapable of competing in an increasingly sophisiticated global economy. This finding resulted in a myraid of corporatized, commercialized, marketized reform efforts designed to improve student achievement and performance (images of animals in the circus come to mind here) usually assessed by ritualized testing whereby the test as "examination" has achieved a cold, clinical iconic if not fetish-like reverence (just where is Foucault when we need him?) devoid of any human warmth and exclusive of anything smacking of affect, emotion, or personalization. Moacir Gadotti and Paulo Freire (Freire, 1993, p. 90) lament the continuing separation, the lack of dialectical unity between the cognitive and affective domains in which traditional pedagogy ignores the determining nature of the affective in constructing cognition, a finding that seems to me to be a more recent reiteration of the work of confluent educators some 30 years previously (Brown, 1971). Most of current school change frenzy, lacking this unity, is usually jazzed up with a strong paean to the doctors of technological rationality who prescribe computers with a strong dose of e-mail to cure us all. Jennifer Smith, an English teacher in an urban Chicago high school, rejects the diagnosis: "I wish I, like the current administration, could believe that if we just had connections to the Internet, all of my kids would become honor students" (1998, p. 32). Technology, testing, national and state standards, narrow positivism, vouchers, privatization, and control of teachers' work (although not usually defined as such) still dominates much of the chitchat about education. Although many are apt to take umbrage with the use of the term "chitchat" as disengenous, I disagree, for most talk about education within schools (and we include the university here as well) is like, as Freire often said, "mosquitoes running across the water" rather than plumbing the depths of authenticity, dialogue, and ideal speech (where is Habermas when we need him?). Elmore (1996, pp. 1-27), along with others (Sarason; 1982, Tye, 2000), argues convincingly that although there has been massive changes in institutional surface structures, the core of educational practice—the deep structure—remains virtually impervious to change in all but a small fraction of American schools and classrooms. The core for Elmore consists of understandings about the nature of knowledge and learning, structural arrangements of schools such as physical space, student grouping practices, relations between teachers and teachers and students, and processes for assessing and communicating student learning. Missing from this keen analysis, however, is an understanding as to what end the core should be directed, what is its ultimate aim? I would argue that the answer must be democracy. The cement that binds, or should bind, the elements of the core together is a conscious attention devoted to the development of a democratic culture, thereby trumping the nation-at-risk thesis.

I do believe that there are cracks, small cracks, in the impervious wall. Although the outcome is far from clear, it is within this democratic grounding of the core that things are perhaps looking up. The rhetoric, the "espoused theory" of which Argyris (1990) speaks, is being matched by practice. The bald-faced functionalism and narrow positivistic implications of the nation-at-risk hypothesis is under siege by a dialectical counterattack formed from notions of ethics, community, voice, and empowerment. For example, an ERIC search using key words "democracy and schools" revealed 705 documents (Wilson, 1997). Solid examples do exist of democratic schools or programs (Apple & Beane,1995; Goodman, 1992; Levine, Lowe, Peterson, & Tenorio, 1995; Meier, 1996; Mosher, Kenny, & Garrod, 1994; Power, Higgins, & Kohlberg, 1989; and Wood, 1992, 1998). As well, the Coalition of Essential Schools, after some 15 years of virtually ignoring any direct discourse to democratic education (Malarkey, 1998; Wilson, 2000a), has recently added a tenth common democratic principle to its statement of purpose:

> The school should demonstrate non-discriminatory and inclusive policies, practices, and pedagogies. It should model democratic practices that involve all who are directly affected by the school. The school should honor diversity and build on the strengths of its communities, deliberately and explicitly challenging all forms of inequity.

Yet, it is premature to come to a conclusion that these sources, impressive as they might be, signify democratic changes on any broad scale. I find myself agreeing with Buras (1999, p. 73) that:

> ... progressive struggles have had an impact on schools, (yet) such gains have not significantly transformed curricular content and pedagogical practice overall ... (and) ... on the whole, traditional curricular and pedagogical forms remain intact, and progressive practices are more often the exception rather than the rule.

The Elmore thesis still seems to hold in the context of the totality of American education.

Before proceeding with a concrete description of still another democratically based program that might have bearing on urban education, I need to ground my suggestion by laying out some ideas about the relationship among the individual, ethics, and democracy itself.

Dewey (1888) made the connection between ethics, the individual, and democracy over 100 years ago when he wrote ". . . democracy is an ethical idea, the idea of a personality, with truly infinite capacities, incorporate with every man. Democracy and the one, the ultimate, ethical ideal of humanity are to my mind synonyms" (p. 248).

Notice the power of Dewey's phrasing. Democracy, an "ethical idea," is at the same time an "idea of personality"—the ideal of democracy therefore exists in every person. At the same time, there is an extension beyond the individual to all of humanity. The person is sacrosanct, yet only in concert with others. But how can this be, how does one be one and still be the other? One answer is in the conceptualization of a democratic, transforming personhood.

Transformation is taken herein as a complicated, slow, interactive, developing process that occurs over the span of a lifetime. Development is not a fixed entity to which one aspires, but rather is a phenomenon that plays out in daily existence. I see as its goal Dewey's (1893) sense of self-realization as a moral ideal anchored in concrete activity, of a ". . . notion of a working or practical self" (p. 44) as opposed to ". . . the self as a presupposed fixed *schema* or outline" (p. 43) to be filled in. Development centers on the now rather than the future. It certainly is aware of the future, but its emphasis is upon the present self rather than the ". . . attainment of a remote ideal self" (p. 49).

For Dewey (1888), the potential of democracy, as an ideal, exists in every personality and thus final responsibility rests with the person:

> In one word, democracy means that *personality* is the first and final reality. It admits that the full significance of personality can be learned by the individual only as it is already presented to him in objective form in society; it admits that the chief stimuli and encouragements to the realization of personality come from society; but it holds, none the less, to the fact that personality cannot be procured for any one, however degraded and feeble, by any one else, however wise and strong. It holds that the spirit of personality dwells in every individual and that the choice to develop it must proceed from that individual . . . (and) . . . the idea that personality is the one thing permanent and abiding worth, and that in every human individual there lies personality. (p. 244)

Dewey's stress upon ultimate individual responsibility seems close to the Greek notion of *eudaimonia* wherein self-knowledge is essential for its intrinsically rewarding and actualizing properties. Norton (1991) writes " . . . according to eudaimonism, persons innately possess not only potential excellences (the aretai that inhere in their ideal personhood, or *daimons*), but aspiration to actualize these excellences" (p. 3). And such desire is, at the root, ethical. To be human is ". . . to bear the moral responsibility to discover and progressively actualize this worth" (p. 107).

Thus, democratic programs need to focus on individual personality, on personhood and its moral and actualizing potential in terms of students' current development. Although sensitive to future development, it can only work with individuals as they present themselves in the present. Democratic personhood development is a "do-it-yourself job" that one works on actively in day-to-day practice. This notion of individualism, however, is not one of self-centeredness, it is not one of "selfishness and egoism" (Miller, 1979, p. 5). Nor is it as described by Tocqueville:

> . . . a mature and calm feeling, which disposes each member of the community to sever himself from the mass of his fellows and draw apart . . . so that . . . he willingly leaves society at large to itself. . . (which "throws" the individual) . . . back forever upon himself alone and threatens in the end to confine him entirely within the solitude of his own heart. (Miller, 1979, p. 5)

Rather, individualism/personhood is akin with what Miller, drawing from Marx, calls individuation, a process ". . . whereby human beings become distinctive, autonomous, and self-conscious agents, each capable of purposefully reshaping the natural world and of independently evaluating moral claims" (p. 5). Yet, in a seemingly paradoxical manner, such agency can only be realized in equal concert with others in community. Gilbert (1990) states the case in terms of a dynamic interrelationship among individualism, moral personality, and capacity:

> In modern terms, it may be helpful to think of capacity for moral personality as a capacity for individuality. The former involves a self capable of fair cooperation with others, a centrally ethical agent; the latter additional features relevant to living one's own life. This dialectical combination of egalitarianism social relationships and individuality is what Marx and Hegel might have called *social individuality* . . . (and) . . . the human capacity for mutual recognition and individuality is inherently relational . . . . (p. 2)

I feel relatively confident that the development of democratic persons as conceptualized above has, in large, not occurred within nor been served by existing school education programs and certainly not by the corporatized school reform efforts that have placed us under surveillance and close scrutiny these past 20 years. Thus, my conclusion that the school's direct impact upon the democratic formation of its charges is, in general, far from adequate and in specific instances negative, still holds (Wilson, 1974/1975). Whereas many conditions might be cited as to the causes of this finding, a major contributor, to a large extent, is the schools' failure to break out of a culture of psychological reductionism. The marking of the student and increasingly the parents (often as the identified patients) as *the* variables, as atomistic entities, within a narrow analysis of existing school authority structures and classroom patterning drives out attention paid to the total educational environment. The almost 30-year gap between Sarason's (1971) "structural regularities" and Tye's (2000) "hard truths" forceably call our attention to the restraining prison of the persistent, static organizational core. It remains as Levin wrote in 1960:

> . . . the school as a *total environment* provides little opportunity for the young to learn or practice social responsibility, moral judgement, or any cognitive or skills requiring the exercise of critical independent judgement . . . (and) . . . so long as schools continue to function primarily as custodial institutions it is hard to be optimistic about the prospects for the success of any program of social or moral education within the school. (1960, p. 89)

Democratic formation involves much more than mere manipulation of teaching method and content. What is necessary is an emphasis upon the culture of educational experiences in which the entire environment, the *weltanschauung,* the democratic core becomes the means by which development is affected. Within this context, what if students could be freed from the existing restrictions, what if they had extensive time to engage in making major decisions about themselves and their own educational process? What indeed if there could be:

> . . . room for the private vision, for the playful, even passionate, reordering of felt reality. There are images of reality that lie outside the domain of analytical thought. To put them to the tests of logical or empirical proof is to threaten that fragile sense of the uniquely valid in one's own perceptions that is so essential to selfhood. . . . In short, (the) . . . classroom should be at once a labora-

tory, a studio, and a forum, a place where the rationale and the romantic can exist side by side as equally valid categories of understanding, where the two cultures of science and art find common ground. (Whitmore, 1970, p. 283)

What if the entire environment altered and the student/teacher authority relationship became transformed? What if the entire process changed in accord with the situation Maslow discussed in which teachers and students:

> . . . behaved in a very unneurotic way simply by interpreting the whole situation differently, i.e., as a pleasant collaboration rather than a clash of wills, of authority, of dignity, etc. The replacement of artificial dignity—which is easily and inevitably threatened—with the natural simplicity which is *not* easily threatened; the giving up of the attempt to be omniscient and omnipotent; the absence of student threatening authoritarianism; the refusal to regard the students as competing with each other or with the teacher; the refusal to assume the "professor" stereotype; and the insistence on remaining as realistically human, as say, a plumber or a carpenter; all of these created classroom atmosphere in which suspicion, wariness, defensiveness, hostility, and anxiety disappeared. (1956, pp. 190–191)

Now if this call seems cut from the fabric of the late 1960s and 1970s, the reader is correct (the dating of the citations herein may have been a clue, of course). Such a program at the high school level existed in the heart of Orange County, California, in 1972-1973. I believe its relevance for current educational practice, urban or otherwise, is as strong now as it was then. Therefore, to flesh out the bones of my suggestion, I will describe a community-based education program, the Newport Plan (NPP), that I, as an assistant high school principal, and my teacher and student colleagues developed. Next, I will reflect upon that experience in light of its shortcomings in terms of my own subsequent understandings and close by arguing that the NPP plan has much to offer as a dialogue of hope for both urban and general education.

NEWPORT PLAN

Initiated in 1972, the overarching purpose of the Newport Plan (NPP) (Wilson, 1975) was to establish a public school, alternative educational program in which secondary school students spent the majority of their time within the local (and at times distant) community using the resources of the community as *the* fundamental curriculum. Although not stated explicitly at the time, its retrospective and essential goal was to test John Dewey's (1916) general notions that students are capable of significant learning drawing from their own strengths and interests in an experiential manner. To this end, the NPP assumed that secondary school students could take major responsibility for such an endeavor outside the confines of the school itself and the normal school day.

It was further hypothesized that NPP students would demonstrate development towards a theoretical construct of the democratic person when compared with students in the best of existing programs *within* the existing school curriculum. Whereas democratic personhood was conceptualized as consisting of open-minded/nondogmatic belief systems, political efficacy, higher stages of moral reasoning, and self-actualization, only open-mindedness (Rokeach, 1960) and political efficacy (Campbell, 1964; Easton & Dennis, 1967; Hess, 1971; Lane, 1959) were directly addressed.[1]

The existing school's impact on the democratic development of students was examined and found to be lacking. It was assumed that the cultural patterns, the almost exclusive emphasis on a priori curricula, the ignoring of affective concerns, the lack of conscious attention paid to the concept of community, and the absence of organizational self-examination within the traditional school blocked the development of democratic students. The requirement was for a new ethos, a democratic environment in which Kurt Lewin's $B=f\ (p,e)$ wherein behavior is a function of the person and the environment could play out (Conway, Vickers, & French, 1992). This new environment, the NPP, was characterized by certain conditions in which direct attention was paid to:

1. The development of democratic personhood (originally labeled political development).
2. The integration of personal and environmental changes with emphasis on student-generated, community-based curriculum and shared control of the program's organizational structures and governance.

---

[1]This notion of the democratic individual has been refined to form an expanded construct of democratic personhood (Wilson, 1998) and now includes the constructs of democratic congruence (Argyris, 1990), terminal value systems (Rokeach, 1973), care (Noddings, 1995), and critical consciousness (Freire, 1997) as well as the original conceptualizations of moral development, self-actualization, openmindedness, and political efficacy.

3. The creation of a TORI educational community characterized by trust (T), openness (O), realization (R), and interdependent authority relationships (I) (Gibb, 1972).
4. Organizational renewal using the theory and methods of organization development (Margulies & Raia, 1972).

OPERATIONAL DESIGN

The program, consisting of 45 second-semester junior students, male and female, ran from January 1972, through January 1973. Three basic phases constituted the program: a three-week orientation, a 30-week tutorial "in the community" cycle, and a six-week community action-culminating activity. Overall coordination of the program was the responsibility of codirectors, a credentialed teacher, and myself. The directors were assisted by four student teacher interns who were fifth-year students working on teaching credentials from institutions of higher learning. Students volunteered for the program with parental consent. This was necessary because students were to be on their own for long periods of time in the community. Meetings were held in a normal classroom which soon became known as the "Newport Room." Students had complete responsibility for the general decor, furnishing, painting, and upkeep of the room. Table 4.1 indicates the year-long schedule including the orientation, the tutorials (student subject matter groups of 15 students each), and the community action phases of the program.

Table 4.1. Newport Plan Year Schedule

Jan. 1972	Feb.-June Summer Sept.	Dec. Jan. 1973
Orientation	Tutorials in the Community	Community Action
← 3 wks →	← 30 wks →	← 6 wks →

Students spent three weeks together for orientation. Eighteen weeks were devoted to being in the community. Some students continued to work during the 12-week summer vacation on projects begun during the Spring of 1972. Community involvement continued for 13 weeks in the Fall 1972 term. The final 6 weeks were devoted to the development and implementation of community change projects.

The three-week orientation was an intensive effort to create an initial thrust in which the philosophical premises of an emergent, five-aspect TORI education community could become a reality. The TORI community education model becomes clear by contrasting it directly with what Gibb calls the "constraint-fear" model as in Table 4.2.

Table 4.2. Model of Education Community

Aspects of Community	Constraint–Fear	Emergence–Trust
Curriculum	Comes from the system, from sources external to the learner inquiry	Comes from the learner and the requirements of inquiry
Values	Comes from culture and authority roles; serve as constraints; stabilizers of community	Are changing, emergent processes; are releasing rather than constraining
Evaluation	External, performed by authority roles against system; creates success or failure	Residual or internal in process; may be used by learner in terms of own criteria, not the central educational process
Cognition/ knowledge	Central to education; knowledge a significant value and outcome as an end	Significant, adjunctive process inquiry; growing as a means
Affect/ emotions	Not central to education; can be aberrant, disruptive; not functional	Significant, adjunctive or central process in inquiry and living

The effectiveness of implementing the TORI model was the major concern during the orientation phase. Such effectiveness, according to Gibb, is most apt to be caused by a change in the dynamics of the system itself. It became necessary, therefore, to establish quite early in the life of the NPP certain criteria drawn from Gibb to guide the movement toward democratic emergence.

1. *Availability of warmth*. Learners learn when they feel warmth, love, and acceptance. In the TORI community this

is characterized by a dramatic increase in the physical and verbal warmth, uncontaminated by extrinsic evaluation, manipulation, or rewarding and punishing behavior.
2. *Personal responsibility.* Learners assume increased responsibility for self. "I can learn what I want to learn. I can create my own life and learning style. I am responsible for me and what happens to me."
3. *Feeling of one's own competence.* Learners increasingly recognize their own potentialities. This comes from de-emphasis on success or failure and the emphasis on personal responsibility. As the learner assumes greater responsibility for his own goals, her own needs, his own evaluation, she becomes more competent.
4. *An experience with the organization of the immediate future.* Learners experience the TORI community itself as an emergent, high lateral mobility, temporary system. The system is function-related with "flat" structures, and movement around tasks rather than role, and around information rather than power. In McLuhan's terms, the "medium is the message," the TORI community is that which is communicated.
5. *Awareness of interdependence.* The learners experience both their own resources and the resources of others; resources become closer to them. The community makes people available to teach and to learn from each other.
6. *Experience with a more adequate theory of learning.* Learners are able to integrate affect with cognition, knowledge into a total learning process. Changed behavior results from showing feelings rather than talking about them, and from doing things rather than thinking about or observing them.
7. *Integration of sensory experiences into learning.* Learners increasingly trust their own perceptions about themselves and others. A movement begins toward integration of one's "organic whole" rather than around an external world of reified knowledge, cultural impositions, and irrelevant skills.
8. *Humanizing the adult.* Adult learners shed their role expectations as "teacher or administrator" and begin to interact as people, regardless of age, engaged in a shared venture.
9. *Reducing the roles.* Learners discover that when warmth and direct communication are established, formal rules become less and less necessary. People begin to behave responsibly toward each other from trust; thus, rules

become increasingly irrelevant. "A rule is always a poor substitute for communication and human interaction . . . and is a symptom that communication has broken down" (Gibb, 1972, p. 84).

10. *Learning trust.* Learners learn to trust both themselves and others. Trust signifies that people are worthy, capable, and contain potential, and can learn and be self-motivated. Once again, "the medium is the message," and a trusting structure will produce trusting people.

Orientation, therefore, consisted of activities selected to make these criteria work for the students. They included small group processes, structured experiences in human relations training, role playing and simulations—all methodologies that were believed to be effective in producing change. Samples of each type include:

1. Small group process skills in both verbal and nonverbal communication, giving and receiving feedback, interpersonal influence, and *JOHARI* window: a means to analyze individual and group dynamics (Pfieffer & Jones, 1973, p. 116).
2. Structured and gestalt/confluent education experiences in risk taking, trust, fantasy, competitive and/or cooperative modes of behavior and team building. (Brown, 1971; Jourard, 1971).
3. Role playing, utilizing video tape playbacks, to increase student self-awareness as well as to increase student interviewing competencies.
4. Simulations, such as *Star Power*, to examine power relationships, interdependency and group behavior (*Star Power*, 2001).

In all activities, the interns and codirectors participated with the students on a first-name basis. This was to initiate the movement from dependency to interdependent authority relationships. To give more specificity to the activities employed, the first week's agenda is presented in Table 4.3.

Table 4.3. Newport Plan Activity Schedule—First Week

Monday, January 31

    Activity No. 1: Establishing Home Base

    Activity No. 2: Testing
        a. Dogmatism
        b. Political Efficacy
        c. Value Ranking

    Activity No. 3: Warm-ups
    (Value Ranking and Sharing/Self-Disclosure)

Tuesday, February 1

    Activity No. 1: Theory X—Theory Y (Lecturette based on McGregor)

    Activity No. 2: Communication Skills
        a. One way—Two way
        b. Broken Squares (an exercise in nonverbal communication)

Wednesday, February 2

    Activity No. 1: Divide into Tutorials

    Activity No. 2: "Positive Stick-ums" (feedback and self-disclosure)

    Activity No. 3: Decide Disciplines

    Activity No. 4: "Brainstorming"
        a. What do I want to learn?
        b. How am I going to do it?

Thursday, February 3

    "Come and See"

A further sense of these activities is provided by giving a more detailed description of "value ranking" and "sharing/self disclosure" conducted on Monday, January 31, Activity 3.

Value ranking was drawn from the work of Milton Rokeach (1973). Participants (students, codirectors and interns) were given the now classic list of 18 values.

1. A Comfortable Life (a prosperous life)
2. A Sense of Accomplishment (lasting contribution)
3. A World at Peace (free of war and conflict)

4. A World of Beauty (beauty of nature and the arts)
5. An Exciting Life (a stimulating, active life)
6. Equality (brotherhood, equal opportunity for all)
7. Family Security (taking care of loved ones)
8. Freedom (independence, free choice)
9. Happiness (contentedness)
10. Inner Harmony (freedom from inner conflict)
11. Mature Love (sexual and spiritual intimacy)
12. National Security (protection from attack)
13. Pleasure (an enjoyable, leisurely life)
14. Salvation (saved, eternal life)
15. Self-Respect (self-esteem)
16. Social Recognition (respect, admiration)
17. True Friendship (close companionship)
18. Wisdom (a mature understanding of life)

Each participant then individually ranked each value in terms of its importance to him/her with the most important placed first, the second most important placed second, and so on, with the least important value placed in last or 18th position. When all participants were finished, they met in small groups of five or six to share their own value rankings and to experience from others in the group the different value ordering possibilities. During the second phase of the warm-ups, all participant value rankings were collected, tabulated, and an entire Newport Plan value matrix constructed. After the termination of the second phase of warm-up, this matrix was made public to allow each participant to check his/her ranking with the entire group ranking.

Sharing something of one's self is an exercise somewhat modified from the original developed by Herbert Otto (1970). In this activity, participants share with members of the small group—again five or six—something about themselves. Each member is "given" two minutes of time in which he/she is to talk about him/herself, using anything he/she wishes as a topic. The two minutes are sacrosanct in that if one cannot think of anything to say after having talked for perhaps 80 seconds, he or she still has 40 seconds of time to "use," regardless of whether such time is filled with talk. No one may interrupt or ask a question during the entire 120 seconds; only the "sharer" may speak, and even if he or she falters, he or she may not be "rescued" by a question. Only after all members of the group have had their allotted time may questions and general discussion occur. The intent is severalfold:

1. It forces individuals to make a personal, uninterrupted statement about one's self. In this sense, it becomes a first experience for many in "self-disclosure" (Jourard, 1971).
2. It establishes a condition wherein listeners really begin to listen, for by preventing questions, there is no responsibility to respond.

An additional intent of the orientation phase was to have students remain with each other over an extended period of time, thereby altering the time structure; activities became the standard governing time, rather than time the standard governing activity as is the usual case within a traditional period-by-period school schedule. Thus, the orientation phase was an extensive developmental effort, directed toward both personal and structural change in starting the growth of the emergent TORI education community.

Tutorials became the basic instructional and growth unit of the program. Each of three tutorials were assigned fifteen students and an intern (with one tutorial having two interns). The basic functions of the tutorials were to provide for (a) a mutual support group for counseling and growth, and (b) a concentrated academic study in one of three subject areas (social studies, science/ecology, and career education/vocational education). Initially, an attempt was made to include other subject areas; however the English, Physical Education, and Art Departments refused to participate. They believed the NPP to be "soft," and without the "rigor" of their own programs, a conclusion certainly open to serious examination.

Approximately every ten weeks, students rotated to a different tutorial, thereby allowing each student to participate in each of the tutorials during the life of the program. Students were randomly assigned to their first tutorial during the orientation phase. During each week, the students attended regular school for the first two periods, then spent the remainder of the day—Monday through Thursday—in the community or in group development activities, including play. On Friday, after the first two periods, the three tutorials met at school for analysis of the previous four days' activities, planning for the next week, general debriefing, and most importantly, to continue with the educational community development begun during orientation. Table 4.4 summarizes the rotation schedule and daily/weekly schedule.

Students, within the broad subject area of each tutorial, selected and developed their own curricula based upon their own interests. This could be accomplished either individually or in concert with another student or students. The community outside of the school (people, places, activities) became the basic resource for such

Table 4.4. Newport Plan Tutorial Rotation

Subject	Jan. 72	Feb.	Mar.	Apr.	May	Jun.	Sep.	Oct.	Nov.	Dec. Jan. 73
Social Studies	O R I E N T A T I O N	A	A	A	B	B	B	C	C	C	Community Action
Science		B	B	B	C	C	C	A	A	A	
Career/ Voca- tional		C	C	C	A	A	A	B	B	B	
		Rotation I			Rotation II			Rotation III			

B. Newport Plan Daily/Weekly Schedule

School Period	Mon.	Tues.	Wed.	Thurs.	Fri.
1 2	Students at Newport Harbor High: PE, Electives, English, Independent Study				
3 through 6	All Tutorials in the field with interns and associate director periods 3 through 6 plus evenings as required			Tutorials at Newport Harbor High School, recap, evaluation, governance, organization and personal development	

Table 4.4 shows the rotation schedule of the three tutorials (A, B, C) through three academic subject areas (social studies, science, career/vocational exploration) during the program year. The tutorials consisted of approximately 15 students each. Approximately every ten weeks, students rotated to a different tutorial. Note that students concentrated upon a single subject for the ten weeks rather than the period per day for a school term as in conventional scheduling patterns.

study, thereby freeing the students to leave the campus on their own to seek out and utilize such resources during the four periods of the NPP, thus moving education to the community at large. This design again alters the structural arrangements. This point should be re-emphasized. The NPP directly questioned the concept that learning occurs best through teacher/student interaction within the confines of square cubicles called classrooms. It questioned whether or not this vehicle—the classroom—was the best educational situation, for it seemed to emphasize "place" rather than activity. Additionally, the "place" syndrome was clearly correlated with scheduling conventions. Students take one hour of this, then one hour of that, then one hour of still something else. Learning in such a mode is a fragmentation of subjects, and education is apt to become a bunch of disconnected bits. Wilson (1969) quotes Harold Taylor that:

> ... the organization of knowledge becomes a matter of administrative convenience rather than of educational imagination and little attention ... (is) ... given to the natural ways in which students can to enter the experience of the arts and society and can form their own conclusions about what they find there.

Of equal significance was the development of the TORI community itself as an educational good, valuable and yes, beautiful in its own right regardless of any future instrumental use. Such contention receives support from Lee, Byrk, and Smith (1993, p. 228) who write:

> The social interactions of schooling are not simply a mechanism for accomplishing some other aim, but rather are education itself ... (and) ... in the distinctive work place of the school, social relations among adults and students are much more than just a factor to be manipulated in the pursuit of academic performance.

One would hope that students might make a connection between the NPP and their later lives, but if not, the experience can stand alone as deeply meaningful.

RESULTS AND EDUCATIONAL SIGNIFICANCE

Results of the first year's operation of the program demonstrated that there was a significant movement towards democratic personhood (in particular, greater openmindedness and a higher sense of political efficacy) within the NPP students than within the contrast groups. As well, NPP students indicated more positive responses to specific semantic factors constituting a "good" but not particularly structured educational program as well as being judged by an impartial jury as an emergent TORI educational community. These findings were supported by descriptive, more qualitative evidence drawn from informal questionnaires, participant interviews, unsolicited responses, student academic and intellectual work, and other program artifacts. The total informational gestalt leads to the conclusion that the NPP was indeed qualitatively different than the traditional school and this difference was the contributing factor to the subsequent democratic personhood development of the NPP students.

After the first year of operation, there was a change in teacher leadership and in school leadership at the principal level. Whereas the original principal had been most supportive, if not tenacious in protecting the program, his replacement was far less so. Because this was his first principalship, it became clear that he did not have the understanding necessary to act as a buffer between the NPP and district administration, which continually expressed doubts about its efficacy. Additionally, the financial impact of California's Proposition 13 with its attending reduction of financial support gradually moved the NPP from its community-based ethos to an atomistic, idiosyncratic, individualized, academically soft, feel-good, self-esteem driven, and alas, an overpsychologized phenomonen, and by 1980, it was gone. (And so was I.)

Beyond its historical effects, the plan's educational significance, as opposed to an overly reductionistic statistical significance needs to be examined for its current relevance. Whereas an extensive literature exists concerning the general impact of schooling upon adult economic and social success (Ekstrom, Goertz, & Rock, 1988; Pedersen, Faucher, & Eaton, 1978) and the role of schooling in the life-courses of students (Pallas, 1993) there is a much smaller literature on retrospective analysis of the impact of specific alternative schools and programs (which we now might label "restructuring") on students' subsequent adult life (Carini, 1982; Willis, 1961).

One of the questions asked in 1974 (Wilson, 1974, p. 250) was " . . . will the NPP be perceived by its participants as being significant to them in the future (one year, five years, ten years)?" Well, how about 29 years later? Currently, there is underway a study to answer this question. Although the study is far from complete at this writing, former students have been asked through interviews to ascertain their retrospective reactions and remembrances of the program. Initial impressions indicate that the program had high personal meaning and salience for them.

An unanticipated finding is the declaration by several NPP graduates in recent conversation that if it had not been for the program, they would have dropped out of school.

If further analysis supports these first-blush findings, then in terms of democratic personhood and life success, school transformation efforts need to be directed toward deep structural changes in core educational practices that are grounded in an ethic of student democratic development. Students should have major responsibility for self-selected but accountable curriculum as well as for large portions of unsupervised student learning time spent in the community. At this writing, because there seems to be no major differences between the NPP and contrast-group findings in relation to later life conditions other than the joy of the NPP itself—no small factor—then it is difficult to argue about the results in terms of direct superiority/inferiority. There is so much more that contributes to "the course of human lives" than specific school curriculum experiences (Pallas, 1993).

This retrospective study, therefore, at least at the high school level, brings into question the current rhetoric about the necessity of common core curriculum, prescribed/accepted/received truth, time on task, national standards, precise accountability measures including the fetish of testing, and student control measures. It runs counter to most local, state, and national restructuring movements, which have virtually excluded the historical notion of the schools' responsibility for the development of democratic culture and personhood (Gibboney, 1994; Wilson, 2000b). Along with the previously cited examples, the NPP becomes an exemplar of critical democratic possibility within the discourse of curriculum development and school change. It provides for experiences that move curriculum from a function of place to a function of community life and activity. In true Dewey fashion, life and learning become part of the same ongoing process. The dualism of which Dewey (1916, pp. 333–339) speaks and rejects, the distinction between school and society, becomes blurred and diffused. The community becomes the classroom and the life of the community emerges as the curriculum; submerging students in such a milieu does not seem to place them at any subsequent life risk.

With the advantage of hindsight, I now want to offer three program shortcomings of the Newport Plan. Implicit within these shortcomings are possibilities to meet current exigencies and further its democratic potential for not only urban schools but for schools in general.

1. Although students had major responsibility for the selection of curricula content within very broad academic limitations, there was little attempt to foster rigorous examination of oppressive cultural conditions. Paulo Freire's (2000) notion of reading, reflecting, and acting upon oppressive cultural reality, of the specific development of his notion of

critical consciousness, was not in any strong evidence. It was not until about 1972 that I discovered Paulo Freire through reading *Pedagogy of the Oppressed*. In this sense, the program was just not sufficiently focused to deepen student understanding of and agency in what Michele Fine calls this "mess called democracy" (cited in Fairbanks, 1998). A healthy dose of a deconstructed, "rethinking" curriculum (Levine, Lowe, Peterson, & Tenorio, 1995) would have brought to bear a penetrating critical eye on student-generated studies.

2. The original NPP students were all white save one or two, and for the most part, middle to upper class. Although issues of race and to a lesser extent class were not neglected, they were approached in a form that I now recognize as liberal naiveté. Racism was perceived as a malady corrected by assuming color-blind postures to color differences. Our assumption, teachers and students alike, was ". . . that to notice colors other than White would be to stigmatize non-white students" (Thompson, 1998, p. 524). Such color-blindness thus becomes, as Thompson states, " . . . parasitic upon racism: it is only in a racist society that pretending not to notice color could be construed as a particularly virtuous act" (p. 524). There were virtually no direct attempts to deconstruct white racism and white class position and societal privilege that both students and teachers brought to the program. How could it be otherwise in the absence of a necessary critical consciousness?

3. In connection with the above, the plan should have sought out vigorously opportunities to bring its participants in meaningful and continual contact with nonwhites. In this, I accept Blum's (1998) lament of the public retreat from racial integration as a moral problem. Any democratic intervention in school requires direct attention being paid to community development characterized by explicit commitment ". . . to racial justice as an internal and external ideal" (p. 10). To this, I would add ethnic, gender, and class justice. The task here is to place students of divergent trajectories and histories together in relatively small community contexts to work collaboratively on common goals without denying the differences that different histories bring. It never dawned on us in the Newport Plan to expand it to the Newport/Santa Ana Plan, which could have brought African-American and Hispanic students from the adjacent city of Santa Ana into a common enterprise.

With all of the above firmly in mind, a final and perplexing query remains. The question becomes this: In this fractured time of ours, to what degree are the democratic lessons learned from the NPP relevant for our current multiethnic, multicultural, multiracial, and class-based American society? Is it possible that similarly designed and executed collaborative school programs, urban or otherwise, would be equally as effective, even in the face of the oppression, discrimination, and repression that seems to continually press upon us all? My answer is yes. A new, more critical, justice-oriented NPP may be framed as a "pedagogy of hope" (Freire, 1995), which, in remembrance of Freire, calls out to us eloquently, forcefully, and continually.

This paean to hope, however, needs to be tempered by a few additional caveats. First, we should perhaps call a moratorium on the necessity for more and more research on urban education unless that research is participatory in nature. What if the energy, time, and expense of academic, narrowly conceived, and often reductionistic research could be diverted to collaborative and participatory research with and within schools? As stated previously, I believe we have solid enough examples and working knowledge of good, democratic schools and programs, including the NPP, devoted to much more than an education for students characterized by narrow academic achievement and the production of competitive consumers.

Second, we should be continually on guard against doing harm when we mean to do good. Fry and Pasmore (p. 273) draw from medicine a notion of allopathic processes that treat symptoms without a concern for the whole system. The result is an iatrogenic or doctor-caused illness. Similarly, a pedogenic condition can exist whereby the school can cause democratic deficits in students in spite of the school's best intentions. Third, we should resist any missionary zeal to insist that any specific template be the intervention for schools other than our own, urban or otherwise. Paulo Freire, in Horton and Freire (1990, p. 145), calls our attention to this caution:

> ... the more people participate in the process of their own education, the more the people participate in the process of defining what kind of production to produce, and for what and why, the more the people participate in the development of their (*sic*) selves. The more the people become themselves, the better the democracy.

I cannot dictate as an outsider in urban educational situations. However, this does not mean that I remain on the side waiting for things to happen, I cannot be neutral. From Freire (2000, p. 75), the revolutionary educators cannot wait, for their

> ... efforts must coincide with those of the students to engage in critical thinking and the quest for mutual humanization ... (and) ... to achieve this, they must be partners of the students in their relationship with them.

What I can do is be available as a critical friend to provide assistance and perspective when requested, as I hope I have done.

And fourth, we need to be continually mindful that the school alone cannot be the solitary agent for social transformation. George Counts' question, "Dare the Schools Build a New Social Order?" (1969) must be answered no, not by themselves. Yet, the schools cannot divorce themselves from deep engagement in the process. And such engagement demands utopian thinking, which is virtually absent for the discourse of school and social change. Although not referring to education directly, Russell Jacoby (1999, pp. xi-xii) writes of the "end of utopia," in which utopia means

> ... in its widest sense, and least threatening, meaning; a belief that the future could fundamentally surpass the present. I am referring to the notion that the future texture of life, work, and even love might little resemble that now familiar to us. I am alluding to the idea that history contains possibilities of freedom and pleasure hardly tapped.

I dream that my suggestions, as utopian as they might seem, have merit and attractiveness for true educational transformation characterized by enlightenment, energy, and justice. It is as Blum (1998, p. 29) forcefully reminds us: "... what a grievous loss it is to a society if it is unable to create some semblance of interracial educational communities...." And these communities, in turn, need to be perceived not as ends in themselves but as means to achieve a future state, an utopia now largely unimagined and more sensed than known.

What we need is not another study of urban education or "inner-city children at risk" but rather a sustained focus on " ... the flaws of American society—flaws rooted in historical inequity and long standing cultural stereotypes" (West, 1993, p.3). The development of critical, democratic persons through ethnoracial student communities drawing from a radically rethought Newport Plan might just become at the least, a partial antidote for our world of which John Fowles in *A Maggot* (1985 p. 388) writes: "... where once again a sense of self barely exists; or most often where it does, is repressed; where most are still ... characters written by someone else than free individuals in our comprehension of the adjective and the noun."

REFERENCES

Apple, M., & Beane, J. (Eds.). (1995). *Democratic schools.* Alexandria, VA: Association for Supervision and Curriculum Development.
Argyris, C. (1990). *Overcoming organizational defenses: Facilitating organizational learning.* Boston: Allyn and Bacon.
Blum, L. (1998, November). Race, community and moral education. Lawrence Kohlberg Memorial Lecture delivered at the Association for Moral Education annual conference, Dartmouth University, Hanover, NH.
Brown, G. (1971). *Human teaching for human learning.* New York: Viking.
Buras, K. (1999). Questioning core assumptions: A critical reading of and response to E. D. Hirsch's *The schools we need and why we don't have them. Harvard Educational Review. 69*(1),67-93.
Campbell, A. (1964). *The American voter.* New York: Wiley.
Carini, P. (1982). *The school lives of seven children: A five year study.* Grand Forks: University of North Dakota.
Conway, T., Vickers, R., & French, J. (1992) An application or person-environment fit theory: Perceived versus desired control. In D. Bargal, G. Martin, & M. Lewin (Eds.), The heritage of Kurt Lewin: Theory, research, and practice. *Journal of Social Issues, 48*(2), 95-107.
Counts, G. (1969). *Dare the schools build a new social order?* New York: Arno.
Dewey, J. (1883). Self-realization as the moral idea. In J. Boydston (Ed.), *The early works of John Dewey, 1882–1898* (Vol. 4, pp. 42–53). Carbondale: Southern Illinois University Press.
Dewey, J. (1888). The ethics of democracy. In G. Axtelle, J. Boydston, J. Burnett, L. Haln, W. Leyes, W. McKenzie, & F. Villeman (Eds.), *The early works of John Dewey, 1882-1898* (Vol I, pp. 227-249). Carbondale: Southern Illinois University Press.
Dewey, J. (1916/1944). *Democracy and education.* New York: Free Press.
Easton, D., & Dennis, J. (1967). The child's acquisition of regime norms: Political efficacy. *American Political Science Review. 61*, 25-38.
Elmore, R. (1996). Getting to scale with good educational practice: Working together toward reform. *Harvard Educational Review*, 1-27.
Ekstrom, R., Goertz, M., & Rock, D. (1988). *Education and American youth: The impact of the school experience.* London: Falmer Press.
Fairbanks, C. (1998). Nourishing conversations: Urban adolescents, literacy, and democratic society. *Journal of Literacy Research, 30*(2), 187-203.
Fowles, J. (1985) *A maggot.* London: Cape
Freire, P. (1993). *Pedagogy of the city.* New York: Continuum.
Freire, P. (1995). *Pedagogy of hope: Reliving pedagogy of the oppressed.* New York: Continuum.
Freire, P. (1998). *Pedagogy of freedom: Ethics, democracy, and civic courage.* Lanham, MD: Rowman & Littlefield.
Freire, P. (2000). *Pedagogy of the oppressed.* New York: Continuum.
Fry, R., & Passmore, W. (1983). Strengthening management education. In S. Srivastva & Associates (Eds.), *The executive mind* (pp. 269-296). San Francisco: Jossey-Bass.

Gibb, J. (1972). Trust and role freedom: A TORI innovation in educational community. *Journal of Research and Development in Education, 5,* 76-84.
Gibboney, R. (1994). *The stone trumpet: A story of practical school reform: 1960-1994.* Albany: SUNY Press.
Gilbert, A. (1990). *Democratic individuality.* Cambridge: Cambridge University Press.
Goodman, J. (1992). *Elementary school for critical democracy.* Albany: SUNY Press.
Hess, R. (1971). The acquisition of feelings of political efficacy in pre-adults. In G. Abcarian & J. Soule (Eds.), *Social psychology and political behavior* (pp. 59-78). Columbus, OH: Charles E. Merrill.
Horton, M., & Freire, P. (1990) *We make the road by walking: Conversations on education and social change.* Philadelphia: Temple University Press.
Jacoby, R. (1999) *The end of utopia: Politics and culture in an age of apathy.* New York: Basic Books.
Jourard, S. (1971). *The transparent self* (2nd ed.). New York: Van Nostrand Reinhold.
Lane, R. (1959). *Political life.* New York: Free Press of Glencoe.
Lee, V., Byrk, A., & Smith, J. (1993). The organization of effective secondary schools. In L. Darling-Hammond (Ed.), *Review of research in education* (Vol. 19, pp. 171-267). Washington, DC: American Education Research Association.
Levine, D., Lowe, R., Peterson, B., & Tenorio, R. (1995). *Rethinking schools: An agenda for change.* New York: The New Press.
Levin, M. (1960). *The alienated voter: Politics in Boston.* New York: Holt, Rinehart, and Winston.
Malarkey, T. (1998). Personal correspondence, Bay Area Coalition of Essential Schools, Oakland, CA.
Margulies, N., & Raia, A. (1972). *Organization development: Values, process, and technology.* New York: McGraw Hill.
Maslow, A. (1956). Self-actualizing people: A study of psychological health. In C. Moustakas (Ed.), *The self* (pp. 190-191). New York: Harper and Row.
Meier. D. (1996). *The power of their ideas: Lessons from a small school in Harlem.* Boston: Beacon Press.
Miller, J. (1979). *History and human existence: From Marx to Merleau-Ponty.* Berkeley: University of California Press.
Mosher, R., Kenney, R., & Garrod, A. (1994). *Preparing for citizenship: Teaching youth to live democratically.* Westport, CT: Praeger.
Noddings, N. (1995). *Philosophy of education.* Boulder, CO: Westview.
Norton, D. (1991). *Democracy and moral development.* Berkeley: University of California Press.
Otto, H. (1970). *Group methods to actualize human potential: A handbook.* Beverly Hills, CA: Holistic.
Pallas, A. (1993, Winter). Schooling in the course of human lives: The social context of education and the transition to adulthood in industrial society. *Review of Educational Research, 63*(4), 409-447.
Palmer, P. (1998). *The courage to teach.* San Francisco: Jossey-Bass.

Pedersen, E., Faucher, T., & Eaton, W. (1978). A new perspective on the effects of first-grade teachers on children's subsequent adult status. *Harvard Educational Review, 48*(1), 1-31.

Pfieffer, W., & Jones, J. (Eds.). (1973). *The 1973 annual handbook for group facilitators.* San Diego: University Associates.

Power, C., Higgins, A., & Kohlberg, L. (1989). *Lawerence Kohlberg's approach to moral education.* New York: Columbia University Press.

Rokeach, M. (1960). *The open and closed mind.* New York: Basic Books.

Rokeach, M. (1973). *The nature of human values.* New York: The Free Press.

Sarason, S. (1971). *The culture of the school and the problem of change* (2nd ed.). Boston: Allyn and Bacon.

Thompson, A. (1998, Winter). Not the color purple: Black feminist lessons for educational caring. *Harvard Educational Review, 68*(4), 522-554.

Smith, J. (1998, Summer/Fall). Dangerous minds: Experiences in Chicago's west side high schools. *Democracy & Education, 12*(3), 31-32.

Star Power (2001).[On-line] Available:www.stsintl.com/schools/star_power.

Tye, B. (2000). *Hard truths: Uncovering the deep structure of schooling.* New York: Teachers College Press.

West, C. (1993). *Race matters.* Boston: Beacon.

Whitmore, R. (1970). By inquiry alone? *Social Education, 34,* 280-285.

Willis, M. (1961). *The guinea pigs after 20 years: A follow up study of the class of 1938 of the University School Ohio State.* Columbus: Ohio State University Press.

Wilson, T. (1969). *Final report: EPDA summer institute: Constitutional issues and ethnic conflict* (Report No. OEG-0-9-141850-1788-725). California State Polytechnic University, Pomona, CA.

Wilson, T. (1974/1975). An alternative community based secondary school education program and student political development (Doctoral dissertation, University of Southern California, 1974). *Disseratation Abstracts International, 35*(9), 5797A.

Wilson, T. (1997) ERIC and democratic schools key words. Unpublished raw data.

Wilson, T. (1998, April). *Democratic personhood.* Paper presented at the annual meeting of the American Education Research Association, San Diego, CA.

Wilson, T. (2000a). Comparing discourses: Democracy, the coalition of essential schools and the eight year study. In M. Leicester, S. Modgil, & C. Modgil (Eds.), *Politics, education and citizenship* (pp. 173-182). London: Falmer.

Wilson, T. (2000b, April). *Democratic personhood: Preliminary ideas.* Paper presented at the annual meeting of the American Educational Research Association, New Orleans: LA.

Wood, G. (1992). *Schools that work.* New York: Dutton.

Wood, G. (1998). *A time to learn: Creating community in America's high schools.* New York: Dutton.

5

The Curriculum of the Self: Critical Self-Knowing As Critical Pedagogy

Jeff Sapp

*Once upon a time there was a little boy
named Sorrow and Fear
Sorrow and Fear had no friends
And lived all alone.
At night the Death Dragon came to him and, by force,
stole days from Sorrow and Fear's life.
The "taking" as he called it, was terrible.
Our words can't describe it.
You'd need another language,
the language of song.
But not songs with words like we know songs.
Just songs with sounds.
And Sorrow and Fear had no voice.
("The Death Dragon"—the first story I penned in my personal journal)*

I moved from rural West Virginia, my home state, to what my Mother calls "that big evil high-falootin City of Angeles" in 1993. I was seeking community and, specifically, a gay community. Having recently Come Out, I felt alienated because I had never really seen myself reflected in people around me. I moved to Los Angeles and began teaching at Occidental College.

Moving into the urban environment reminded me of that old science experiment where you put a frog into a pan of cold water and then turn on the heat. The frog simply isn't aware that the water is getting hotter and hotter and, finally, it boils to death. Stress in the urban environment is just like that. It sneaks up on you. It begins with the simple suggestion of a friend that you need to get a "Club" (a device that locks the steering wheel of your car and prevents theft). "Rent an upstairs apartment . . . it's safer," they say. The noises of the City itself are a stress factor: the traffic, the car alarms, the neighbors fighting at two in the morning, and the sheer density of people trying to live together.

Training new teachers in schools in urban Los Angeles created new situations for me. I remember one of my student-teachers, Debra, and the time a student shot another student outside her door and the bleeding student stumbled into her classroom for safety and help. Debra, gifted even as a novice, was focused on things like writing a good lesson-plan, implementing a fair classroom management system, and making literature relevant to her students. Nowhere in her training had she been informed that a student who had just been shot might enter her room. There was the time when ten of our student-teachers were in a local middle school. A man murdered his wife and then turned the gun on himself. The children of these two were students of most of my student-teachers. Crisis-intervention had become a major part of our curriculum. The water in the pot was getting hotter and hotter.

I saw the frog boiling recently, though. I just last week talked to Jennifer, a student-teacher I had four years ago. I immediately asked her about a recent stabbing at her school between an Armenian student and a Latino student—these two groups have quite a bit of racial tension between them. I had heard about the stabbing on the news. Her response? "Ah . . . it wasn't that bad. Would you like another cup of coffee?" Columbine shocks us. Paduka shocks us. When these things happen in Los Angeles and other urban centers people simply ask you if you'd like another cup of coffee. We have gotten so used to the hot water, it seems, that we don't even give it a second thought anymore.

I don't think we realize the stress we live under in urban environments. Only recently, in our own department, we had a colleague go "postal" on us. It was very traumatic and resulted in a psychologist who specializes in work violence coming to do some sessions with those who experienced this violence. A different colleague of mine is losing her hair. Each morning she actually touches up her hair with some type of cosmetic paint that is made for just this purpose. I could spend pages and pages going on with multiple examples of both subtle and blatant stress stories like this. They have become, sad to say, the norm. How do we train future teachers to live in an environment that is filled with such Sorrow and Fear? What kind of a model do we give new teachers who are training to live in this environment?

Let me tell you a story of how my personal search for freedom changed my teaching. Maxine Greene said that a teacher in search of her/his own freedom may be the only kind of teacher who can arouse other people to go in search of their freedom (Greene, 1988). John Dewey stated that we are free "not because of what we statically are, but in so far as we are becoming different from that we have been" (Dewey, 1928/1960). Freedom is to be found in the continuity of developing experiences (Dewey, 1938).

I will tell you a story of voicelessness to Voice. Like most people who begin journaling, it was crisis and desperation that brought me to the blank page. My desperate crisis was dealing with my sexual orientation and Coming Out. I thought if I could just write it all out and look at it that perhaps I could learn something about myself. I started by telling my stories to myself on the blank page. Isak Dinesen said, "All sorrows can be borne if you put them into a story or tell a story about them" (Keen, 1989, p. 1). I could hardly bear hiding from my sexuality anymore. I didn't know what to do and so I picked up black ink and blank page and began to decipher myself.

> I do not know and so I start with a blank page. I do not know and so I pick up an ink pen. I do not know and so I look at what is in front of me and I write about what it teaches me. I do not know if I am the tattered and marked up book I am reading for the third time. I do not know if I know my story line or plot. I do not know what chapter I am in. I do not know what my title is. I do not know is the one thing I know most. I do not know why knowing that compels me to pick up blank pages and scribble with black ink onto them. I do not know why I have to write so much. And I did not know that somewhere in the liquid white empty pages I would start to know. And understand. I did not know that. (personal journal, p. 3598)

Each day as I wrote myself onto the page in an attempt to deal with my sexuality, I became more and more clear. I had lived my life letting others define me. I was an unhappy wreck and suffering from a terrible bleeding ulcer. I understood the hopelessness that gay and lesbian teenagers feel, the hopelessness that leads to ever-increasing rates of teenage suicide (McConnell-Celi, 1993).

My research methodology for my dissertation was a critical point in saving my life. I chose a qualitative research paradigm, heuristic research, for my dissertation. Moustakas (1990) states that in "heuristic research, the investigator must have had a direct, personal encounter with the phenomenon being investigated." In a very real way, all research is autobiographical. The researcher must have experienced the phenomenon being studied in its entirety. My primary task as the researcher is to recognize whatever exists in the consciousness of the participants and myself as a fundamental awareness, to receive and accept it, and then to dwell on its nature and possible meanings (Moustakas, 1990). In heuristic research there is an unshakable connection between what is out there and what is in the investigator in reflective thought, feeling, and awareness (Moustakas, 1990). The truth is that what is "out there" and what is "within" the researchers cannot be separated. The heuristic process challenges the researcher to rely on her/his thoughts, feelings, senses, and intuitions (Moustakas, 1990). I also drew from Denzin's (1989) work on interpretive interactionism. Interpretive research has, as one of its main criteria, the reality that research begins and ends with the biography of the researcher. The focus of interpretive research is the epiphany—a life experience that radically alters and shapes the meanings people give to themselves.

I had this sudden moment of revelation: "Everything I know about being gay I've heard from white, conservative, heterosexual males! No wonder I'm messed up. How is it possible for someone who is not me to name and define me?" I immediately made a commitment to begin reading material written by gay people for gay people. Likewise, I realized that I was the greatest authority on my own life. The revolution had began.

> In my writing I am sniffing myself out. I am rooting through the dense forest of pages seeking my scent. Sniff, sniff, sniff. So many things have smeared their goop all over me to hide my authentic humanity. Society. The church. My family's expectations. No wonder it's taken me so long to catch wind of myself. Suddenly I write something so randomly in the path of myself and wham! The hound dog in me catches a whiff! I grow excited and begin to run with it. Ink flying through the pages. The smell getting stronger and stronger. Finally I get it treed. Here in the pages that were wood and bark and leaves before this blank whiteness.

> My beagles self flips through the pages scent seeking. I discover that I am incense and offer myself up to the Universe as an offering. (personal journal, page 3564)

If you came to my home you would find a wonderful Pinocchio puppet hanging from my ceiling. If you came to my office you would find a large Pinocchio book standing up on my shelf. They are there to remind me of how incredible it is to finally be Real. I have spent most of my life being unreal and I want to be reminded every day of how incredible it is to finally be Real. The sacred Journal was the instrument with which I loved myself to Realness by becoming, like the archetype Pinocchio, a teller of Truth. "We teach who we are" (Palmer, 1998, p. 1). I moved from West Virginia to Los Angeles in 1993 and began teaching at Occidental College. Occidental College is right in the greater Los Angeles area and, as teacher-educators, we were training teachers to work in the urban schools within and around one of the largest cities in the world. When I entered the urban environment, I simply brought with me stories of my journey to Realness. I brought with me a love of black ink and blank pages. I brought with me a great love of reflection. My first day of class I told Occidental College student-teachers about the teacher-as-reflector. I held in my hands my own instrument of transformation. I opened it and read to them from the "Curriculum of my Self."

I read to them of teaching from who they were . . . and that they could find themselves in the blank page as I had.

> When I was a small child in the rural Appalachian Mountains of West Virginia, my childhood friends and I would spend the lazy, hot summer evenings catching fireflies. We ran like banshees collecting them one-by-one-by-one. Soon, after imprisoning several dozen, we'd have nature's flashlight to guide us through the dark forest to home. Keeping a journal is like that. One-by-one-by-one you set free the celestial moments of your life. And after collecting dozens and dozens of them you begin to see the light—the patterns and themes of your life. Captured in your Journal Jar. Together they bring illumination to your dark journey through the forest and back home to yourself. (personal journal, p. 1118)

I read to them about social justice.

> Sometimes I write in red. I write in red when those who once loved me as a liar don't speak to me anymore now that I speak my Truths. So, I write in red. I wrote in red last Tuesday when Dan died of AIDS. And each letter I wrote in red stood for a thou-

sand-thousand Dans. So I wrote in red and I capitalized all my letters and underlined all my words. There was another gang killing of an innocent child this week. So I wrote in red. I wrote in red the day I heard a teacher speak a mean word to a student. And I wrote in red the day my brother stopped speaking to me because I was gay. I write in red a lot these days. Well . . . truth is I actually make it a point to write in red at least once a day now. There is, after all, so much to write about in red. (personal journal, p. 1127)

And I gave them loving warnings.

But I should warn you before you go on. If you fall in love with ink and blank pages it will change everything you have known. Sooner of later it will be time for you to write your own authentic version of yourself. And the people who are used to doing the editing for you may not like it. That one thing alone will tell you that you are on the right path. When people get nervous. (personal journal, p. 3564)

As an act of social justice, I simply wanted to use my newfound Voice. I wanted to speak about reflection and how it had changed my life. I wanted to be identified as my authentic self, an aspect of which was my gay identity. I wanted to break the silence that some homosexual people feel and that gay educators particularly feel. I wanted to end some stereotypes and educate. I wanted to model that my journey to my Real Self had drastically changed who I was and, thus, how I taught. Social justice is not only about the acts we do in the world. I believe that social justice is about being a reflector and critical thinker of myself, my place in the world, and the way I act in the world. When the person is transformed, the teacher that the person is likewise is transformed. I wanted to tell my story. Little did I know that I was entering my Voice into a 20-year legacy and joining colleagues who had set the precedent 20 years earlier. Gay and lesbian professors met in New York City in 1973 for the first conference of the Gay Academic Union (D'Emilio, 1992, p. 127). They wrote in their statement of purpose words I would honor 20 years after their ink had dried:

As gay men and women and as scholars, we believe we must work for liberation as a means for change in our lives and in the communities in which we find ourselves. We choose to do this collectively for we know that no individual, alone, can liberate herself or himself from society's oppression. . . . We assert the interconnection between personal liberation and social change. We seek simultaneously to foster our self-awareness as individuals and, by applying our professional skills, to become the agency for a critical examination of the gay experience that will challenge those generalizations supporting the current oppression. . . . Our hope is that by pooling our experiences and sharing our expertise, we will be able to begin the arduous job of challenging the sexiest myths that now dominate pubic discourse and influence private association.

Story had changed my life and, honestly, I just wanted to let student-teachers in on a good thing. Thus, a cornerstone in my teaching philosophy is that good teachers know who they are and that knowing affects everything about their teaching. I saw that the student-teachers who were struggling were ones who had a weak sense of themselves or no sense of themselves. They were overcome by their woundedness and often perpetrated it upon the children in their classrooms. For instance, those student-teachers with a low sense of self-esteem often relied heavily upon getting their sense of self from how their students responded to them. They did not have self-esteem, they had "other-esteem." Their sense of self was explicit. They fed upon their students. They were powerless and looked to their students for power. In contrast, I saw student-teachers with a strong sense of themselves who inspired students from the overflow of self-power they had to freely give those students. Every chance I could get I would weave a story into the curriculum that was from what I called the "curriculum of my Self." I began to wonder what impact my personal transformation might have on my students and my research. My original intent for this chapter was to ask former students if an Out gay professor had any impact on their current teaching experience. I e-mailed former students this question.

Certainly I saw an opportunity to make a dent in the institutional homophobia that permeates schools. McConnell-Celi (1993) states that "Lesbian and gay adolescents have one of the highest suicide rates, one of the highest drop out rates, and one of the highest substance abuse rates in the country." One out of ten teenagers attempts suicide. A third of these do so because of concern about being homosexual. That means that in every statistical classroom across the country there is one young person in danger of dying for lack of information and support concerning his or her sexuality. In his book, *Telling Tales Out of School: Gays, Lesbians and Bisexuals Revisit Their School Days*, Kevin Jennings (1998) writes that "Our stories are our best weapons in the fight against homophobia."

I found that my story did a great deal of educating for diversity. Tina speaks of her total shock at finding out that she had a gay professor:

> I still remember that first night of class and someone asked how your winter break was. You mentioned that you had visited West Virginia and something about ". . . ever since I Came Out." I felt shock immediately—a gay professor! I could not believe it (and you were open about it). I remember feeling disgust—the idea of two men together repulsed me. However, as time went on, I saw you as a person, a good person, a good educator and I did not care whether you were hetero/homosexual because that did not influence the way you taught (directly at least). I developed respect for you and soon admired you for being honest with yourself as well as with your students. You are courageous because you do not hide from the truth and do not care what people think. Having an "open" professor was a wonderful experience for me because I have lived a somewhat sheltered life and after meeting you, I learned to look beneath, to look at the spirit.

Very recently I received an e-mail from one of Tina's high school science students. She was upset by a negative article on homosexuality in her school newspaper. Tina had given her my e-mail address so that she could gather some information and write a rebuttal. Three years ago Tina and I wrote our stories together and, now, her student adds her voice to our conversation.

Carlos shares about his concern about having a gay professor. "Initially I might have had reservations about the nature of your class because of your gay orientation. I knew some about you because my girlfriend was in your class before. I never have seen her take such an interest in any professor's class before. I lost any reservations within weeks because I learned so much information about education and about you." There were many students, like Willow, that talked about how my being gay had little impact upon them except that it continued to deconstruct societal stereotypes of what is meant by being gay. "On a personal level it was good to get to know someone who was gay on a more intimate level and keep reinforcing the idea that stereotypes of someone who is gay are just that . . . stereotypes."

When we tell our stories to each other, we both find the meaning of our lives and are healed from our loneliness and isolation (Keen, 1989). Every I is a we. When you tell your story, I am able to see some of myself in it. When I tell my story, you see your reflection. Is this not, simply, what Freire wrote of when he spoke of the importance of dialogue? bell hooks (1994) states that "As a classroom community, our capacity to generate excitement is deeply affected by our interest in one another, in hearing one another's voices, in recognizing one another's presence" (p. 8). She goes on to say that "any radical pedagogy must insist that everyone's presence is acknowledged." There is universal truth and wisdom in story. To understand yourself is to understand all people. Story changed every aspect of how I taught.

Certainly, my being an Out gay professor who is training teachers is an act of social justice. I believe, though, that any time any of us speak our Truths it is an act of social justice. hooks (1994) calls this "engaged pedagogy." Engaged pedagogy is to educate as the practice of freedom. It is to believe that not only is it our job to share information with students, but that it is our privilege and responsibility to "share in the intellectual and spiritual growth of our students" (p. 13). hooks states that we must teach "to transgress those boundaries that would confine each pupil to a rote, assembly-line approach to learning" (p. 13). Engaged pedagogy is an act of political activism in and of itself. Surprising to me, though, was that most of the responses students e-mailed me were not about the affects of my being Out. Instead, it was the "Curriculum of my Self" that seemed to have left the larger impact. Mary says, "I am not sure if my educational experience was really in any way affected by your being gay. It was strongly influenced by who you are." Carlos stated:

> You know what I really gained from you? It was seeing you model everything. It was your showing me and my peers about you—the Jeff Sapp who taught my class, the Jeff Sapp—the person. Who you were. Where you were from. What you were about. Before this I wouldn't tell my students anything about me. If I modeled poetry writing, vignette writing and journal writing I would make up the entry/experience and I would tell them that. After Sapp, I opened up and related every one of my "modelings" to my life. To what I was about. Where I was from. Me. This is the greatest gift you gave me. You modeled for me how I could open up to my students and make myself more of a person and not just a figure in front of a classroom setting.

Indeed, it was the sharing of the "Curriculum of the Self" that deconstructed the traditional power paradigm of teacher and student in the classroom. Students saw my sharing of my sexual orientation as the sharing of an intimacy. One student wrote: "One way that your being gay might have affected your role as a professor was that it was something very personal that you shared with us. It was like a confidence you trusted us with (not meaning that it was a secret or anything). It was a way of bringing in your personal life to the course." Education typically divorces the self from knowing and, in doing so, creates a power struggle where people only have two choices: be a person who forces their distortions on others or be a person who has succumbed to others' distortions of themselves (Palmer, 1983). Donna demonstrated the theme of the deconstruction of power when she stated that "I am mildly embarrassed to say that it was quite late in the term before I even realized you were gay. Being a good Jewish mother, my first reaction was, 'How do I go about introducing my wonderful gay professor Jeff to my beloved gay cousin Joel?'" Donna didn't see her relationship with me in traditional teacher-student parameters. Instead, she saw me as someone she would want as a member of her family.

Let me tell you a story that is an old story, but one that bears repeating. Dewey (1938) stated 65 years ago that "education is essentially a social process." He wrote about how democratic social arrangements promote a better quality of human experience. "Enforced quiet and acquiescence prevent pupils from disclosing their real natures. They enforce artificial uniformity. They put *seeming* before *being*" (Dewey, 1938). I still find that the most amazing indictment about many schools today . . . putting *seeming* before *being*. I just this day finished reading a set of papers in which preservice teachers interviewed children. One of the typical questions they asked children of all ages was "What is a good student?" Even the first graders had already mastered the art of *seeming*. They replied, "Someone who sits quietly, sits straight, and has their hands folded on their desk and does what the teacher says." Dewey said that "the non-social character of the traditional school is seen in the fact that it erected silence into one of its prime virtues" (Dewey, 1938). I agree with Freire (1990) that "innumerable cultures of silence still exist; there are numbed, hungry, and compliant populations everywhere." Freire goes on to say that those who are oppressed must see examples of vulnerability from the oppressors so that a contrary conviction can begin to grow in them. I believe that sharing stories from the "Curriculum of the Self" can do just this. "When professors bring narratives of their experiences into classroom discussions it eliminates the possibility that we can function as all knowing, silent interrogators. It is often productive if professors take the first risk, linking confessional narratives to academic discussions so as to show how experience can illuminate and enhance our understanding of academic material" (hooks, 1994, p. 21). Sharing our stories creates a place where "freedom can sit down" (Greene, 1988). It is a way of being co-present with each other.

The "Curriculum of my Self" is only the model. What I really want to do is redirect students' attention away from my voice and to each others' voices. I am deliberate about this. I even go as far as to begin each class session with what is known as a Gratitude Walk (Jenson, 1999). Students take a ten-minute walk with each other and share with each other the GLP of the Gratitude Walk. The GLP helps them remember the three questions they share with each other during their walk: What are you *G*rateful for in your life right now? What are you *L*earning (in class or in life)? What is a *P*romise you can make to yourself today? The Gratitude Walk becomes one of the best loved practices in our learning community because, as students walk with a different class member each time, they are invited to become a real part of each others' lives. "How much does the possibility of freedom depend on critical reflectiveness, on self-understanding, on insight into the world? How much does it depend on being with others in a caring relationship? How much depends on actually coming together with unknown others in similar predicament, in an 'existential project' reaching toward what is not yet? How much does it depend on an integration of the felt and the known, the subjective and the objective, the private and the public spheres?" (Greene, 1988).

I have a running joke with my students that at any given moment I may make them stand in a circle, hold hands, and sing "Kumba-ya." We always chuckle together at this. It is after the chuckle that I embed the story that I have just shared with them into the theory and practice of teaching. I know that people are suspicious of teachers talking too much about themselves. After all, who didn't have that old teacher in high school that you baited with a story about his experience in World War II so that he'd go on and on about himself and you wouldn't have to do any work in class that day? The danger in telling our stories is that our ego can get out of control. Dewey (1938) said that "the road of the new education is not an easier one to follow than the old road but a more strenuous and difficult one." I think he knew that his dear Deweyian midway—the balance between the cognitive and the affective—was a hard-won accomplishment. "There is no discipline in the world so serve as the discipline of experience subjected to the tests of intelligent development and direction" (Dewey, 1938). Freire also wrote about this when he penned that for dialogue to be liberatory it had to be infused with love. "Because love is an act of courage, not of fear, love is commitment to other people. No matter where the oppressed are found, the act of love is commitment to their cause—the cause of liberation. And this commitment, because it is loving, is dialogical. As an act of bravery, love cannot be sentimental; as an act of freedom, it must not serve as a pretext for manipulation. It must generate other acts of freedom; otherwise, it is not love" (Freire, 1990). We do not share our stories with each other so that we can wreak emotional havoc on each other and manipulate each other in our preordained directions. We share our stories so that we may enter into communication with each other in states of being, not seeming. It is as Buber (1958) said when he stated that we could interact with each other as objects in an I-It relationship, or as subjects in an I-Thou relationship.

In his now classical work, *To Know as We Are Known: Toward a Spirituality of Education*, Parker J. Palmer (1983) talks about the origins of our knowledge. History suggests that there are two primary sources for our ways of knowing. One is curiosity. The other is control. Curiosity is knowledge as an end unto itself. Curiosity can kill. Control is knowledge as a means to a practical end. Our desire to control has put deadly power is some very unstable hands. Another word for control is power. These ways of knowing are the "objective" ways of knowing that schools so value. The Latin root of "objective" means "to put against, to oppose." In German its literal translation is "standing-over-against-ness" (Palmer, 1983). Objective knowing, in and of itself, puts us in an adversary relationship with each other and with the world. It has made us enemies of ourselves. Objectivism believes that the knower and the objects that are to be known are apart and independent from each other. I believe this is really about power. As long as I can remove myself from what I do and hide behind my larger mastery of content area knowledge, I remain more powerful than my students. It is when I step out from behind the podium of fear and reveal myself to my students that I become a colearner with them. I am heartened by Maria Harris' (1987) extension of Buber's I and Thou. She extends the I-Thou relationship to include what we'd normally see as lifeless objects—the physical arrangements of our classroom, chairs, and spaces between us. They are not an I-It—lifeless. They are an I-Thou—alive and mediating.

Palmer states that there is a third way of knowing though and it is the knowing that Freire spoke of—a knowing that originates in compassion and love. The goal of this knowing is "the reunification and reconstruction of broken selves and worlds . . . a knowledge born of compassion aims not at exploiting and manipulating but at reconciling the world of itself" (Palmer, 1983). hooks (1994) speaks of how Thich Nhat Hanah, the Buddist monk, informed her pedagogy. He "offered a way of thinking about pedagogy which emphasized wholeness, a union of mind, body and spirit. His focus on a holistic approach to learning and spiritual practice enabled me to overcome years of socialization that had taught me to believe a classroom was diminished if students and professors regarded one another as 'whole' human beings, striving not just for knowledge in books, but knowledge about how to live in the world" (p. 14). Palmer (1983) states that this way of knowing is an "act of entering and embracing the reality of the other, of allowing the other to enter and embrace our own. In such knowing we know and are known as members of one community." Palmer reiterates what Dewey and Freire have said. He states that this kind of knowing is "not a soft and sentimental virtue; it is not a fuzzy feeling of romance." Instead, it is a "tough love" that calls us to involvement, mutuality, and accountability. Consequently, I would say that this communal knowing is what keeps ego in check. It is in relation to others that I can live out (or discover that I am lacking) my ways of knowing.

It is the teacher that is the mediator between the knower and the known ... between the learner and the subject to be learned. We may teach our students about democracy (the subject being learned, the known) but if we merely tell them about democracy and run a classroom in a Hilter-esque fashion then, trust me, we have not taught them a thing about democracy. They have learned the "Curriculum of the Self" of that teacher (the knower). "I am forming students who know neither how to learn in freedom nor how to live freely, guided by an inner sense of truth" (Palmer, 1988). What I am really teaching is a mode of relationship between the knower and the unknown. I am teaching a way of being in the world (Palmer, 1983). More is caught than taught. In his book, *The Courage to Teach*, Palmer (1998) states that "Teaching, like any truly human activity, emerges from one's inwardness, for better or worse. As I teach, I project the condition of my soul onto my students, my subject, and our way of being together" (p. 2).

The root meaning of "to educate" is "to draw out." I cannot imagine a teaching that does not want and need to hear the stories of students. We teach people, not content. If we see ourselves as the holders of an objective truth that needs to be deposited into our empty-bank students, we are working from an unbridled ego. The humanist, revolutionary educator's "effort must be imbued with a profound trust in people and their creative power. To achieve this she/he must be partner of the students in her/his relations with them" (Freire, 1990). Power in the form of knowledge is not the property of any one individual. Students know when a teacher works from ego and power. Myss (1993) states that "when an individual is focused upon the acquisition of any form of external power, it is indicative of what is absent internally in that person. The stronger the obsession, the greater the lack of authentic power" (p. 12).

In his book *The Seat of the Soul*, Gary Zukav (1999) says that authentic power is aligning "our thoughts, emotion, and actions with the highest part of ourselves" (p. 26). Sadly, most schooling does not model for students what authentic power is because, as hooks states, "the objectification of the teacher within bourgeois educational structure seems to denigrate notions of wholeness and uphold the idea of a mind/body split, one that promotes and supports compartmentalization" (1994, p. 16). Dewey said that "children are more sensitive to the signs and symptoms of this difference than adults are" (Dewey, 1938). He also said that when education is based upon experience and educative experience is seen to be a social process, that the teacher loses the role of external boss and takes on the role of leader of group activities. Greene (1988) says that freedom shows itself when people come authentically together without masks, pretenses, and badges of office. I heard the story once of a first night of class introduction activity. Everyone was going around telling their degrees, their experiences, and their titles. The introduction came to an African-American woman and she spent a half-hour telling the class about her family, their roots, their hopes and dreams. Not once did she ever mention what she did. We must come together to be affected by each other, to be involved with each other. "Realities ultimate structure is that of an organic interrelated, mutually responsive community of being. Relationships—not facts and reasons—are the key to reality" (Palmer, 1998). One of today's leaders in brain-compatible teaching told me that the number one factor in a brain-compatible classroom is its relationships (Jenson, 1999). I loved how Martin Buber, in his classic work titled *I and Thou*, states that "In the beginning is the relation" (Buber, 1958, p. 69).

I think we are afraid. Of each other. Of ourselves. Of coming together in vulnerability. I recently sat in a meeting where we were developing a new MAT program (Masters in Teaching). Some of my colleagues were concerned that people who had only been teaching for a few months were going to be getting a Masters degree. "What can they offer in reflective practice and research with such limited experience?" they said. I considered this Deweyan/Freirian heresy. I told them as much. Dewey assumed "that amid all uncertainties there is one permanent frame of reference: namely, the organic connection between education and personal experience." Ron Scapp (hooks, 1994, p. 148) states that "when one speaks from the perspective of one's immediate experiences, something is created in the classroom for students, something for the very first time. Focusing on experience allows students to claim a knowledge base from which they can speak." hooks states that:

> ... more radical subject matter does not create a liberatory pedagogy, that a simple practice like including personal experience may be more constructively challenged than simply changing the

curriculum. That is why there has been such critique of the place of experience—of confessional narrative—in the classroom. One of the ways you can be written off quickly as a professor by colleagues who are suspicious of progressive pedagogy is to allow your students, or yourself, to talk about experience; sharing personal narratives yet linking that knowledge with academic information really enhances our capacity to know. (1994, p. 148)

The founder of Foxfire (Wiggington, 1991) said that "To make our education effective, we must start with the real-world reality of our students' lives, be it centered around raccoons, ginseng, a little tavern, McDonald's, or a ghetto street—accept that, build on that, and broaden that. Otherwise, we demean that reality, or negate it. We imply that nothing they've learned in their lives is valid or has relevance. We deny their past, deny their present, and proceed from the assumption that they're ignorant and deprived and that we must correct the situation or they're doomed." Freire (1990) stated:

> How can I dialogue if I always project ignorance onto others and never perceive my own? How can I dialogue if I regard myself as a case apart from other men—mere "its" in whom I cannot recognize others I's? How can I dialogue if I consider myself a member of the in-group of "pure" men, the owners of truth and knowledge, for whom all non-members are "these people" or "the great unwashed"? How can I dialogue if I start from the premise that naming the world is the task of an elite and that the presence of the people in history is a sign of deterioration, thus to be avoided? How can I dialogue if I am closed to—and even offended by—the contribution of others? How can I dialogue if I am afraid of being displaced, the mere possibility causing me torment and weakness? Self-sufficiency is incompatible with dialogue. Men who lack humility (or have lost it) cannot come to the people, cannot be their partners in naming the world.

The problem is that, in education and in urban classrooms, the focus is always outward. These huge books contain the realities that we deem important and anything inside the teacher or the students is suspect. A teacher talks about how he or she has experienced these outside realities and tries to relate that to students—or even worse, relates how someone else has related to outside realities and then tries to relate that to students. Palmer says that the student becomes the spectator and is "sitting in the far reaches of the upper grandstand, two or three times removed from what is happening on the field" (Palmer, 1983). Yes, involvement has its problems, but is detachment the solution? It seems logical, as we enter a new millennium, that we move toward a balance of teaching to the whole person. We must recognize "that no human can live happily when one part of his being is nurtured at the expense of another. In doing so (teaching to the whole person), we will be better equipped to nurture more than just the minds and bodies of the students within our schools and will as well begin our work in rediscovering and caring for the lost souls in American Education" (Lawrence, 1996, p. 229).

Plain and simple, we need teachers who have done "inner work." How can we expect to teach transformation when we do not even understand what is meant by the word? Thich Nhat Hahn believed and called for healers, teachers, therapists, and those in the helping professions to first heal themselves. He said, "If the helper is unhappy, he or she cannot help many people" (hooks, 1994, p. 15). "The transformation of teaching must begin in the transformed heart of the teacher. Only in the heart searched and transformed by truth will new teaching techniques and strategies for institutional change find grounding" (Palmer, 1983). I am calling not only for the "teacher as reflector" of their practice, but for the "teacher as reflector" of themselves. We can blame the "system" only so long and we have been doing so for decades.

Dewey said that there was something immoral about how things have stayed exactly the same for so long. I am a great fan of the history of education and teach a foundations course on the subject. I find irony in showing students quotes from the Quintilian in 95 A.D. that say the exact same things about curriculum that we are still saying today. I watch their mouths gape in astonishment. At some point we must realize that institutions are only projections of what is going on in the human heart.

For things to change, I must change. This is not California New Age mumbo-jumbo. We simply teach who we are. A wounded person teaches woundedness. A person in search of her freedom teaches others how to search for their freedom. You can't teach liberation. You have to *be* liberation. "If professors are wounded, damaged individuals, people who are not self-actualized then they will seek asylum in the academy rather than seek to make the academy a place of challenge, dialectical interchange, and growth" (hooks, 1994, p. 165). Nel Noddings (1984) said that the caring teacher must struggle with students as subjects in search of their own projects, their own ways of making sense of the world around them. I spent 30-some years teaching from my unknown self. I was teaching fear, voicelessness, and conformity. It wasn't until I began to journal in search of my own liberation that I began to be a participant in liberatory, emancipatory education.

Dewey, like the existentialist thinkers, didn't think that the self was complete. He said that the self was "something in continuous formation through choices of action" (Dewey, 1916). We create ourselves by going beyond what exists and bringing something new into being (Sartre, 1943/1956). We must always be birthing ourselves. "Education as growth and maturity should be an ever-present process" (Dewey, 1938). Freire spoke about an education that affirms people as being in the process of becoming—" . . . as unfinished, uncompleted beings in and with a likewise unfinished reality" (Freire, 1990). Indeed, he even stated that "The joy of being human is our unfinishedness." I am reminded of Paulo Freire writing that we all have the same profession and it is the "humanization" of each other. We must affirm each other as "subjects of decisions" instead of "objects." We must all strive for our own completion and this is a striving that can never end (Greene, 1988). hooks states that "I celebrate teaching that enables transgressions—a movement against and beyond boundaries. It is that movement which makes education the practice of freedom" (hooks, 1994, p. 12). I started this chapter with the first story I had ever written, "The Death Dragon." I will end the chapter with its conclusion.

*One day, after Death Dragon had stolen years
and years and years and years from Sorrow and Fear's life,
he heard other songs.
They were different songs but they were the same.
Sorrow and Fear was scared at first,
but then decided to find the other Singers.
He found them gathered at The Holy.
And there they sang. Some alone. Some together.
Taking turns singing about their Dragons.
And there were no words. Just sounds.
And Sorrow and Fear understood all songs.*

*It seems that there were other Dragons about.
He hadn't been alone.
Terrible Dragons.
Hopeless Dragon. Shame Dragon. Despair Dragon. Guilt Dragon.
And the worst Dragon of all . . . only known as "Conquered."
Some of the songs were about Singers who had been silenced forever.
Sorrow and Fear wept. But still he listened.
The Singers had other songs. Songs that told of horrible battles.
Of Dragons chained. Of Dragons Slain.
Of Singers freed. Of Singers changed.
And Sorrow and Fear felt The Happy spring up in him for the first time.*

*And still he listened.
And sometimes he sang along. And all rejoiced when Sorrow and Fear found his voice.
And one day Sorrow and Fear sang alone.
And Singers wept, but Happy-weeping, not Sorrow weeping.*

*And when Sorrow and Fear ended his song the Singers told him that now they had to change his name because he had found his voice.
And so they called him
Courage and Hope.*

I once read "The Death Dragon" to Joseph Campbell's successor-of-sorts, Jamake Highwater. When I finished the story Jamake said, "You have written your myth." We must all live the hero's (and shero's) journey, the search for the Holy Grail of ourselves. I believe in the transformative power of story more than anything. When Czeslan Milosz won the Nobel Prize for literature he said, "In a room where people unanimously maintain a conspiracy of silence, one word of truth sounds like a pistol shot." Dewey called for the education of the whole child and I, likewise, am calling for the education of the whole teacher. Urban education can be enhanced, but it's not going to be enhanced by endless political reforms. Palmer (1998, p. 6) states that "to educate is to guide students on an inner journey toward more truthful ways of seeing and being in the world. How can schools perform their mission without encouraging the guides to scout out that inner terrain?" I believe that the way to seriously work for the transformation of schooling is to vigilantly work for the transformation of Self. Yesterday, as I put my finishing touches on this chapter, there was yet one more violent school shooting here in Los Angeles. A man walked into a daycare center and fired upon five- and six-year-old children, sending several wounded children to the hospital. It has been the most common image we have had of education and schooling this year. We need images of hope to diffuse these images of horror. I believe that the images of hope will come from the transformed hearts of teachers. It is the only way to turn Sorrow and Fear into Courage and Hope. And it is why I start each class session with the phrase—Let me tell you a story. . . .

REFERENCES

Buber, M. (1958) *I and thou* (Ronald Gregor Smith, trans.). New York: Collier Books, Macmillan Publishing Company.

D'Emilio, J. (1992). *Making trouble: Essays on gay history, politics, and the university.* New York: Routledge.
Denzin, N. K. (1989). *Interpretive interactionism.* Newbury, CA: Sage.
Dewey, J. (1916). *Democracy and education.* New York: Macmillan Company.
Dewey, J. (1960). Philosophies of freedom. In R. Bernstein (Ed.), *On experience, nature, and freedom.* New York: The Liberal Arts Press. (Original work published 1928)
Dewey, J. (1938). *Experience and education.* New York: Collier Macmillan.
Freire, P. (1990). *Pedagogy of the oppressed.* New York: Continuum.
Greene, M. (1988). *The dialectic of freedom.* New York: Teachers College Press.
Harris, M. (1987). *Teaching and religious imagination: An essay in the theology of teaching.* San Francisco: Harper.
hooks, b. (1994). *Teaching to transgress: Education as the practice of freedom.* New York: Routledge.
Jennings, K. (1998). *Telling tales out of school: Gays, lesbians, and bisexuals revisit their school days.* Los Angeles: Alyson Books.
Jenson, E. (1999, July 11-16) Six-Day Workshop on the Brain. San Diego, CA.
Keen, S. (1989). *Your mythic journey: Finding meaning in your life through writing and storytelling.* New York: Putnam.
Lawrence, T. A. (1996). *Lost souls: A cry to recapture what is disappearing from American schooling.* Battlecreek, MI: B's Hive.
McConnell-Celi, S. (1993). *Twenty-first century challenge: Lesbians and gays in education.* Red Bank, NJ: Lavender Crystal Press.
Moustakas, C. (1990). *Heuristic research: Design, methodology, and applications.* Newbury Park, CA: Sage.
Myss, C. (1993). *The creation of health: The emotional, psychological, and spiritual responses that promote health and healing.* New York: Random House.
Noddings, N. (1984). *Caring: A feminine approach to ethics and moral education.* Berkeley: University of California Press.
Palmer, P. J. (1983). *To know as we are known: A spirituality of education.* San Francisco: Harper Collins.
Palmer, P. J. (1998). *The courage to teach: Exploring the inner landscape of a teacher's life.* San Francisco: Jossey Bass.
Sartre, J.-P. (1956). *Being and nothingness.* New York: Philosophical Library (Original work published 1943).
Wiggington, E. (1991). *Foxfire 25 years.* New York: Doubleday.
Zukav, G. (1999). *Seat of the soul.* New York: Simon & Schuster.

III

UNIVERSITY FACULTY IN THE SCHOOLS

6

Reworking Urban Educational Leadership Through Naming and Narrative Inquiry

Penny S. Bryan

"Tell me your story." In many ways we come to know the world and ourselves by using words to name the things and ideas in it and by telling stories about our own experiences and those of others. When the specific stories connect to some larger aspect of reality, language becomes a powerful mediator between experiences and meaning; how we name things and tell stories are quite important to how we view the world. If there are stories in urban education that go unheard and unheeded, then human beings and organizations exist but cannot flourish.

The chapter begins with factual data to support a critical stance for redefinition of the terms "urban," "community," and "educational leadership." After justifying and redefining key vocabulary, the second part of the chapter develops a revisited conceptualization of urban educational leadership. I argue that narrative inquiry, when connected to critical inquiry, provides a kind of learning that is powerful and moral. However, it is only when these redefinitions connect explicitly to lived experiences that a legitimate use of the narrative as a mode of inquiry comes into existence. In order to connect the parts necessary for validity, I then invite the reader to look at a real story of this re-formed urban educational leadership at Pio Pico Elementary School in Santa Ana California. The chapter ends with a brief summary and personal reflection. The epistemological aim is that these narratives, including that of the researcher-as-storyteller, are integrative. They can form a legitimate mode of inquiry research and result in an effective construct for contextualized knowing and understanding that can impact future action. The premise is that critical, narrative storytelling can be a form of truthtelling; it can serve as a research vehicle whose purpose is to raise consciousness, deepen understanding, both descriptive and normative, and to inspire wise actions. Insiders are therefore key inquirers into their own practices and perspectives.

Human speech, connecting sounds and experiences, probably began in caves and around campfires. Storytelling is a basic part of being human in most cultures. It implies an awareness of time other than the present. It infers that what happened in the past can influence what happens in the future. Greek stories centered around mythical, idealized, and fixed heroes. The Jewish tribes of Ur were among the first in Western civilization to include personal human identity and story as part of their history (Wolpe, 1992). The notion is that human beings and cultures can develop. There is life-time. Some ordering, of what is otherwise chaos, is made conscious through reconstructions of events as a way of making sense, assigning power, and defining both ourselves and the world for future reference and action. Life is not a predetermined wheel to which we are only collectively and endlessly shackled; we have free will, choice, and the possibility to develop.

Individual, cultural, and institutional narratives are, however, incomplete texts. They are partial mixtures of knowledge—some public, some private, some known by others but not to ourselves, and some unconscious to self and others. Based upon the epistemological assumption that we can never know the whole because we are embedded in it, we can, however, move toward a deeper understanding of ourselves and others by closely scrutinizing whom we sanction as the official storytellers and by what meanings and motives we ascribe to the words that describe our worlds. This enhanced understanding, even though not complete, is necessary for human and community development.

This choice of a narrative research perspective conveys three important beliefs: first, the primordial relationships among experience, language, and story; and second, the usefulness of the critical and social constructivist theories to guide us in making wise judgments; and finally, the courage required to take such actions in the world. I believe that there is *phronesis,* Plato's term for practical wisdom (Heslep, 1997), to be gleaned from critical inquiry into connections that are particular to individual and collective lived experiences and how they are voiced, in this chapter, in urban educational settings. Each of the other chapters in this book contains a powerful narrative that offers the reader some understandings and hopefulness. All are specific and concurrently transcendent of single experience. What may be unique in this chapter is not the separate theoretical postures, but the attempt to understand the integration required for *phronesis* or practical wisdom, when trying to build leadership capacity in schools with urban features.

As the faculty coordinator of the Ed Leadership and Administration programs, I have led the efforts to design our curricula and programs in a model of shared leadership. We have labored collaboratively to address the political and moral aspects of leadership practice and the impact both have on instructional design, organizational structure, and implementation. In writing this book chapter, I began by seeking some understandings among certain ideas and actions. Convinced of the possibilities of constructivist theory aligning leading and learning (Lambert et al., 1995) and its application to the ideas for building leadership capacity in schools (Lambert, 1998), how could I adapt this lens so that it connected in meaningful ways to a critical stance and social justice? I wanted to explore words like "urban," "community," and "leadership," that when viewed from a postmodern lens might shift their significance; traditional schema could become open for critical examination, perhaps take on new and multiple meanings and expand the stories as codifications that can inform our personal and institutional consciences.

While seeking connections to the themes of this book, we faculty authors have been meeting at our university campus in the heart of Orange County, California. The vital writing process dialogues with university colleagues have reminded me to find the meaning in context (Mishler, 1979), my own and those of others, to back up and question the terms: urban, social justice and building leadership capacity, before exploring any possible relationships among them. I need to know the meanings, shared and discrepant, that *the participants* make of these concepts, because if we believe in building leadership capacity for a whole community, such theories-in-use shape important decisions made in the educational environments in which we live, conduct inquiry, and work (Argyris & Schon, 1978; Senge, 2000).

Orange County, California has been tenaciously characterized by many since the 1950s as homogeneous (white, conservative) and suburban, but is that rendering still accurate? And if those descriptors don't fit for me and others, then what alternative choices do confirm our lived experiences? What implications does a reconceptualization have for the theory and practice of leadership in our public schools? What are the visions and challenges of trying to build leadership capacity, community, and knowledge in ways that promote social justice and care? And finally, why does this strand of inquiry matter so much to me?

IDENTITY AND GEOGRAPHY: FROM POST-WORLD WAR II-SUBURBAN TO POSTMODERN-URBAN

One day, rugged sierra, the next tamed suburbia . . . all this growth is troubling to Orange County dwellers, who said they have grown intolerant of an increasingly urban life, even while they enjoy some of the economic rewards, according to a Times Orange County poll. . . . "There's been a hardening in the attitudes," said Scott Bollens, chairman of urban and regional planning at UC Irvine. "We're back where we were in the late 1980s in terms of people being concerned about and opposed to growth. . . ."

*Three new residents arrive each hour, two of them Latino and the third of Asian descent. That's about 70 people a day, everyday for 20 years.
*One new housing unit will be built at least each hour—as many as 9,000 a year into the 2000s—to handle them.
*And nearly a million new jobs are on the way, or 90 new hires every day. With somebody new clocking in every 15 minutes, it will add to the congestion, because there will not be enough housing for them all.

There is a lava flow of humanity and economy coming to Orange County, and even if they wanted to, there isn't much anyone can do to stem it. . .

Orange County surpassed Los Angeles in population density per square mile during the late 1960s, according to state Department of Finance figures and now ranks among the most populous counties in the nation. With about 3,450 people per square mile in 1998, Orange County is ahead of counties that are home to places such as Denver and New Orleans and just behind Detroit, Milwaukee and Bergen County, NJ. Larger and larger portions of the County are dense, more urban, socially diverse. . . .

Some experts don't believe Orange County's older communities, which were among California's early suburbs, were designed with longevity in mind. . . . The communities of the '50s are in danger of becoming the slums of the '90s. (Ourlian, 1998, p. A16)

DENSE, DIVERSE, DISTURBING TO SOME . . . URBAN?

Who, where, and when is urban? Why does it matter? Why do older images persist and what does urban mean? I believe that in critical ways for education, urban is increasingly us, right here and now, a state of mind, not geography. And Orange County, California is not alone. Many "suburban" areas of the United States are dealing with previously labeled "urban" issues of immigration, housing, jobs, youth, and crime. If so, then what might this renaming with such terms as "postsuburban or metropolitan suburban" (Klein, 1988) mean for places that have characterized themselves since World War II as suburban? Why should we bother with language; what's in a name?

In the worlds and words of postmodern reflection, everything in education is political (hooks, 1994) and is referenced to power. Those in power define knowledge, make the rules about legitimacy, and chronicle the official version of history. A look at state-level involvement in curriculum through frameworks, standards, and high-stakes testing supports that much important decision making about the content of what is taught in schools is not inclusive of all voices. We need to begin to acknowledge the locus of power by naming our situations, because in that process is the possibility that we can imagine the world in which we live more freely and fairly. In that process is the power to use language to plan and act in ways that will build infrastructures of physical and moral support and the hope of meaningful participation and social justice for all the inhabitants. Only through the naming or codifying and decodifying (Freire, 1985) our present situations can we begin to understand how to distribute power more equitably, so that we can recreate the future cultures and architectures in which all the peoples of an educational community work, make meaning, and learn. Only through the naming can we possibly face the oppressive politicization, polarization, and demonization of ideas and persons, with whom we disagree or fear.

> There is an illusion that poverty, social instability and community decline stop at the central city borders and that US suburbs are monoliths of affluence, social harmony and political unity. In truth, the suburbs are diverse—and as plagued with problems—as the central cities they surround. . . . Disturbingly this diversity too often means that communities within a region are growing farther and farther apart, resulting in social and economic polarization. (Orfield, 1998, p. M1)

Writers (Canada, 1995; Kozol, 2000) describe urban as having an economic underclass, marginalized individuals, and subgroups based upon race, religion, gender, sexual identity, and language identities. Urban areas contain streets and formally prescribed neighborhoods of cultural and racial sameness that are multigenerational and densely populated with wide disparities among physical and fiscal conditions. By modern post-World War II standards, urban U.S. inhabitants live closely together with ethnic and racial neighborhoods tightly juxtaposed to one another. Local border crossings can mean moving from one block to another. These are small, well-defined lines of safety and risk for local denizens.

Less visible and larger are the postmodern movements of some urban transient populations back and forth across national borders that can be charted like the daily ocean tide schedules. Only blue jeans, franchises, and other artifacts of commodification appear to be global. People have emigrated to developed countries because of economic and social opportunities, but still remain significantly connected to their nations of birth and ancestry. They enter this country and gravitate first to areas where they find others like themselves. Such enclaves, which used to mean the central cities, now characterize areas defined as metropolitan suburban or "edge" cities. In addition, the fastest growing population is that of racially and culturally mixed children. And then add subcultures of gangs, life revolving around the neighborhood church, and an "urbane," educated middle class made up of artists and professionals, who choose to remain or return to the setting because of its very "color," resources, culture, and inspiration. There is a sense of freedom of identity within the comfort and belonging to a subculture with its shared history, rituals, and customs.

In summary, the urban portrait is strikingly complex. Such demographics and characteristics describe more and more of what was previously labeled homogenous and suburban. Many of the communities in which our university campuses and local school districts are located increasingly manifest urban characteristics. Not to name these features where we know them to be is to ignore, to design error

(Argyris, 1990), however ingenuously or unconsciously. The result of such ignore-ance is to perpetuate its concomitant inequities. Excluding parts of an image or people may succeed for a little while, despite the distortion, sense of malaise (Argyris, 1990), and/or emergence of alternative systems. Eventually, what serves to repress feelings and alienate groups sows the seeds of unrest and violence that rupture when there are no legitimate vehicles for participation and expression.

The language of an ideal vision of urban social justice in schools would mean that when mirrors are held up to the collected faces, power is equitably distributed and everyone finds him or herself fully included in the reflection. In one case study of Turin, a multiethnic urban high school, researchers expressed that

> ... both teachers and administrators acknowledged the value of what they were learning from the students they had come to teach. ... Within this perspective cultural ethnic and racial diversity appeared not just as a resource for academic engagement, but as a stimulus to moral development of teachers, students, administrators, parents and other community members.
>
> As a Turin parent noted: This decade is the crucial time to be prepared to effectively understand the changes in our community. Many are giving lip service, rather than doing something constructive. I recognize that we are asking a lot from the schools, but I couldn't think of a better place to face the challenge than in our schools today. (Wagner, 1998, p. 98)

Affirming a critical stance requires more than "lip service." Naming that most of our neighborhoods have urban characteristics, then, has serious implications for a kind of moral codevelopment (Wagner, 1998) for leadership in education, pre-K through postsecondary.

> [T]here is yet a third perspective toward power and ethnicity emerging among the teachers at Turin High School. This third perspective differs from both the academics and students engagement perspectives in two key respects: First, it acknowledges that Turin students are facing cultural, moral and political challenges that may be more complex than those faced by Turin teachers and administrators in their own adolescence. Second, it acknowledges the value to adults—including teachers, administrators and parents—of learning with and from students about how to face these

> challenges constructively. Within this perspective—which I call moral codevelopment—teachers and administrators are also learners and students are also teachers. (Wagner, 1998, p. 93)

Having acknowledged the change in thinking, marked by shifts in language, from modern to postmodern and from urban/suburban to metropolitan urban context, I find that educational leadership also needs redefinition. The demographic shifts and urban characteristics have substantively changed the identity and context in which we work. In order to collectively become who we want to be, we need to first name the situation or chaos (Wheatly, 1994) in which we find ourselves now. There is the potential alignment of energies necessary to learn, self-organize, and transform ourselves and the systems, if we have the courage and will to first name them (Freire, 1985). There is less homogeneity than ten years ago in the populations of most of our schools and there will be less in the future. Only by acknowledging that we currently exhibit many of the features of urban education and comprehensively describing the collective and inclusive "we," can we get "unstuck" and let go of older mental models, action theories, and schema (Argyris, 1990; Lewin, cited in Johnson & Johnson, 1957; Senge, 2000) of who we were. We can then begin to dream and imagine ourselves anew in a world big enough to sustain every one of us.

> Leadership then becomes an act of release, as well as transformation. Persons are free to envisage what might be and what should be, even as they are supported in their efforts to devise their projects in an always ambiguous world. (Greene, 1995, p. ix)

There is no greater requisite of *democratic personhood* (Wilson, 1996) than the freedom to know, the freedom of ideas that supports human growth and development. There are powerful fears and reductive categorizing that all constituencies tend to construct regarding "others." These defensive images of identity need to be named, explored, and reframed. As diversity and proximity increase, so do the probabilities of prejudicial reasoning, conflict, and blaming others—Freire's naïve consciousness. When we talk of developing the leadership capacity that has to explore diversity and politics in order to codevelop a moral vision, this is a considerable feat of psychological and sociopolitical understanding and the will to act courageously.

POSTMODERN URBAN EDUCATIONAL COMMUNITY AND POWER

Most noticeable are the diversity of populations and constituencies and the varied manifestations of the values and beliefs they hold. The complex webs of relationships within and among individuals and subgroups can significantly help or inhibit the tasks that we need to do. As a traditional bureaucracy, much of the work that educators have done has been organized in cell- or hive-like constructs (Lortie, 1975) that are isolating and structured for competition. Legitimate knowledge is defined by the powerful. The roles, rules, structures, and processes support the assumption that some people will have power and control over others. Max Weber (1947), in the name of being fair and democratic, originally conceived of the bureaucracy as a vehicle for rewarding merit and knowledge, not patronage. As the bureaucratic organization became the dominant institutional form in education and in our culture, it became more hierarchical, inflexible, and inequitable. Federal, state, and local governmental bureaucracies have fought for control and power in education alongside organized labor and special interest groups. We must remember, however, that these groups are not monoliths; serious power plays for control also exist within each group, complicating any analysis or attempt to understand the dynamics. This need to describe what happens as we live our lives in the real world has given rise to micropolitical case studies and case stories, which look more closely at the power and ethics of implementation (Blase & Blase, 1998).

Dangerously, the move to standards has become a call for standardization based exclusively upon mainstream ideals. Accountability and excellence have become euphemisms for punishment (Evans, 1999) and perpetuating a culture of victimization.

> [A] diagnosis of failure encourages simplistic and even punitive rhetoric about "solutions" to the problem. What's the stated goal of change? It is to send more people to "reformed" schools! "Make teachers (*and other marginalized participants*) accountable" is another example of a popular punitive slogan that ignores the reality of how change—or learning—happens. Pressure in the form of increased test scores may get the attention of some teachers, but it will not create the organizational learning required to obtain significantly better results. As in a good constructivist classroom, the challenge in the change process is to create significantly higher expectations without the crippling anxiety that thwarts risk-taking and learning. (Wagner, 1998, p. 513)

Critical authors, such as Giroux (1997) and others, have focused our attention on the preservation of the status quo of those in power and marginalization of whole groups of others, who look, speak, or experience their realities in their own ways. Different has come to mean deficient and disenfranchised. To be remediated has meant to be assimilated based upon the assumptions, values, and norms of the dominant group. Citizenship has come to mean obedience.

COMMUNITY, BELONGING, AND CARE

We have been told that a primary responsibility of educational leadership is to develop a community of learners (Senge, 2000) and that to do that we need a shared vision. How do we share a vision and build a community while affirming differences? Acknowledging differences uncritically seems only to exacerbate them, encourage bipolarized categorization, and sound-bite communications.

> In trying to build community there is the danger; . . . to recreate sameness as a basis for community is anachronistically modernist and probably futile. Normative/constructive postmodernism offers a new metaphor for community, a global community that represents an interconnected web of persons across cultures and a new sense of community—acceptance of otherness and cooperation within difference. . . . When community is used in a modernist sense, it may unwittingly serve as a dividing practice or as a tool of social control. (Furman, 1998, p. 311)

What Furman so eloquently argues for is a critical concept of community that shifts power and perspective, connects to constructivism and moral codevelopment with all the participants engaged in educational learning and building leadership capacity.

> [A] post modern concept of community might be this: Postmodern community is community of difference. It is based on the ethics of acceptance of otherness with respect, justice and appreciation and on an interconnected, interdependent web of persons engaged in global community. It is fostered by processes that promote among its members the feelings of belonging, trust of others and safety. (Furman, 1998, p. 312)

Noddings (1992), Gilligan (1982), and Beck (1994) have written about care, the latter placing reciprocity of care as an even higher value than universal justice. They argue for an ethic of care that engenders belonging and trust and as a way of being in the world on a daily basis. This would seem an antidote to Willower's (1994) claim that postmodernist educational leadership languishes in the theoretical, devoid of practical application. In fact, just the opposite seems to be the case. This transformative kind of leadership requires personal responding and remaining in relationships that democratically negotiate and resolve conflicts across differences. Such leaders assign power and respect for the individual equitably. Critical and constructive postmodernists believe that being actively engaged in the world is what will constitute leadership and movement in any direction. I would add that the goal is movement toward moral codevelopment by the citizens who are "building a community of virtue" (Ryan & Bohlin, 2000, p. 309), and humanization of the institutions of schooling.

Care is necessary for educational leadership, but even here there is reason to pause and examine whose definition and assumptions are used as the foundational norm.

Audrey Thompson (1998) has written compellingly that the literature on an ethic of care has been colorblind, using an exclusionary white feminist perspective as the universal standard. Thus, those authors are guilty themselves of an universalistic position they criticized in redefining Lawrence Kohlberg's (1981) male-centered work on the stages of moral development. Thompson urges educators to explore black, feminist lessons for educational caring that she believes are different. When "colortalk" is suppressed as not nice, there is no naming of racism and therefore no possibility of problem posing and transformational change of individuals or whole systems in order to nurture democratic personhood (see the chapter by Wilson). Chris Argyris (1990) would claim that in such an embarrassing or threatening situation, defensive reasoning occurs, reinforced by organizational routines and unacknowledged through covering up and then covering up the cover up!

What do educational leaders need to know when trying to instill "the three C's ethic of care, concern and connection," such as Martin describes in her work "Schoolhome" (1985, 1992). Most significant is that despite intentionality, the participants' responses may be framed in terms of their own racial or cultural identities, thus universalizing and perpetuating a fourth C, colorblindness. For examples, let's use the terms "home" and "family." First, if we use Martin's term "schoolhome," whose definition of the perfect home prevails? Thompson (1998) promotes the notion of "home" as a safe, sacred place as a white social construct. Second, multiple conceptions of what constitutes "family" coexist within communities largely without mainstream acknowledgment or acceptance of any configuration other than the modern nuclear family. Thus, regardless of how some experience life differently, the words used by those with power become the "real" version. Difference or other is defined by relation to some accepted norm. Postmodern thought shifts this notion to accepting multiple variations *without one being the normal one against which variations are considered "other."*

> In sum, most of the research generated by White theorists of care has worked within a framework limited by the theorists' own distinctive cultural and class assumptions and by information from largely White, middle- and upper-middle-class respondents. Even when studying students of color, White researchers have tended to look for the culturally White practices and values that they and their theories-already recognize as caring. (Thompson, 1998, p. 531)

Definitions drawn from lived experiences of what constitutes moral and ethical behavior may be quite disparate. Particularly those with power need to examine what they assume are universal definitions and understandings in common. Minority stories may exist but remain invisible to those in power. This has important implications for building leadership capacity and community.

BUILDING LEADERSHIP CAPACITY IN SCHOOLS, A SHARED RESPONSIBILITY

What might the nature and practice of educational leadership look like as we consider it in the context of building the postmodern, urban community, one committed to social justice? As the patterns have become ever more complex and the thrust of change less predictable and accelerated, having one leader with authority at the top of the organizational pyramid no longer functions very well. It becomes apparent that for our changing landscape and scope of difference, no one person can most effectively lead alone to accomplish important desired outcomes. One response, then, is to begin to reconceptualize leadership from the role of a single individual to the shared function of a community, a capacity for the citizenry to learn to build.

> Roles determine how we interact with each other, what we talk about and don't talk about. Attempts to break out of our established roles can be threatening to others and can be frightening to ourselves. This is part of what makes shared leadership so difficult. In order to share leadership, we're redefining what it means to be a teacher, to be a principal, a parent or student. In order to create relationships which are different, roles must be re-defined and becoming a full participant and a leader requires relationships which are authentic and support our growth and the growth of others. Becoming a full participant requires that we are learning our way into new definitions of ourselves and our work. (Lambert, January 1997)

In this shifting pattern, constructivist leadership means "the reciprocal processes that enable participants in an educational community to construct meanings that lead toward a common purpose about schooling" (Lambert et al., 1995, p. 29).

How do we establish a common purpose across deeply embedded epistemological differences? Leadership becomes viewed as a dialectical process, one which seems to exhibit competing values. "Leadership as a dialectical process is the willingness to face the ambiguities and subjectivities of choice and consciously acknowledge that with any choice there are potential opposites of equal value" (Carlson, 1996, p. 166). Constructivist learning and leadership seem to fit well, because the premise and promise is that knowledge is actively co-constructed inclusively by the learners/leaders and others in social settings. They make the distinction between the role of the leader with singular authority and functions of leadership distributed among the members of the group. When this process of leadership is democratized, the possibilities for achieving greater social justice in the institution are enhanced, but not assured. Active commitment to the critical perspective and criteria are what prevent hegemony and maintenance of the status quo.

LANGUAGE, A POWERFUL TOOL TO UNDERSTAND THE POLITICS, DIVERSITY, AND URBAN LEADERSHIP IN SCHOOLS

Shared understandings are mediated and communicated largely through language. Whose language and whose meanings for words and ideas then become critical, whether it is in the classroom, administrative office, or school board meeting. Language can mediate across differences and conflicts, but only through conversations as dialogue around inquiry into multiple meanings, definitions, and problematizing. In genuine dialogue, conversations require examining and listening to ourselves and others. In other words, the conversations allow a match and expression of experience and the language to describe concrete situations from multiple points of view (Anderson & Jones, 2000). From isolated participants of various subgroups, an aggregate of people whose purpose is education need to make time and safety for self, group, and whole institutional reflection, examining practices, values, and assumptions. We need to be willing to listen and able to construct meanings that come from different lived experiences, different semantics and syntax, and begin to move toward purposes that respect a variety of stories.

I think of one of my graduate students, Alma, an Hispanic female teacher in a highly urbanized district, who finally got fed up with the snide remarks the mostly Anglo teachers made about the Latino students. She said that staff would do so right in front of her, not recognizing that she was Latina. Her perception was that as professional colleagues, they saw her as like them; her ethnicity was invisible. After being patronized, literally patted on the head at a faculty meeting by an administrator, she finally organized a meeting of Hispanic teachers. They met at school one afternoon and after venting their frustrations around inequities, they began to dialogue about change. They focused upon a possible solution for a more equitable way to participate on school committees. They were beginning to see that with voice comes risk and shared leadership responsibility to make change. In the process they have the power to transform themselves and the system. Alma was chastised by an administrator for having an exclusive meeting, only for certain Latino teachers, and told that she was not politically correct. In spite of this, the group is just beginning to reflect and codify together their current reality. The process may open them to the possibility for visualizing a process of change.

THE MORAL POWER OF NARRATIVE

The stories we are and the stories we tell are powerful ways to use language to convey ideas and build leadership in human relationships. Credibility and trust come from coherence between the two versions. Both kinds of stories can confer meaning, answer important questions, and bind or destroy community by defining a shared heritage, its challenges, triumphs, and injustices.

We look at the stories people tell in order to persuade others and the stories embodied in the ways they lead their lives. During presidential impeachment discussions in 1999, the lawyers for President Clinton were trying to persuade the legislators and public that this difference and probable contradiction within stories was not reason for impeachment from the highest leadership office in the country. Such an event illustrates a specific pedagogical dimension of the narrative—its moral power for teaching and learning.

One of the most powerful ways to lead in creating an ethic of care is through narrative story telling. We need to name the differences; this means bringing to mainstream white consciousness, stories such as Audrey Thompson (1998) describes that have previously not been told (see Dolores Gaunty Porter's chapter). And then, including the stories of each group, appreciating the subtle differences in style and structure among them, and that each is normed by its own original tradition. Teachers can implement subgroup-inclusive as well as learner-centered curricula (Boyd & Arnold, 2000).

Administrators can facilitate dialogues that challenge their own assumptions as universal and support asking the questions that result in the whole community reflecting upon the assumptions upon which they filter their own stories and those of others. Varying definitions and diverse stories are resources upon which to build, not problems to be feared, ignored, or repressed. They become an important part of naming the current situation and shared decision making.

Thompson believes that there is a special kind of story telling that is communal truth telling about the ways of black women being in the world. They act in ethical ways that dispel myths of the mainstream culture. ". . . it is a matter of creatively reshaping experience so that what is revealed is not simply what is already known, but rather what is there but not understood" (1998, p. 538) There is also the recalling of history, bringing the past into the present narrative. Whereas black male authors focus on the struggle with whites, the women tend to focus upon relationships within the black culture. Freire (1985) would call this storytelling of our own situations, a naming or codifying, a problem posing that is necessary for transformational change of individuals and systems. Social justice provides the moral compass for the change narrative. Chris Argyris (1990) moves this concept into the democratic organization, where he advocates making our espoused theory our theory in use, individually and as a learning community.

Having taken a stance for a redefinition of vocabulary around concepts such as urban and educational leadership and the power of story as inquiry, I want to tell you a story. . . .

PIO PICO: A POWERFUL STORY OF LOVE, HOPE, AND PHRONESIS

There is a year-round elementary school called Pio Pico, in the same Orange County urbanized district where Alma works. The principal, cadre of teachers, and others have tried to put the ideas expressed in this chapter into practice from the school's beginning. It was to this principal leader, Judy, one of the original teachers, Emily, and some of the others in the community that I turned for some ways to understand the application of practical wisdom or phronesis. Every Pio Pico participant has a story to tell. I have been fortunate to have multiple contributions to this narrative composition.[1]

Pio Pico is named after the last territorial governor under Mexican rule. He was a mulatto with a colorful life. Not literate in English, he once mistakenly signed over all of his land to pay a gambling debt. He helped to found the first school in Los Angeles and later served as a city councilman. There is a mural of his life story, in the multipurpose room. The children learn his story, including the need to be literate in Spanish and English.

Pio Pico fits the profile defined at the beginning of this chapter as postmodern urban. Twenty-six thousand children, 18 years of age and under, reside within one mile of the school. Founded in 1991 to alleviate overcrowding in the "mother school" of 1,635 students, this K-5 school population is now over 900. This was Judy's first assignment as a principal and Emily's fourth year as a teacher. Judy recruited the initial ten teachers "with a vision of doing things differently, working together *with* the community and pushing the edges of curriculum. I remember sitting in Judy's backyard with these teachers, many of whom were outstanding educators in the district and thinking, 'Wow'!" (Interview with Emily 8/5/99). Those recruited were not only interviewed by Judy, but by committed members of the community as well, who were already naming a stance of empathy and match of philosophy.

Pio Pico has as its mission statement: *"To become the 'hub' of the school's community. This entails broadening our repertoire of instructional strategies and developing our thinking and meaning-centered curriculum upon the real-world needs of our students and families."*

---

[1] I am most grateful to Judy Magsaysay, Emily Wolk, Manuel Ballestro, and Nita Walker at Pio Pico, for being true "critical friends" and for giving this chapter such thoughtful consideration, narration, and careful editing. They honored me by sharing their stories so full of love, hope, and phronesis, so that I, too, could become a Pio Pico storyteller through them.

The education of the principal and teachers and the story of the school took a turn when Judy and her teachers led an initial meeting with the parents in the community to share the school's mission and academic program.

> During this well attended meeting, parents made it clear that their first concern was for the safety of their children. The school building was to be located on a block that was "owned" by gangs and drug dealers. Parents and community members pointed out that open drug deals and drive-by shootings were common along the block. The staff adjusted its priorities, making the first order of business not curriculum and instruction but rather cleaning up the neighborhood. (The Benchmark Study Update, 1998, p. 1).

Together Judy and her staff listened, a deliberate choice that has become an embedded pattern at Pio Pico. They responded by working with families to set up a Neighborhood Safety Committee. "The process empowered the community, created shared leadership and established the school as a force in the community" (p. 1).

> The Parent Safety Committee soon evolved into the Pio Pico Neighborhood Association. Anyone who lives, works or owns property within the neighborhood is invited and encouraged to attend; to listen, to contribute, and to problem solve. Each month, following the tradition of the Parent Safety Committee, updates are presented by the city and police officials. A specific problem or issue impacting the health, safety or well-being of the neighborhood is addressed. Examples of such topics are: Street lights shot out, sprinkler systems never finished, and a detailed factual update of neighborhood murder. Folks get the "straight scoop" and can debrief. (Judy, conversation 8/20/99)

Judy shares the community's Latin roots through her Italian mother, who helps out at the school. Judy has integrated so well into this community that she has made it her own. She shares the same religious views of the community and many of the cultural rituals and beliefs seem quite comfortable to her. She speaks Spanish fluently. Change has come about, through listening and leading conversations that have respected both the language and stories of the community and by building alliances across differences that operationalize the mission statement. Formal partners include: the police, local universities, the Korean American Association, and the Boys and Girls Club. Over 200 representatives of business and government work with children one-by-one around literacy, under the guidance of a Mentor Advisory Board on which I currently serve.

The first year, according to Emily, the ten teachers began with lofty purpose and little else. Resources were scarce. Rather than taking custodial time from the host site, they assumed the responsibility for keeping the school clean. "We began with no library and no books, just four walls and a key," said Emily. There were some hurt feelings of abandonment because four of the ten teachers had left the larger school. These teachers tried to be sensitive and ameliorate relationships with former colleagues. A sense of mission was formed around "equity for our kids," a population that seemed unwanted and shoved to the side. Seeking social justice was the glue of common purpose.

They brought in innovative curriculum expertise from the County Department of Education, learning about new findings in brain research and democratic classrooms. They set about creating a thinking- and meaning-centered curriculum, one that included the language and stories of their population. Emily was later able to "name" the school's critical or Freirian stance from her Master's Degree work at Chapman University with Tom Wilson.

Each year, since the beginning, teachers, students, and some parents select action-based culminations of science, social studies, or health units of study. These projects reach into the neighborhood to address student and family concerns. Examples include: A Health and Safety Fair, A Poison Control Campaign, Operacion Limpieza, A Home Library Building Program, Pedestrian Safety (see the chapter by SooHoo), and a Fotonovela that was designed to lower the incidence of preschoolers being hit by cars in the area.

One of the most difficult challenges has been the tremendous growth and the changes that the growth required in trying to build and sustain community. They went from ten classroom teachers to over 40. Teachers went from sitting around a table for listening, deliberating, and making decisions to needing systems and a representational form of governance. They went from a tight group, bonded by their initial history, to the felt tension of seeing new hires and asking, "Who is that?" There were usually six to eight new staff each year. They became a High Performance Learning Community School and went to educational retreats to learn and strengthen their knowledge base. Would the culture of inclusive community and the modeling of citizenship be able to survive such accelerated growth and change?

The governance system that the teachers and administrators developed this past year has three parts: Leadership Team, Steering Committee, and Staff Advisory. After brainstorming all the leadership responsibilities, the staff found that most issues fit within one of these areas. Someone then took on the assignment of being the chief "worrier" for each one. Leadership Team membership is determined by default; it is the resource teachers, who do not have classroom responsibilities, and the two administrators. They meet daily and have equal voice. The Steering Committee is comprised of one teacher at each grade level, members of the Leadership Team, and representatives from the School Site Council. They are responsible for curricular planning, implementation, and assessment. They raise issues and problem solve to enhance curriculum, staff development, and mentoring new teachers. Planning meeting time for each level is built into the schedule weekly by "banking" time and early dismissal each Wednesday. All teachers actively participate in their grade level planning teams and support each other. Nita Freire visited the school and met with the teachers. Emily remembers that she shared two important lessons from critical pedagogy, "(1) Always teach from love and call attention to when it is not happening, and (2) You must reflect on practice alone and together" (Emily, conversation 8/8/99). This is what they aspire to for learning and leading at Pio Pico.

Emily, as "worrier" for the Steering Committee, listens closely and solicits ideas for the agendas so that they are topics in response to teachers' needs to better serve students. The Assistant Principal is the head "worrier" for the Staff Advisory, the group that deals with school operations such as lunch and discipline. One teacher from each grade level also serves on this committee.

The School Site Council consists of seven teachers and seven parents. As the community issues are increasingly listened to and addressed each year, engaging parents in instruction and assessment has expanded. They are moving now to make stronger links between families, curriculum, and what is going on in the classroom. For example, parents did sample exercises from the state tests in order to better understand them. With a focus on math now, parents have requested to know more. The school listened; the text publisher is conducting in-service sessions for parents. Each year, more parents help in the classrooms.

With this representational democracy in place and operational leadership shared among the staff, what then is the principal's role? Most importantly, she continues to provide the moral imagination and space for moral codevelopment and constructivist learning. In her communication she emphasizes the shared responsibility for leadership. This happens through a pattern of listening and an inclusive cultivation of voices through dialogue and action. With teachers like Emily and staff and families genuinely sharing this work, Judy can concentrate more of her efforts on the symbolic and political needs of the school. She can continue to work with the district, city, and state groups in partnerships, alliances, and gaining resources. The deep structure of schooling is constantly pulling innovation back toward the mainstream status quo (Tye, 2000). It is both the story of who she is and the story she tells that communicate the collaborative vision and stay the course toward new possibilities at Pio Pico. She reflects her confidence and trust in them as she leaves more of the daily operations to her staff, who in turn become empowered as they plan, implement, and reflect upon their decisions, without the demoralization of top-down management or the imposition of one leadership voice. The school stories are many, because the storytellers are many.

The school mascot and vision were chosen through democratic deliberation and conversations among the whole community. The mascot that they chose is the *paloma de paz*, dove of peace. They have a school song about the *palomita blanca de paz* and a copper dove on their school tower. The vision, developed first in Spanish, reads:

> "Mar mentes inquisitivas, listas y preparadas para hacer contribuziones positivas hacia una comunidad diversa y mundial."
>
> "To develop lifelong thinkers and learners, who are eager and well-prepared to make positive contributions in a diverse, global community."

When I asked Judy what sustains her, she says that it is this genuinely co-constructed vision that she "feels in every fiber of her being. . . . When I go to speak about Pio Pico I often start with the vision statement, first in Spanish, then in English. It reminds me. The connections to the families mean everything to me, seeing families that have never engaged in any system before. I see the whole, the tie-in between community modeling and engagement. The children see that their parents have voices. This is what citizenship looks like" (Judy, conversation 8/20/99).

Does this sound utopian? Well, from the insiders' voices comes a loud, "This is hard!" They struggle daily with the internal and external forces impacting their vision and processes of change that work towards social justice. Its challenges, ambiguities, and needs for constant attention and high energy are stressful. Each of the staff must constantly ask not only how hard is it humanly possible to work, but for how long do I want to keep up this pace? Some have left for these reasons. Some have moved on to positions of leadership, taking their story of this experience with them. Of the original ten staff, only three and the principal are still at the school, and only one teacher is still in the classroom full-time. After a particularly divisive political struggle to become a charter school this past year, Judy took a short leave. The distancing has given everyone time to reflect. Both Judy and Emily believe that they will undoubtedly revisit their vision, listen to each other, and reinvent their plans for moving toward it. This is Pio Pico, a powerful story of love, hope, and phronesis.

SUMMARY

In summary, there is a need for a new kind of educational leadership, especially in urban educational settings. Such leadership is committed to shared power and webs of relationships that build care, connections, and concerns among diverse constituents in urbanized educational settings. As they go about the daily business of schooling, they consciously use inclusive and emancipatory language to communicate information and narrate individual and collective stories. One literate tradition is not the single norm around which any other version is referenced as "other". One sanctioned leader is not the single voice around which any other story must conform. A major constraint to building community in a postmodern urban school context is that there are multiple variations of schema around notions of urban, education, leadership, and social justice. There are colorations of meaning affected by personal experiences and filtered through subgroup affiliations of race, gender, and cultural identities. Choice of language and use of language play key roles in the legitimized meanings and narratives of a group and whether or not it becomes a community. As Linda Lambert (1998) says, it is the job of leadership to facilitate and deepen such conversations.

The sociolinguistic, organizational, political, and moral concepts in this chapter may not be new to the reader. The significance may be the shifting or contesting of the concepts and the requisition of definitions that are more inclusive and in concert with a variety of lived experiences. A critical consciousness in individuals plus the will to engage in democratic change processes, both with self and others, have the power to transform the relationships and structures of a group. This is a way into changing "conventional wisdom" and the "deep structures of schooling" that resist (Tye, 1999) efforts to build educational communities that value social justice. The implications of this confluence are that there is a need to support a different paradigm (Anderson et al., 1994; Anderson & Jones, 2000; Capra, 1982).

Participant discourse and leadership that can examine, affirm, and navigate across contradictions and differences will be necessary in order to understand, build, and sustain leadership capacity and community in urban educational settings.

> Story was used not only to contribute to the theorization of her data but also as a way to facilitate professional learning with her staff. She suggests that as administrators begin to experience the contradictions between their values and their actions, their need to resolve these contradictions drives their research. She states the following: "I believe that my values lead my actions in moving towards a more fulfilling and satisfying way of life for me, and for those with whom I work. I am driven to change my practices because I recognize that they do not reflect fully my values, and I therefore feel ill at ease with myself. . . . I am taking part in educational inquiry to get in touch with and live more fully my values about being a deputy head and supporting teaching and learning. It is educational because I act to change myself according to the values to which I am committed." Evans is quick to add, however, that she cannot do this alone. "I need a group of people to challenge my thinking, to put alternative points of view, to point out inconsistencies in my thinking, to make problematic the assumptions I have taken for granted." (Evans' dissertation in Anderson & Jones, 2000, pp. 445-446)

PERSONAL REFLECTION

What in my personal story resonates with the theme of social justice in my professional life as an educator and leader? There were biographical influences of family, personality, religion/culture, and experience. Like Judy, I was highly influenced by the "60s". I grew up on the East Coast in the post-World War II modern suburbs with two parents and a younger brother. My childhood in many ways reflects the post-World War II suburban image that perseverates today, but no longer exists in many communities. My family's immigrants, two or three generations back, fought many of the battles against prejudice and poverty, so that I was afforded many privileges and opportunities to achieve that came with third-generation assimilation.

It is the stories, however, that are etched in memory, shaping my values and beliefs. Both my parents were from large families, and I grew up listening to stories, often told with great humor, animation, and dialect. I sat quietly at gatherings, so that the adults wouldn't notice my presence. I heard one pattern of tales that separated us and them. I came to understand that this flavor to the grown ups' talk had to do with "us" being Jewish and "them" being everyone else. Safety was inside the group; danger existed outside the boundaries, and they told stories of prejudice and injustice to reinforce the notion. Scariest of all, however, were the stories of the Holocaust, vivid and personal retellings of the horrors of Hitler and Nazism. I grew up with frightening memories of stories, for which I had no direct experience. I identified closely with Anne Frank. Second-hand violence, the anticipation of victimization at any moment, was a powerful motivation to seek the safety of assimilation. Upon reflection, I am sure that it influenced my choice of political science and history as an undergraduate and has shaped my determination to seek social justice for oppressed groups as an adult.

This fear and mistrust has had little confirmation in my own adult lived experiences. As far back as five or six, I believed in myself as a leader and agent of change. What prejudice I encountered was balanced with opportunity, fairness, and the rewards of curiosity and genuine caring relationships with others. I have married someone of a different background and sought bridges and friendships that brought people together. In the late 1960s, I worked toward civil rights and a world without war, one that nurtured social responsibility. It was a world that I thought was worth fighting for as a new mother, teacher, and active citizen. Coming from a religious tradition scapegoated for centuries and being of the generation that survived World War II genocide, equity of access and success for knowing the worlds and knowing the words seem right and fair "in every fiber of my being," as Judy says.

I do not like to define identities, including my own, limited by labels and categories; but I have come to see that group memberships are also part of our human stories. When we make something in others invisible, however well intentioned, we deny it power and legitimacy. When we deny it in ourselves, it also can become a self-imposed limitation, a magical powerlessness that contributes to a culture of silence and perpetuation of oppression. Without personally acknowledging and publically affirming human diversity, there can be no building of hope and community. Without genuine hope and trust in community, there can be no progress towards social justice. Without social justice, what is the purpose of building democratic leadership capacity and the point of public education?

REFERENCES

Anderson, G., & Jones, F. (2000, August). Knowledge generation in educational administration from the inside out: The promise and perils of site-nased, administrator research. *Educational Administration Quarterly, XXXVI*(3), 428-464.

Anderson, G., Herr, K., & Nihlen, S. (1994). *Studying your own school*. Thousand Oaks CA: Corwin.

Argyris, C., & Schon, D. (1978). *Organizational learning, a theory of action perspective*. Reading, MA: Addison-Wesley.

Argyris, C. (1990). *Overcoming organizational defenses: Facilitating organizational learning*. Needham Heights, MA: Allyn and Bacon.

Beck, L. (1994). *Reclaiming educational administration as a caring profession*. New York: Teachers College, Columbia University.

Blase J., & Blase J. (1998). *Handbook of instructional learning*. Thousand Oaks, CA: Corwin.

Boyd, D., & Arnold, M. L. (2000, March). Teachers beliefs, antiracisim and moral education: Problems of intersection. *Journal of Moral Education, 29*(1), 23-46.

Canada, J. (1995). *Fist, stick, knife, gun*. Boston: Beacon Press.

Capra, F. (1982). *The turning point*. New York: Simon & Schuster.

Carlson, R. (1996). *Reframing and reform: Perspectives on organizational leadership and school change*. White Plains: NY: Longman.

Evans, R. (1999, February 3). The great accountability fallacy. *Education Week*, pp. 52-35.

Freire, P. (1985). Politics of education: Culture, power and liberation. In P. Freire & H. A. Giroux (Eds.), *Critical studies in education series*. New York: Bergin and Garvey.

Furman, G. (1998, August). Postmodernism and community in schools: Unraveling the paradox. *Educational Administration Quarterly, XXXIV*(3), 298–328.

Gilligan, C. (1982). *In a different voice: Psychological theory and women's development*. Cambridge, MA: Harvard University Press.

Giroux, H. (1997). *Pedagogy and the politics of hope: Theory, culture and schooling*. Boulder, CO: Westview Press.

Heslep, R. (1997). The practical value of philosophical thought for the ethical dimension of educational leadership. *Educational Administration Quarterly, 33*(1), 67-85.

hooks, b. (1994). *Teaching to transgress*. New York: Routledge.

Johnson, D., & Johnson, F. (1997). *Joining together: Group theory and group skills* (6th ed.). Needham, MA: Viacom.

Jones, A. H. (Ed.). (1998). *Teacher Education Quarterly*, Twenty-Fifth Anniversary Issue. A publication of the California Council on the Education of Teachers. San Francisco: Caddo Gap.

Klein, N. (1998, November 15). Opinion: Salvaging suburbia. *Los Angeles Times*, Orange Co. Edition, p. M1.

Kohlberg, L. (1981). *The philosophy of moral development: Moral stages and the idea of justice.* San Francisco: Harper Row.
Kozol, J. (1991). *Savage inequalities.* New York: Routledge.
Kozol, J. (2000). *Ordinary resurrections.* New York: Crowne.
Lambert, L., Walker, D., Cooper, J. E., Lambert, M. D., Gardner, M. E., & Slack, P. J. F. (1995). *The constructivist leader.* Thousand Oaks, CA: Corwin.
Lambert, L. (1997, January). Can constructivist leaders reframe leadership roles (Prf. Dev. Brief #6). California Staff Development Council.
Lambert, L. (1998). *Building leadership capacity in schools.* Alexandria, VA: Association of Supervision and Curriculum Development.
Martin, J. R. (1992). *The schoolhome: Rethinking schools for changing families.* Cambridge, MA: Harvard University Press.
Mishler, E. (1979). Meaning in context, is there any other kind? *Harvard Educational Review, 49*(1).
Noddings, N. (1992). *The challenge to care in schools: Alternative approaches to education.* New York: Teachers College Press, Columbia University.
Orfield, M. (1998, November 15). Opinion: How to stop communities from growing farther and farther apart. *Los Angeles Times,* Orange Co. Edition, p. M1.
Ourlian, R. (1998, September 21). Unpopular development. Data from Times Orange County Poll by Baldassare Associates, *Los Angeles Times,* Orange Co. Edition, p. A16.
Pounder, Diana G. (1998). *Restructuring schools for collaboration.* Albany: State University of New York Press.
Ryan, K., & Bohlin, K. E. (2000). *Building a community of virtue. The Jossey-Bass reader on educational leadership.* San Francisco: Jossey-Bass.
Senge, P. (1991) *The fifth discipline.* New York: Doubleday.
Senge, P. (2000). Give me a lever long enough . . . and single handed, I can move the world. In *The Jossey-Bass Reader on Educational Leadership.* San Francisco: Jossey-Bass.
Senge, P., Cambron-McCabe, N., Lucas, T., Smith, B., Dutton, J., & Kleiner, A. (2000). *Schools that learn.* New York: Doubleday Dell.
Thompson, A. (1998, Winter). Not the color purple: Black feminists lessons for educational caring. *Harvard Educational Review, 68*(4), 522–554.
Tye, B. (2000). *Hard truths: Uncovering the deep structure of schooling.* New York: Teachers College Press, Columbia University.
Wagner, J. (1998). Power and learning in a multiethnic high school. In Y. Zou & E. T. Trueba (Eds.), *Ethnic identity and power, cultural contexts of political action in school and society.* Albany: State University of New York Press.
Weber, M. (1947). *The theory of social and economic organization.* New York: Oxford University Press.
Wheatley, M. (1994). *Leadership and the new science.* San Francisco: Berrett-Koehler.
Willower, D. (1994). *Educational administration: Inquiry, values, practice* (rev. ed.). Lancaster, PA: Technomic Publishing.

Wilson, T. (1996). *Education for democratic personhood: A curriculum for ethical and critical democracy*, Unpublished paper.
Witherall, C., & Noddings, N. (Eds.). (1991). *Stories lives tell: Narrative and dialogue in education.* New York: Teachers College Press.
Wolpe, D. L. (1992). *In speech and in silence.* New York: Holt.

7

Crossing Cultural Borders Into the Inner City

Suzanne SooHoo

> *The white, middle-class, university student's eyes widened with fear as I informed her of her student teaching assignment at an inner city school. "I can't go there she proclaimed with an emphatic emphasis on the word there. "Why?" I asked. "It's dangerous!" she declared. I asked, "For whom?"*

The inner city, "a holding space for blacks and browns no longer of use to the larger economy" (Hamilton, 1991, p. 1). High poverty neighborhoods, commercial abandonment, drug economy, inadequate police, lack of job opportunities, web of negative influences—these are the descriptors portrayed by everyday media, newspapers, televisions, advertisements. The "inner city," the code word politicians and bureaucrats use to signal the deficit framework imposed on subordinate groups. This deficit model, commonly referred to as "at-risk," reduces the value and status of people who live in the inner city and conjures up images of the poor, illegal immigrants, English deficiency, and people of color. Research in the inner city of "those problems" frequently reproduces a social structure to further affirm these distorted images that promote public fear. The perpetuation of these images as reality is one way that dominant groups exert their power over subordinate groups. The inner city as darkly described is not a place but a state of mind (Freire, 1987).

As a teacher educator and researcher, I have a responsibility to "deghettoize" these misconceptions through critique and lived experiences; through coursework and fieldwork. Questions I asked myself: Just how far from the mainstream is this place called inner city? How could a research team made up of insiders and outsiders facilitate an alternative description of urban education? Like a river and its tributaries, it is at the edges, where the water cuts the shoreline, that the river is defined.

INTELLECTUAL METIZA

This chapter describes a collaborative action research project conducted by urban elementary school students, a community member, a teacher researcher, and a university researcher. It focuses on significant cultural exchanges between the students, teacher, community member, and the university member of the research team. I describe my journey as an outsider who makes entry into the borderlands of the inner city school and share community members' reactions to my involvement as the only outsider on the research team.

My intent was to gain an understanding of how cultural identities influence the various dimensions of the research project. I had hoped to acquire, through our interactions together, a greater awareness about how cultural identities could facilitate the collection of data and evoke more culturally significant interpretations of the action taking place. I expected to bring to the team my own experiences as a fellow member of a subordinate group, respecting our respective differences as historically inscribed. How could my identity as an Asian woman inform the research project? What happens when an "Other" is a researcher? How could the cultural identities of the collaborative action research team inform the data and the process of collaborative action research?

As a cultural activist, I claimed a genealogical, cultural and political set of experiences, which I speculated, to some extent, was shared with other people of color. We are defined by our marginalization. "The Other, however we are named, have a presence in the

Western imagination, in its fibre and texture, in its sense of itself, in its language, in its silences and shadows, its margins and intersections" (Smith, 1999, p. 14).

My history of marginalization and the marginalization of my Chinese ancestors have helped me identify with other subordinate groups. I, too, have been colonized, but I also recognize that as an educated and sanctioned member of the academy, I am also the colonizer (Villenas, 1996). Thus, I must routinely interrogate myself about how my own marginality and privilege inform the research. I am both friend and foe.

I use both an inside and outside stance to become what Anzaldua (1987) calls the intellectual metiza, a border crosser (Giroux, 1993; Rosaldo, 1993) who is culturally competent in multiple cultural contexts. By putting my cultural difference on the table, I could search for how this subjectivity interacted with the data (Scheurich, 1997) and look for "those unintentional, multicultural spaces—sometimes called 'common ground'—where disparate cultures meet; where the people living on these peripheries discover cultural parallels . . ." (Anzaldua, 1987).

My goal was not to be a cultural tourist in the inner city but an action researcher committed to a long-term relationship with school and community folks. The work described in this chapter was embedded within a three-year intimate relationship with the school, students, and teacher researcher. Sometimes this meant a whole semester of daily presence. Other times, this meant maintaining my weekly office hours at the SooHoo-designated lunch table in the quad. Being part of the daily life of the school was a critical prerequisite to establishing a collaborative action research team. A long-term relationship with a community can eventually make an outsider an insider (Villenas, 1996).

METHODOLOGY: WHY COLLABORATIVE ACTION RESEARCH?

The research project came out of a deep conviction to participate at the local level in socially responsible citizenry. Like other participatory researchers (Brice Heath, 1983; Freire, 1995; Park, 1997; Wigginton, 1985), the critical inquiry was shaped by an emancipatory interest in transforming educational communities to achieve equitable opportunities for all their members. The teacher researcher and I chose a research approach that was aligned with these philosophical underpinnings. Collaborative action research, characterized by its power-sharing feature, challenges the dominance hierarchical relationships model of research where there has been a "tendency for Western researchers to impose even their most enlightened cultural constructs on Others . . ." (Stanfield, 1992, p. 176). Instead, this project was designed by the teacher, students, community member, and myself to benefit the students and their community. Each of us was held accountable for the work and the way the research was disseminated to others. Prior to submission for publication, drafts of this chapter were sent to fellow team members for their feedback and changes. Our multivoiced narrative has been presented at several conference presentations.

There would be many good reasons for this Latino school community to be suspicious of nonindigenous researchers because traditionally those from the outside of urban communities have assumed a position of cultural superiority. Consequently, urban schools and its constituents have often been described as "at risk," powerless, and unable to cope with life's problems. This social pathology approach (Bishop, 1996) has promoted ethnocentric assumptions and racist practices and attitudes.

> Researchers are in receipt of privileged information. . . . They have the power to distort, to make invisible, to overlook, to exaggerate and to draw conclusions. They have the potential to extend knowledge or to perpetuate ignorance. . . . (Smith, 1999, p. 176)

There has been a history of assault by dominant society researchers who have colonized communities by using research solely for the benefit of the outside researcher. Smith quotes one community member's assessment of research "being done on" Maoris.

> We have a history of putting Maori under a microscope in the same way a scientist looks at an insect. The ones doing the looking are giving themselves the power to define. (Mita, 1989)

Commonly, non-dominant groups have been studied and interpreted by dominant researchers who also have the market on conceptual frameworks for research (Stanfield, 1992). Therein lie the reasons why indigenous people are skeptical or hesitant to give access to outsiders.

Some communities have openly challenged the research community about this colonizing perspective (Smith, 1999). There have been communities—for example, Maoris (Bishop, 1996)—that have gone as far as prohibit outside researchers, believing that research should be led and undertaken by their own people only. They have "argued that only those researchers emerging from the life worlds of their subjects can be adequate interpreters of such experiences" (Stanfield, 1992). This position represents the felt need to fight back against the invasion of their communities by academic and corporate interests. But this act of resistance is also an act of self-determination to think about and carry out research for their own purposes from their own perspectives (Smith, 1999).

Particular care and attention are necessary before a nonindigenous researcher enters an indigenous community.

> Researchers, policy makers, educators, and social service providers who work with or whose work impacts on indigenous communities need to have a critical conscience about ensuring that their activities connect in humanizing ways with indigenous communities. It is a very common experience to hear indigenous communities outline the multiple ways in which agencies and individuals treat them with disrespect and disregard. (Smith, 1999, p. 149)

One should assume a position of participatory consciousness (Bishop, 1996) and be willing to work within a power-sharing context. The first beneficiaries of the research must be the community members themselves. They must be assured that all intellectual and cultural property resulting from the research will not contribute to the exploitation, colonization, or devaluation of their people. In New Zealand, the charter of the Indigenous Tribal Peoples of the Tropical Forests signed in 1993 states in article 45, "all investigations in our territories should be carried out with our consent and under joint control and guidance" (Smith, 1999, p. 119).

> What happens to research when the *researched* become the researchers?
> (Smith, 1999, p. 183)

By requesting the presence of community members on the collaborative action research team, those beneficiaries act as invaluable resources to cultural norms and protocols and can access information differently than an outsider. Furthermore, as a member of the research team, they demystify the research process for the rest of the community and are in key position to oversee the representation and dissemination of the research findings. When constituents affected by the project participate on the research team, it becomes a democratic project. What is needed is an emancipatory model of research where those on the inside and those on the outside work and shape the research together.

SETTING: YOU HAVE BE "THERE" TO KNOW "THERE"

Situated in the second most densely populated square mile in the United States (by children under the age of 18 years), Pio Pico School has a student population of approximately 1,000 students, 97% Latinos and 3% Other. The city's population is approximately 70% Hispanic, 30% Other. There are five elementary schools in one square mile—urban artifacts of the multimember extended families who populate the small bungalow homes and many large apartment complexes. Most of the families are blue-collar workers. Eighty-five percent have emigrated from Mexico just 80 miles away. Fifteen percent have come from Central America. Students in the school learn to speak both Spanish and English. The street that runs alongside of the school is extremely dense with foot and car traffic. It was this road that eventually became the focal point of our collaborative action research project.

In the spring of 1998 I worked at this local elementary school that was only two exits down the freeway. Although my university and the school are in the same county, we are culturally and economically worlds apart. My school is both a liberal arts and professional degree university made up of primarily white, middle-class students.

The collaborative action research team consisted of approximately eight fourth and fifth grade students, with a monthly turnover of about 20%, a 12-year veteran, bilingual Spanish teacher who was biracially Japanese and Anglo, and a local Spanish bilingual Boys Club director who was a former gang member. Student researchers have met regularly with the teacher and professor over the past couple of years on other research projects. In the past, graduating student researchers have presented their projects to other classrooms, school assemblies, and PTA meetings, which not only provided a forum for the research team to share their findings but also served as recruitment for future student researchers each year. The teacher and the professor have a long-term relationship from other collaborative action research projects and both are members of a local teacher research group, Collaborative Action Researchers for Democratic Communities.

Our research question was, "What are the problems in our community?" The initial data collection came from our community walks. After school, equipped with notebooks and cameras, we walked up and down the streets, capturing community life. The apartment balconies crowded with plants, laundry, and bicycles were rich photo opportunities.

Upon reviewing their pictures and research notes, student researchers wondered if they had gotten the full picture of their community and posed the question, "Who are our Community Experts?" Three names came up: the "Lady in the Pink House" who gave community members advice about how to make their homes beautiful; a student's father, because he lived in a house that was centrally located in the community; and a Boys Club director and former gang member who "knew a lot of people in the community." All three were invited to an interview in the school library. Adults brought cookies and punch and students set up tables.

Team members were very excited about the new data and the perspective these experts offered to the team. Shortly after the interviews, it became clear to the researchers that the life credentials of these community experts qualified them to join our research team. An invitation was made to both the Boys Club counselor and the father to join us on our research team. The father declined due to work schedule conflicts, but the Boys Club counselor graciously accepted the offer, acknowledging that the project had piqued his curiosity.

As evidenced in this project, collaborative action research can be a microcosm of democracy in the way it brings interested constituents together to work on projects to improve a community. Our purpose was to bring forth all voices, all interested parties to engage in mutual inquiry as equal partners with equal status. In this way, collaborative action research addresses the conventional hierarchical relationship of the researcher collecting data "on subjects." By inviting subjects to participate as coresearchers, data is collected "with and by subjects."

This research is different from the typical "zoo visit" research in urban settings, where "outsiders" come in to study phenomena among subordinated cultural groups. This research team's composition, by design, intended to acquire both insider and outsider perspectives. From inside of the cultural circle (Freire, 1995), the project solicited community voices that were typically devalued because of their marginalized sociocultural positions. From the outside, both teacher and university professor offered their professional expertise in teaching and learning, their lived experiences, and their own membership in other subordinated groups. Together the research team brought their multifaceted resources to the project.

As cultural outsiders, the teacher and I were careful to not become colonialist researchers who take voice away from the people. We were conscious of limiting our school authority voices so as not to dominate the project with our scholarship. bell hooks (1990) cautioned us when she sarcastically projected herself as a colonizing researcher: "No need to hear your voice when I can talk about you better than you can speak about yourself."

A PROBLEM IN OUR NEIGHBORHOOD
THE RESEARCH PROJECT

After analyzing the notes taken in our research notebooks about our community walks and interviews with community members, the research team identified an intersection adjacent to the school as "the problem" in the neighborhood. Heavy traffic prevented students and their families from crossing the streets safely. Cars did not observe the speed limit nor adjust their speed as they approached the yellow cautionary street signs. In addition, the intersection was not aligned perpendicularly, which meant pedestrians were crossing traffic in a diagonal configuration that confused motorists.

Students and adult researchers collected data by setting up beach chairs at the four corners of the intersection. They tabulated the number of cars going in each direction before and after school. One day, in a ten-minute period, 148 cars were recorded going southbound, 174 northbound! Several accidents had occurred at the intersection as reported by community members. City Hall was called to obtain the exact number of accidents reported at the intersection. We found a discrepancy between the official records and the community memory. The crossing guard's interview and the school nurse's log confirmed that the city did not have accurate records of the problems at that intersection. We decided to report this discrepancy to the City Engineer. We invited him to one of our research team meetings.

In preparation for this meeting, the research team designed a plan to galvanize support for the project, anticipating that the City Engineer might dismiss the data collected because of the student membership on the research team. Petitions were circulated throughout the student body to galvanize peer support. Student researchers also presented our research project to the PTA in Spanish and in English, thus garnering parental support.

In addition, we took field trips to identify the different traffic interventions used to slow cars down so that we could make suggestions to improve the intersection. The research team members photographed speed bumps, signs, signals, painted lines, roadblocks, flashing lights, and police cars. During one particular community excursion, we discovered that certain places in the city were safer than others. For example, at the north end of street, the homes were visibly more affluent and there was a permanent roadblock to prevent cars from entering the neighborhood. At hospitals, there was a generous allotment of stop signs and speed bumps, making crosswalks noticeably safe for their patients. Students questioned why people living in affluent areas and hospitals were given more consideration in regard to traffic safety than schoolchildren from a poor neighborhood. This marked the first instance of students' awareness of their own oppression and the demarcation of borders between those who are valued and those who are not.

The research team met with the City Engineer and presented their photo essay to the City Engineer. This seemingly harmless meeting triggered a formal investigation of the intersection by the city. Newspaper coverage followed. Inspection teams made visits. In the end, the dangerous intersection was repainted, crosswalks realigned, and a traffic light will soon be installed. Contrary to custom, this traffic light will not be an urban headstone for the dead. Typically, it is pedestrian deaths that prompt city officials to erect traffic lights. This traffic light is instead a symbol for the living, a light reminding us of our capacity to transform our community.

ENTERING THE BORDERLANDS

The next section teases out the cultural exchanges made between the students and me and between me and the two other members of the collaborative action research team.

Border Crossings With the Students—Declaration of Cultural Authenticity

An Asian-American woman among a Latino student body is as conspicuous as a dragon at a Cinco de Mayo celebration. I felt like a new immigrant in a foreign land and students were noticeably curious about me. They told me they only saw Asians on television and sometimes at the store. I was the only Asian person they could recall who had ever spoken with them.

Examples of questions students asked upon my arrival were: "If you're Chinese, do you know how to use chopsticks." "Do you know how to do kung fu too?" "You don't speak Chinese? Not even a little bit?" It became clear to me through their questioning that the students expected that I wear my ethnic culture on my sleeve. In order to enter these borderlands, I felt students were requesting a cultural visa; a demonstration of ethnic affinity. They were disappointed that I couldn't demonstrate kung fu. I reasoned that I needed to bring into this new community cultural markers to prove my cultural authenticity. I attempted to do so with lessons on how to use chopsticks and simple Chinese words and phrases.

My first lesson with chopsticks was a disaster. Rice crackers danced all over the tables. Marshmallows were not only a better alternative for the second lesson, but also improved my classroom management. I sent the students home with chopsticks to practice with at their dinner meal and to signal parents that I was among their children's daily experiences.

Chinese writing and speaking of simple phrases and numbers followed. Teachers expressed their appreciation of my responsiveness to the children's request and to the cultural exposure I was giving to the students. But the students weren't satisfied with simple language lessons; they insisted on more and became frustrated when I couldn't deliver. "What kind of Chinese person are you anyway?" they demanded.

The question pierced my cultural consciousness, taking me back to the painful recognition of my cultural genocide. Parenthetically, this is the same question my overseas Chinese cousins ask me. These students and my cousins pitied me for losing my native language. I mourned my loss, too. These students and their families had not "assimilated" like mine. After moving away from San Francisco's Chinatown, my family chose to erase many cultural identifiers that separated them from mainstream white America. For me, this meant a white stepfather, a white school, and an English-only speaking family.

These students were different. At ages 10 and 11, they knew the significance of knowing both languages. They shared with me how important it was to have two or more languages and how much smarter they were because they were bilingual. Clearly, they understood how bilingualism conferred one's cultural credibility. Students were sympathetic to my ignorance of my own language. Unlike me, who learned to make my ethnicity invisible, they wore their ethnicity as chest plates with distinct boldness. They motivated me to shed my cloak of cultural ambivalence.

Border Crossings With the Teacher—Eastern Winds

"I thought you were a Latina!" were my first words to the bilingual teacher researcher after she revealed to me that she was bicultural—half-Japanese, half Euro-American. The teacher was a member of the faculty at the school for 12 years and every interaction I have had with her had left me with the perception that she embodied the spirit, the customs, the values, the ideology, as well as the language of this Mexican-American community. Judging from her interactions with students, parents, and fellow teachers, I was certain she was a member of the indigenous community.

The teacher's bilingualism granted her cultural credibility within the school community. She not only knew the language but she was intimately comfortable with the culture. Her successful acculturation to the Latino community was seen in her adeptness in mediating high-context situations, situations saturated with cultural messages that can only be interpreted by someone who is familiar with the values, beliefs, and customs of a group. Whenever people were late for meetings, she reassured me that people would eventually come, and if they didn't, it was because they had very good reasons why they couldn't make it; for example, sick relative, child care, unexpected calls to go to work, and so forth. At agenda-less meetings, she was confident that the agenda would emerge from those who did come. And she was right; preconceived agendas were not useful because group meetings were highly contextual and co-constructed by whoever was there. At several meetings, after waiting 30 minutes, I packed up the refreshments thinking no one was coming. Inevitably, I would be at the exit when people started to arrive.

The teacher researcher enlightened me with a different concept of time. Time clocks did not control schedules here. Working, living, and meeting required flexibility and fluidity. Lateness and/or limited attendance should not be misconstrued as a reflection of intentions. The operating assumption was, "I will come once my children are cared for and my work is done." Have faith and be patient. This I learned while holding a bag of melting ice.

Since then, I have learned from a Hopi man about Western society's preoccupation with time. He claimed that the Western world orients its existence by counting. For centuries, time had been of no importance to the Indian. The sun rose, the sun set. There were changes of the moon, changes of the seasons; but no one counted the hours (Qoyawayma, 1992, p. 176). My recent visit to a Hopi reservation revealed no visible clocks and its people wore no watches. The ages of many Hopi elders were not known because counting was not important. "They lived the days as they came and were not concerned with the length of their sojourn on earth" (Qoyawayma, 1992, p. 104). One is simply born and then one grows small in old age (Qoyawayma, 1992). These lessons have given me permission to release myself from the tyranny of time within particular research settings.

Seat Belt Pragmatics

At one point in the project, tension grew between the teacher researcher and myself. The incident involved the disagreement over the number of student researchers who would participate at the annual 1998 conference of the American Educational Research Association (AERA) in San Diego to present our collaborative action research project. It was not possible for children to arrange their own transportation. The teacher researcher had planned to invite only the number of students for which her car had seatbelts. I had suggested that we needed to do everything we could to find transportation for all of them. For several meetings, she listened to my recommendations but made no attempt to move on them. I saw that she was conflicted. I jokingly suggested that she was blinded by pragmatism. She was not amused. I asked her to weigh her seatbelt pragmatics against voice and participation. She was not talking much to me.

In the end, we were lucky to take any of the students to AERA. Several parents were not willing to have their children cross a border checkpoint between Santa Ana and San Diego for fear of the unknown—anticipated action by Immigration Authorities. The passage of recent anti-immigrant bills has put certain populations in California unfairly on alert. Border guards routinely detained anyone who looks "Hispanic," reported the teacher. Subsequently, only five students were given permission to go to San Diego and we now had enough seatbelts. This situation became the second sighting of our oppression; borders between those who can move freely within the state and those who cannot.

The teacher researcher and I talked about this tension after AERA. She wanted me to understand that she was the school person responsible for the children and she only felt comfortable transporting a small number of students over whom she would have constant oversight. This field trip would be a new adventure for students and she felt responsible for their safety and well-being. I had not realized the seriousness of this issue nor her deeply held commitment to keep her students safe and protect them.

Her honesty further revealed unexpected cultural dimensions in play. She informed me that when I made suggestions, it was particularly difficult for her to disagree with me. She explained that she felt conflicted disagreeing with an Asian elder. The fact that I was both Asian and an elder had initially paralyzed her voice of resistance. She self-disclosed that she could not figure out how to disagree respectfully with me.

Our disagreement had summoned forth something culturally coded from our past and brought forth a dimension in her ethnic identity that was unexpected by me and seemingly incongruous to her Latina persona. It was an honor of Asian reverence, which I was not used to. She had conferred upon me respect that I had not earned, based on our mutual birthrights. This unquestioned respect caused her to defer to my suggestions and to mute her own ideas. I became conscious once again of my own ethnic identity signaling unconscious cultural messages to my fellow team members.

This reflective debriefing helped me see the impact of multicultural identities in action research. In this case, I had misjudged the color of the teacher's ideology by assuming she was exclusively Latina. Her disclosure reinforced the idea that our cultural identities are fluid, ever-changing, and multiple. We are cultural chameleons both consciously and unconsciously, sometimes responding to the same social context with different frames.

Border Crossings With the Community Researcher—Facilitating Voice

Student researchers initiated the idea to invite a community member to join our research team. He was a Boys Club counselor, Latino, and former gang member who had many experiences in the community. Indeed, he had played many roles and was well versed about the problems in the neighborhood. He told the students what the difference was between graffiti and tagging, what the neighborhood was like ten years ago and who the community heroes were. He showed them the scars of an old gunshot wound and gave them advice on how to improve their lives. He was warm and supportive of the students. It was clear they respected him.

All of us considered him the community hero. For him, the students and the teacher were a part of his community, but I was an outsider. At a debriefing meeting months later, we both confessed our initial reservations about our relationship—community member and university professor, Latino male and Asian woman—how would these social identities play themselves out? He admitted that throughout the project he was "checking me out," wondering what I could offer these students. Why was I doing this? I also divulged that I had sensed his careful appraisal of my credibility and had checked him out as well. I wondered if he thought I posed a threat to the community. What would he do to facilitate or obstruct our efforts to work together?

He understood the students with a genuine tenderness as evidenced at a research meeting where students interviewed the City Engineer. Students pressed the City Engineer to explain the discrepancy of accidents reported. City records showed fewer car accidents near the school than the data we collected from the community memory. A shy, quiet, 10-year-old Latina student researcher was having difficulty articulating the frequently practiced interview questions. I recognized the awkward utterances as her first steps of trying to break her language of silence. This young Latina was attempting to cross a cultural border from a place where women are generally silent, particularly in mixed gender situations, to a place of voice, power and influence. She was stumbling. The community researcher intervened. With skillful sensitivity, he framed her questions by gently supplying leading sentences that allowed her to step in when she could find the words. The teacher researcher and I were impressed with his reading of what she needed at that moment. He was there at her side, gently ushering her through this difficult transition. She looked relieved and grateful for his assistance and affirmation.

Many of us from nondominant groups would recognize the painful familiarity of coming to voicedness. As an Asian and as a woman, I, like this Latina, am conscious of how my voice is compromised when I am with dominant groups. Many of us have had mentors to assist us in locating our social and political voices. These mentors help carve a pathway to enter the sociopolitical world of influence. They help members of subordinate groups access the language of power in order to influence the power structures that oppress their communities. One must learn the word in order to read the world (Freire, 1993, 1995). One must use the language of power to deconstruct and transform existing power structures.

MAKING SENSE OF THE CULTURAL EXCHANGES

As an action researcher, I must be able to summon my personal sociocultural knowledge to inform the cultural mediations in the field. My experience in nondominant groups as an Asian and as a woman has equipped me with particular subjectivities to better understand the events in the field. In this research project, the students illuminated for me the differences between Latin and Asian cultures with respect to ethnic pride and bilingualism. Unlike my immigrant grandparents who chose to assimiate, the students proudly and publicly proclaimed their ethnic affiliations. Acknowledging my own cultural loss, it seems like a smart idea to wear one's ethnic chest plate when navigating through their world.

From the teacher researcher, as Latina and Chinese, I learned how easy it was to fall into the trap of reducing individuals into single ethnic identities. I didn't initially recognize what should have been familiar—the role of nonexhibition of cultural identity among Asians—and therefore, wrongly assumed that the teacher was singly Latina. When I finally recognized the multidimensions of the teacher's ethnic affiliations, I realized more fully the complexities of teasing out cultural mediations as a line of inquiry.

Because of our long-established relationship, I was able to go back and examine the tension points in our collaborative work together with the teacher researcher. In so doing, we were able to identify more specifically cultural dimensions in play that had not unfolded in our work together. I found I was unconscious of my own ethnic identity sending us cultural signals.

The momentous occasion between the community researcher and the female student demonstrated how a skillful reading of the contextual clues can facilitate the function of voice in an action research project. The community researcher intervened at "the right moment" as the student's guide to the language of power and influence. As a fellow member of the Latino community, he was intimately familiar with both her spoken language and her language of silence. He read her silence and knew what she needed.

As a fellow member of subordinate groups, I recognized the teacher's silence while recognizing our cultural differences. Our professional experiences were informed by different cultures. Our nexus was a shared ethnic heritage and the accompanying honoring of elders. This recognition of similarity within differences is referred to (George, 1993) as cultural fusion. It is when diverse groups create common ground while continuing to acknowledge important differences (Wellman, 1996).

Border Guards and Border Crossings

Roadblocks and anti-immigrant policies were concrete evidence of the border guards, which protect the outer city from the inner city. Equally oppressive is the frame of mind in which traditional research has been conducted "on" the inner city. Research informed by a white ideology has dominated the conceptual frameworks. Citizens are regarded as subjects to be studied. "The tendency for Western researchers to impose even their most enlightened cultural constructs on Others rather than creating indigenous theories and methods to grasp the ontological essences of people of color, is of course, legendary" (Hill Collins, 1991, p. 176). Research designs and the conduct of the research reflect "patriarchal and hierarchical presumptions and assumptions of male-centric norms and values (that) influence not only the contents of research but, perhaps more important, the conduct of research as a structured power relationship" (Stanfield, 1992).

A fundamental assumption in the convening of collaborative action research teams is the invitation to others with diverse perspectives to act as coresearchers on a research team. In the research project reported in this chapter, students, teacher, and community member acted not only as border guides into the inner-city school community but also as cultural collaborators. They identified cultural context clues critical to the compatibility of the researchers' interest and the research phenemona—for example, Latino time. They facilitated the excavation of culturally embedded data in exchanges between community member and student. And they translated the cultural messages, using their insider/outsider status to inform the action of the team.

Some people have argued that only those researchers emerging from the life worlds of their "subjects" can be adequate interpreters of such experiences. With full respect for this perspective, and until such time as this becomes a research norm, I ask that researchers thoughtfully consider the composition of their research teams to include cultural collaborators as coresearchers. These participants not only balance the power relationships but they can be valuable, resourceful research partners. And at the very least, scholars should resist writing about the inner city without the benefit of the informed wisdom of its inhabitants.

A second border guard to inner-city research is the common practice of depersonalization study in the name of scientific objectivity. Most researchers who have been trained within the traditional canons hesitate to use their subjectivities to inform their work. Working from the assumption that people cannot fully understand another person's marginalization or "otherness" unless they themselves are conscious of their own experiences of otherness (SooHoo, forthcoming), I argue that our own experiences of otherness can be our passports into the borderlands. These subjectivities can evoke sociocultural insights in the emergence and interpretation of data, which are often obstructed in the name of scientific objectivity.

As a researcher of color, I recognize that the research is scarce on how people of color use their cultural identities to inform the work. This chapter was an attempt to mine my own cultural subjectivities as I teased out the cultural dimensions of the research project. It is my hope that other researchers will affirm their own sociocultural identities as valuable research tools, whether they are from dominant or subordinate groups, as a way of "grasping the ontological essences of people of color" (Hill Collins, 1991, p. 37).

I recognize an instinct that we people of color have to assess the degree of affiliation we have to a dominant or subordinate group. This cultural antenna has been finely tuned to determine one's relationship to the white community. This indigenous competency has, in part, contributed to our survival in the white man's world.

"Color is both confining and liberating" (Martinez, 2001). Although my membership in subordinate groups facilitates one cultural learning, it inhibits another. My own Eastern proclivity to silence as a language of choice almost prevented me from recognizing the careful scaffolding and support the community member gave to the student coresearcher in her attempt to speak. Initially, I had difficulty discerning whether the student chose not to speak or was intimidated to speak. Sensitivity to methods and foras that amplify the voices of community members should be a primary objective for cultural border crossers.

IN THE END

As a researcher and teacher educator, I have an ethical responsibility to help aspiring teachers to enter urban borderlands and rename the socially constructed landscapes. Danger lies only in the resistance to engage personally, culturally, and intellectually. Should one call upon one's own social identity and experiences to navigate urban contexts, there are new identities and discourses to be found from both the researched and the researcher.

REFERENCES

Anzaldua, G. (1987). *Borderlands: The new metiza=La frontera.* San Francisco: Spinsters/Aunt Lute.
Bishop, R. (1996). *Collaborative research stories: Whakawhanaungatanga.* Palmerston, New Zealand: Dunmore Press.
Brice Heath, S. (1983). *Ways with words: Language, life and work in communities and classrooms.* Victoria, Australia: Cambridge University Press.
Freire, P. (Personal conversation July 14, 1987).
Freire, P. (1993). *Pedagogy of the city.* New York: Continuum.
Freire, P. (1995). *Pedagogy of the oppressed.* New York: Continuum
George, L. (1993, January 17). Gray boys, funky Aztecs and honorary homegirls. *Los Angeles Times Magazine,* pp. 14-19.
Giroux, H.(1993). *Border crossings.* New York: Routledge.
Hamilton, C. (1991). *Apartheid in an American city: The case of the Black community in Los Angeles.* Van Nuys, CA: Labor Community Strategy Center.
Hill Collins, P. (1991). Learning from the outsider within. In M. Fonow & J. Cook (Eds.), *Beyond methodology. Feminist scholarship as lived research.* Bloomington: Indiana University Press.

hooks, b. (1990). *Yearning: Race, gender and cultural politics.* Boston: South End Press.

Martinez, R. (Personal conversation, March 19, 2001).

Mita, M. (1989, October 14). Merata Mita on . . . *New Zealand Listener,* p. 30.

Qoyawayma, P. (1992). *No turning back.* Albuquerque: University of New Mexico Press.

Park, P. (1997). Participatory research, democracy and community. *Practicing Anthropology, 19*(3), 8-13.

Rosaldo, R. (1993). *Culture and truth.* Boston: Beacon Press.

Scheurich, J. (1997). Coloring epistemologies: Are our research epistemologies racially biased? *Educational Researcher, 26*(4), 4-16.

Smith, L. (1999). *Decolonizing methodologies: Research and indigenous peoples.* London: Zed Books.

SooHoo, S. (forthcoming). *The other side of difference.* Cresskill, NJ: Hampton Press.

Stanfield, J. H. (1992). Ethnic modeling in qualitative research. In. N. K. Denzin & Y.S. Lincoln (Eds.), *Handbook of qualitative research.* Newbury Park, CA: Sage.

Villenas, S. (1996). The colonizer/colonized Chicana ethnographer: Identity, marginalization, and co-optation in the field. *Harvard Educational Review, 55*(5), 711-731.

Wellman, D. (1996). Red and black in white America: Discovering cross border identities and other subversive activities. In B. Thompson & T. Sangeeta (Eds.), *Names we call home.* New York: Routledge.

Wigginton, E. (1985). *Sometimes a shining moment: The foxfire experience.* New York: Anchor Press/Doubleday.

IV

STUDENT VOICES

8

Gatekeepers

Jan Osborn

> *When I was little I wrote silly poems. I was a pint-sized vandal then, writing on the wooden gate of my mother's store with chalk. I saw them dismantle the wooden gate. I saw them replace it with an iron one, with bars instead of a flat wooden surface. From then on the iron gate stood. But it never talked to me, not like the wooden gate.*
>
> (Gaston Santiago, Grade 12
> Pioneer High School, Whittier, California)

Urban schools far too often dismantle the wooden gate of experience, taking away the one surface upon which students can communicate and replacing it with bars, more concerned with keeping out than letting in. Such "keeping out" can take the form of evaluating work before a process is learned, of lowering expectations for second-language learners or students of color or low socioeconomic background, or keeping them out of college-preparation courses, a precursor to university admission. Such institutional policies as tracking certainly replace wooden gates with bars, replace hope for a good future with despair. Educators have the capacity to use the wooden gates of experience, to work from the premise of what students have rather than what they lack. Educators are, indeed, the gatekeepers, with some students kept out of a meaningful educational process.

Gaston's memory has remained a powerful metaphor for me as I work with young people in their literacy development. Having been both a high school and college English teacher and currently working to educate future teachers, I have had to learn ways to open the gate rather than replace it with a new one: inviting students to become fluent in their communication prior to becoming "correct," providing students time and "space" to explore their own thinking prior to "testing" their understanding, ensuring students that knowledge is dynamic, growing from *exactly* where we are to where we want to go, necessary like all growth, in a nurturing environment. The metaphor of the gate was further reinforced recently as I read Jonathon Kozol's book *Ordinary Resurrections* (2001). He uses a gate metaphor (as well as a literal gate) to make a point about Pineapple: "The trouble is that Pineapple could not get through the narrow gate!" (p. 294). Kozol's gate is certainly part of a gate that we must work to open in urban education. He writes:

> There should not be a narrow gate for the children of the poor, a wide and open gate for children of the fortunate and favored. There should be one gate. It should be known to everyone. It should be wide enough so even Pineapple can get in without squeezing. (p. 296)

The idea that educating young people is about removing them from that which they know, replacing it with what *we* know is in their best interest appears, to me, to be the underlying principle in urban education: *Talk the way we talk, read what we read, value what we value.* Certainly, this is not a new idea. John Dewey (1938) expressed this dichotomy: "The history of educational theory is marked by opposition between the idea that education is development from within and that it is formation from without" (p. 17). How can it be that we continue to grapple with this or, worse yet, that our inner-city schools move toward even more rigidity based upon fear of these young people, fear of what they are capable of doing. Everywhere I hear the discussion of more discipline, stricter dress codes, less free time . . . more standardized testing, and, hence, more test preparation, more security, more. . . . Fill in the blank. Where is the "organic connection between education and personal experience" (p. 25) in all of this talk? When Dewey writes, "Any experience is miseducative that has the effect of arresting or distorting the growth of personal experience" (p. 25), I can only catch a sharp breath and think of the "mis-education" I see all around me. We must reach back, allowing students to write on that wooden gate, as a means to move forward.

Without such dualism, I watch students become silent in a second language; I watch them shut down and tune out when they discover "their" interests are not worthy of study; I hear them call teachers "stupid," homework "stupid," class projects "stupid," because they have been made to feel "stupid" trying to communicate on these new iron bars called "school." Again, I hear Dewey in my mind at such moments:

> How many students, for example, were rendered callous to ideas, and how many lost the impetus to learn because of the way in which learning was experienced by them? How many acquired special skills by means of automatic drill so that their power of judgment and capacity to act intelligently in new situations was limited? How many came to associate the learning process with ennui and boredom? How many found what they did learn so foreign to the situations of life outside the school as to give them no power or control over the latter? How many came to associate books with dull drudgery, so that they were "conditioned" to all but flashy reading matter? (pp. 26–27)

How is it that the institution of education continues to turn off the very students we most need to turn on? This is the most pressing issue facing education today. It is imperative that we reach our young people, that they connect education with self, with discovery, with joy. Jacques Barzun, Professor of History at Columbia University, addresses the core of this issue in his lecture, "The Care and Feeding of the Mind":

> We go on spreading culture as if it were peanut butter, through our free libraries and museums, our paperbound books, and our wonderful reproductions of painting and music, but we feel qualms about the result. Despite the unbelievable distribution of good things for the mind, we turn against our school system out of fear that it is producing barbarians, and we turn against our men [and women] of ideas out of fear that intelligence will betray us.

This seeming contradiction is not contradictory at all. Our focus on standardized testing, on conformity is greatest in the inner city. Why? My mind will not allow me to skirt this issue, for I believe we "fear that intelligence will betray us," that intelligence of these young people who do not look like us, often do not talk like us, in many cases are not citizens of this country or purport separatism. Ah ha, we fear that intelligence. Therefore, we create the bars, those which turn students away from the intellect they could develop; we mis-educate by turning students away from their roots, away from the wooden gate upon which they could discover their intellect. Alfred Tatum (2000) confronts such mis-education when he writes about the seven years he has sought to "empower and accelerate the reading achievement of African American adolescents assigned to lower-level reading tracks" in the face of the "current momentum toward minimum standards and high-stakes testing" (p. 570). He reflects upon James Baldwin's essay, "A Talk to Teachers" (1963) and can only wonder what our society intends with such education, for "the whole process of education occurs within a social framework and is designed to perpetuate the aims of society" (Baldwin, p. 679). Tatum sees the iron gate and calls it for what it is:

> curriculum dictates satisfied by test-driven instruction that prevent more comprehensive approaches for teaching reading, thwart critical competencies, and unfairly consign this group to the bottom of the economic, social and political ladder. (p. 570)

Students must be validated for what they bring to school; they must be given the "opportunity to critically examine the society in which they are born. . . . Students should be provided with the possibility to understand who they are in ways that are different from identities formed by the dominant culture" (Tatum, 2000, p. 571).

bell hooks (1994) explains this well when she tells the story of sitting in her living room with two little girls "talking about teaching and writing, telling them about cultural criticism" (p. 2). How to discuss thinking and writing and culture and learning with children is an essential question for all educators. hooks began with what was around her there in the living room, not keeping the children out but letting them in, talking about what they recognized, what they saw: "We talk about everything we see that we like" (p. 2). And slowly the three engage in a conversation about cultural criticism that evolves from looking at where they are: "We practice cultural criticism and feel the fun and excitement of learning in relation to living regular life, of using everything we already know to know more" (p. 2). That idea of using everything we know to know more is thrilling. It values young people, values the stories they have to tell, values the little wooden gates they are writing upon, values their knowledge as a seed for more knowledge. hooks' discussion with the girls is a paradigm we educators could use in our classrooms, inviting our young people into the conversation, asking *them* what *they* know as a means to know more. hooks opened the gate to learning for those little girls; she enabled those students to enter a pedagogical process, uniting where they were with new ideas, uniting recognition and inclusion with growth. There were no judgments that they did not know *enough*. Their place in the world was accepted, honored even. Such acceptance, such validation of the surface upon which they "write" what they know (their wooden gate, if you will) allowed them to begin to learn more. It did not shut them out for lack of the "proper" knowing, it did not intimidate or judge or humiliate; rather, hooks' pedagogy invited, validated, nurtured these young people to more knowing.

It is this process that must be the cornerstone of urban education. Too many urban youth end up behind bars because we replace their wooden gates with bars when they enter the education arena. In *Rethinking Schools,* William Ayers (1998) chronicles the demonization of youth, "backed by legislative proposals such as trying more children and teens as adults, building more youth prisons, and codifying the 'three strikes and you're out' approach even for children" (p. 1). Alex Kotlowitz (2000) sees the demonization of youth in the calls to lower legal age for the death penalty for juvenile offenders (p. 23). He cites David Tanenhaus, a historian of juvenile justice, pointing to, "a general loss of faith in children and the rehabilitative idea" (p. 23).

As we lose faith in children, educational bars become the obstacles to growth. Why the emphasis on evaluation at younger and younger ages? Why label children at five or six because they have not filled a particular box created by those far removed from their lives? It is possible to use what we know as a foundation for what we can know. Focusing upon what we do not know dismantles that gate, takes away any voice at all. Uniting life outside with knowledge in the classroom has been the driving force in my own practice. Gaston's understanding of what happened in his life certainly informed my intellectual work.

As Colleen Fairbanks (1998) stated, "educating students must . . . concern itself with the institutional and political relations that push some students and some schools to the fringes" (p. 187). This push results in a "devaluing of the local knowledge that students acquire outside of school" (p. 189). This seems to me to be a central issue in urban education. When our students become voiceless, when their identity is seen as a negative, something they have to "overcome," "be educated out of," we are confining rather than expanding possibilities. How else can we explain schools full of young people who read below grade level, who write only when forced. They are reluctant readers and writers because what they know and can read and write about is not seen as valuable; therefore, they choose not to participate. The 74% of students at a local high school who read below grade level (whatever that structure may tell you about reading ability) can, for the most part, decode words, but those words are not seen as meaningful, and they stagnate at low levels of reading ability. They choose not to read because it has been an activity with absolutely no connection to themselves; it is an act forced upon them and tested ad nauseum; it is an iron activity rather than a welcoming surface, a wooden gate on which they explore their world. In their commentary, "Reinventing adolescenct literacy for new times: Perennial and millennial issues" for the *Journal of Adolescent & Adult Literacy*, Moje, Young, Readence, and Moore (2000) address the critical need for improved adolescent literacy as determined by the International Reading Association's Commission on Adolescent Literacy:

> Adolescents entering the adult world in the 21st century will read and write more than any other time in human history. They will need advanced levels of literacy to perform jobs, run their households, act as citizens, and conduct their personal lives. . . . They will need literacy to feed their imaginations so they can create the world of the future. (p. 400)

They conclude that "adolescents need spaces in schools to explore and experiment with multiple literacies" (p. 402). Again, we are looking at the wooden gate, a place of exploration, of freedom, of choice.

As I observe students in school after school, I see them restricted by the activities of the day. This is such an odd irony. They enter school believing it will be a means of expanding their knowledge, a place of excitement and exploration and new knowledge. I cannot help but think of Gaston taking his chalk out to that wooden gate, exploring letters and images and ideas in that natural environment, only to have that surface replaced by those iron bars. This metaphor makes sense as I look at schooling. A "keeping out" mentality restricts students from the very beginning. For example, when second-language learners are led to believe that their language is "second-class," "inappropriate," and so forth, they internalize this information, seeing themselves as "second-class," "inappropriate."

Diaz-Rico and Reed (1995) suggest "that a certain bias exists in being bilingual—that being competent in a 'foreign language,' is valuable, whereas knowing an immigrant language is a burden to be overcome" (p. 42). Overcoming these restrictive elements of formal education can be a lifetime battle.

In *The Healing Drum*, Yaya Diallo (1998) writes of his schooling at the hands of colonial teachers in French West Africa in the 1950s, yet his words accurately describe a reality in urban education: "the school made me and my schoolmates, in the eyes of our adults, almost lost souls to the community" (p. 119). This is a statement that urban youth could easily make at the turn of the century. I hear this conversation all the time: "Young people today don't want to learn." "These kids are nothing but a bunch of thugs." "Let's get back to basics, the 3 R's." "What do we do with students who don't care?" Lost souls is the theme here, not far removed from the colonialist attitude Diallo experienced: "They had not come to meet us as human beings with valid cultures of our own. . . . Our parents were not considered fully human by the teachers" (p. 120). The idea that the parents are failing long before their children is not an uncommon thought in urban schooling. Diallo clearly articulates the manner in which the colonialist educators viewed their new students: "In their evangelizing, the teachers saw no place on earth for our 'barbaric, pagan' beliefs and practices" (p. 120). I have heard the same words in Whittier or Garden Grove or Santa Ana, California: "Their parents don't care about education"; "They don't want to learn English"; "All they know is that disgusting rap music." While we condemn colonization on an intellectual level, we practice it in our inner cities.

Such a colonialist attitude infuses urban education with practices that ultimately remove children from the joy of learning, from discovery, from writing on their wooden gates about their lives, their thoughts, their understanding, from finding themselves in literature, in history, in the world of the mind. Robert Scholes (1998) explores this idea in *The Rise and Fall of English*. He cites John Guillory in a discussion of the canon: "in teaching the canon, we are not only investing a set of texts with authority; we are equally instituting the authority of the teaching profession" (p. 27). Forcing "our" canon on students who have not had the same reading experiences can, indeed, take the life out of reading, can promote literature and writing as a domain far removed from life, can replace a gate of honest language with bars, bars that do not talk to the students. Guillory shows how the "safe haven" of teacher texts has become a type of religion with teachers becoming "a clergy without a dogma, teaching sacred texts without a God" (p. 27), with literature itself defined as a place of "interminable analysis" (p. 27). Giving students material to read that has no relation to their abilities or interests and then testing them on that material creates a deadened environment that many students escape.

I appreciate Frank Smith (1986) when he writes, "Children learn constantly—when they have not become persuaded that they can't learn. The time bomb in every classroom is that students learn exactly what they are taught" (p. ix). Children in our inner cities are learning that school negates their culture, that school doubts their abilities, that they need to be disciplined rather than educated. If, as Smith says, "students learn exactly what they are taught," consider the lessons we are teaching. Yes, our students have learned, they have learned that school is a foreign place one must suffer through. They have not learned to think, to question, to read for pleasure, to write as a means of discovery.

When we separate our children from their knowledge, we separate them from themselves in a way that has impacted our society most harmfully. Working within this irony in the inner city educational structure, understanding its corroding power, forces a teacher to look at ways to change, to help teachers and students "use everything we already know to know more."

We (both teachers and students) must not move away from ourselves to grow into whom we may become. In fact, we cannot. Paulo Freire's work is central to this discussion. As explained by Denis Goulet in the introduction to *Education for Critical Consciousness* (1998), the basic components of his literacy methods focus on the need to begin where we are, to "tune in" to the vocabular universe of the people (p. viii). His work asks educators to become "educator-educatee—in dialogue with educatee-educators too often treated by formal educators as passive recipients of knowledge" (p. viii). Students in urban education suffer from this tremendous surge to make them recipients of what the system wants them to receive: Let me tell you what you need to know, let me test you on what I think you need to know, let me tell you that your speech is incorrect, your thoughts are wrong, your very being is flawed. This, I believe, is the message of far too much schooling. Is there any surprise that students drop out or rebel or suffer through simply because they are "supposed to"? In discussing Freire's pedagogy, Denis Goulet (1998) captures the idea at the center of Gaston's gate:

> Paulo Freire's central message is that one can know only to the extent that one "problematizes" the natural, cultural, and historical reality in which s/he is immersed. Problematizing is the antithesis of the technocrat's "problem-solving" stance. In the lat-

ter approach, an expert takes some distance from reality, analyzes it into component parts, devises means for resolving difficulties in the most efficient way, and then dictates a strategy or policy. Such problem solving, according to Freire, distorts the totality of human experience by reducing it to those dimensions which are amenable to treatment as mere difficulties to be solved. But to "problematize" in his sense is to associate an entire populace to the task of codifying total reality into symbols which can generate critical consciousness and empower them to alter their relations with nature and social forces. (p. ix)

A pedagogy of paternalism, of control, is one that negates human experience, one that removes students from meaningful growth as learners. Education is that which is done to them rather than that which they do. Freire calls for people to become "subjects" rather than "objects" of their education. Certainly, we can see the need for such a dialogue in education today. The entire system appears to be one where teachers and students alike are objects of a larger system, involved in preparing for standardized tests legislated by those far removed from any community of learners, cringing at scores published in the newspaper, defending a system for which many have no sense of empowerment. Even students tell me they are taking these tests because they "have to." And teachers say they give them because they "have to." Any sense of ownership, of a nurturing, learning environment has been stripped away. The wooden gates have been replaced by iron bars.

Such co-optation of the educational system, co-optation by bureaucrats without understanding of a larger process of educating, has resulted in schools focused on control, schools focused on test-preparedness, schools determined to give students what they need to be sure the scores get them ranked high enough to ensure a stable real estate market. The picture is big, the means to this end is a removal of the wooden gate of personal experience and understanding to an iron gate unable to talk to children, to listen to children, to allow them to use what they know to grow, separating children from their language, their past, their community. Garret Hongo (2001) writes, "I want the dead beside me when I dance, to help me/flesh the notes of my song, to tell me it's all right". This is Gaston mourning the loss of his wooden fence upon which his poems had a life. The bars, the loss of that fence, the loss of his language, his culture, his experience, represent what school represents for too many children. I want my students to dance, to dance with the dead beside them to nourish the new, the growth, the education. Only when they are nourished as valued human beings can school become a nourishing place:

> *The children passed from hands of parents,*
> *Gathered up root and bone,*
> *Embraced the world with laughter.*
>
> (Wood, 1993)

REFERENCES

Ayers, W. (1998). The criminalization of youth. *Rethinking Schools: An Urban Educational Journal, 12*(2), 1, 3.

Barzun, J. (n.d.). *The care and feeding of the mind.* Columbia University Lecture.

Dewey, J. (1938). *Experience & education.* New York: Collier.

Diallo, Y. (1998). *The healing drum.* Rochester, VT: Destiny.

Diaz-Rico, L. T., & Weed, K. Z. *The crosscultural, language, and academic development handbook.* Boston: Allyn and Bacon.

Fairbanks, C. (1998). Nourishing conversations: Urban adolescents, literacy, and democratic society. *Journal of Literacy Research, 30*(2), 187-203.

Goulet, D. (1998). Introduction. *Education for critical consciousness by Paulo Freire* (pp. vii-xiv). New York: Continuum.

Hongo, G. (2001). O-Bon: Dance for the Dead. In *The river of heaven.* Pittsburgh, PA: Carnegie-Mellon University Press.

hooks, b. (1994). *Outlaw culture: Resisting representations.* New York: Routledge.

Kotlowitz, A. (2000, January, 17). Comment. *The New Yorker,* pp. 23–24.

Kozol, J. (2000). *Ordinary resurrections: Children in the years of hope.* New York: Crown.

Moje, E. B., Young, J. P., Readence, J. E., & Moore, D. W. (2000). Reinventing adolescent literacy for new times: Perennial and millennial issues. *Journal of Adolescent and Adult Literacy, 43*(5), 400–410.

Scholes, R. (1998). *The rise and fall of English.* New Haven, CT: Yale University Press.

Smith, F. (1986). *Insult to intelligence.* Portsmouth, NH: Heinemann Educational Books.

Wood, N. (1993). *Generations. Spirit Walker.* New York: Bantam Doubleday.

9

Expect the Unexpected: A Practitioner's View of Urban

Susie Weston

My name is Susie Weston-Barajas. I have been teaching at the elementary level for 12 years. I am "white," "Caucasian," "Euro-American"—I am not sure which label is politically correct these days. I received a privileged middle-class upbringing. I have blonde hair and green eyes; I look very different from most of my elementary school students. I am a graduate of the Chapman University's School of Education master's program. Three of the authors of this book were my professors when I was in the program. So why am I an author in this book on urban education? Why should you, the reader, read what I have to say? I believe there are two reasons. First, I obtained my master's degree and administrative credential (post-master's work) from Chapman; I have been forever changed by my association with my professors and my experiences in the program. It is my hope that, after you read my chapter, you will see that it is possible for educators at the university level to have a profound impact on their students; students, who will in turn, work toward social justice and equity for all students, especially those in urban settings.

Second, my story of my journey as an educator is one that will hopefully encourage other practitioners to take a stand and contribute their stories and voices to the conversations surrounding urban education. What I am offering in this chapter is what has informed my practice as an urban educator; my experiences are my ways of knowing. These experiences involve every aspect of my life—the workplace, my colleagues, my family, and my friends. Sharing and storytelling are a "legitimate mode of inquiry and effective way of knowing" (Bryan, Chapter 6). I believe that it is only through this sharing of stories, experiences, and multiple ways of knowing that educators can learn from each other and begin to work together for positive change in urban education.

FIRST ENCOUNTERS

I remember the first time I stepped on the Westside (pseudonym) campus. I thought to myself, "There is no way I can work here." I did not think this because the school's population was primarily minority, or because of large numbers of English language learners, or even because of large numbers of students on free or reduced lunch. I couldn't get past the physical plant itself.

The school was run down, poor, ugly, hot, and uncomfortable. The furniture was old and falling apart. The water that came out of the sinks was often brown. Most of the outer walls and surfaces had been painted over to cover up the graffiti. I had never seen a school like it, except on television.

It was such a contrast to the world I had known. I had attended school from first grade through high school in Irvine, California. My schools were beautiful: carpeting, air conditioning, new furniture, water that I could actually drink, and ample materials and supplies. I assumed all schools were like the ones I had attended. I did not expect Westside School to be any different. This was my first real encounter with "urban"; my first realization that educational settings were not equal.

Once I got over the initial shock of these stark differences, I accepted the job of teaching third grade as an intern. (The internship was not through Chapman University, but another highly revered southern California university.) At the time, an intern was someone who received half pay and was fully responsible for a classroom with the assistance of a master teacher who usually had other responsibilities on site. Internships took the place of student teaching experiences. Interns in California now typically receive full pay and often complete one semester of student teaching before the internship.

I had entered the intern program late, so I did not have any other fieldwork experience. As soon as I received my assignment, I asked for all of the third grade materials I could carry home with me, and planned all summer long in isolation. I planned my lessons very carefully. I studied the teachers' editions and followed all of the recommendations. By the time the first day of school rolled around, I had an entire month planned to perfection.

Then the children arrived. Most of my lessons bombed! I went home almost every night crying. I was very angry at the credential program that had supposedly prepared me to teach. The professors never prepared me for the diverse realities; multiple ways of knowing, or students' wide range of knowledge bases. I expected a better education and preparation from a university reputed to be one of the state's major research facilities.

As a result of this poor preparation, I only knew to treat all of my students the same. I only knew one model of teaching and had no idea how to meet the diverse and demanding needs of my students. My master teacher and university supervisor were of some help, but not much. They helped me with classroom management and a few teaching strategies here and there, but I needed so much more. I was frustrated and so were my students. They did not have the tools and knowledge to experience success with my lessons, and I did not have the tools and knowledge to give them what they needed to succeed. I felt like such a failure. How could I get through another week, let alone an entire year?

EARLY DISCOVERIES

My one salvation was my teaching partner at my grade level. She was also a first-year teacher. After a few weeks of comparing notes, we discovered one of the problems in my classroom. The students had been tracked. I had what others referred to as "the low track." The lessons my colleague and I planned together were very successful in her class, but they were a disaster in mine. This made me feel a little bit better because I realized I was not as horrible a teacher as I thought I was. I just didn't possess the best tools to best meet the needs of my students. After this big realization, it was now my job to try and gain some knowledge in order to help my students achieve success.

In my assessment of my knowledge base, I reflected back to my teacher preparation courses and my previous schooling experiences. The one course on multicultural education taught me nothing about how to teach a diverse group of learners. The only thing I really remembered about the class was the instructor. She treated any student with light eyes and light hair unfavorably. I suppose it was her way of "othering" us—attempting to make us feel like the minority, at least temporarily. My affective filter (Krashen, 1994) was very high throughout the class. If there was any content worth learning, I certainly do not remember it.

My experiences as a student were also of no use to me. Although my high school, at the time, was one of the most racially diverse in the country, and my friends reflected this diversity, we all possessed a privileged middle-class upbringing, which meant we were more similar than different. My friends who were people of color were not encouraged by their parents to maintain their traditions, cultures, and languages. These cultural markers were downplayed. Even though racial diversity was present, this diversity did not produce or add to a new knowledge base for me. I did not understand that there were other ways of knowing informed by differences. As a result, I had little to draw upon to help me teach my students. "Teachers can be victims of their experiences" (Gaunty-Porter, Chapter 3). This was certainly true for me.

During my first year, I tried anything and everything I could think of to help my students experience success. I was always trying to come up with lessons that would be hands-on and meaningful to my students. I purchased countless lesson plan books from the local teacher supply, searching for lessons that would benefit my students. Approximately 85% of my students were English language learners, so I tried to focus on vocabulary development. But I was surviving day by day, lesson by lesson. My lessons did not develop sequentially or build upon each other. I taught endless unrelated lessons that the students enjoyed, but there was no "big picture," no real meaning. I was just trying to survive. Teaching was a constant struggle, and I believed I did a terrible disservice to those students my first year.

JONATHAN

My one bright moment was Jonathan. Jonathan was one of my favorite students my first year of teaching. He was Samoan, in the third grade, and almost the same height as me at 5' 1". He sat with Jaime, a Hispanic boy who was also large and about the same height.

I always had to seat them together because I had only one table that was raised high enough for their legs to fit under.

Jonathan was funny and always had a great attitude, but he was also my biggest worry. He had great difficulty with school and was not doing well. Although he tried hard in school, he was not experiencing success. In addition, he often fell asleep in class because he stayed up so late at night. He said this was usually because of late nights spent at church or large family gatherings. I felt like I taught him nothing and failed him.

Jonathan moved after that first year and I never saw him again. I have always worried that Jonathan wouldn't make it; that he would end up hanging around with the "wrong crowd," which would result in gang membership or involvement in the juvenile system. Over the years I have seen so many students turn to this way of life. I was guilty of unityping (Cardinal, Chapter 2). I believed that poverty, his status as English language learner, Title I, and "low track," and his urban surroundings of crime and gangs would define Jonathan and predict his future. Although I always hoped Jonathan would overcome the hurdles in front of him, I realize now I did not believe he would be capable overcoming these "urban" obstacles.

About a month ago, a man came into my classroom. He was about 6' 5" and had a deep and booming voice. I was a little cautious at first; I have had strangers enter my room before who have posed danger to my students as well as myself, and I still had students in my room. Then the voice asked, "I am looking for Ms. Weston?" We both realized at the same time that he was looking at Ms. Weston and I was looking at Jonathan. I jumped up and we hugged. We talked endlessly.

Jonathan was in his first year of college, studying music and doing very well. He told me I was one of his favorite teachers and he enjoyed school when he was in my class. He was also curious about why I always sat him with Jaime because, "We were always getting into trouble." I had to explain about the table accommodating their body sizes.

I realized several things during this discussion with Jonathan. Even though I was not what I would call a good teacher that first year, I did teach something to those students and they did learn. I also learned that teaching is more than lessons, strategies, and assignments. When a teacher puts herself into her teaching—all of her passion, love, and effort—it makes an incredible difference that can have a powerful impact on learning development. It is what made Jonathan come by to visit me after all of these years. And it is what will keep me in this profession for as long as it will have me.

Jonathan represents all of the students who need more than just academic instruction. He represents the students who need love, care, understanding, a sense of belonging and a feeling of being valued. I think of Jonathan almost every day, and remember the lessons he taught me.

A TIME OF TRANSITION

In my second year at Westside School I taught kindergarten and learned some invaluable lessons. The most important lesson was the power of an integrated curriculum; a cross-disciplinary, thematic approach to instruction. Integrating curriculum was one of the first things that saved me. I saw students make connections in curricular areas to their own lives and they showed more interest in learning.

The following year I returned to third grade and implemented a more integrated approach to curriculum and had much more success, as evidenced by student achievement. In the spring of this third year of teaching, I was trained in Project GLAD (Guided Language Acquisition Design; Brechtel, 2001). GLAD is a national academic excellence program that works to meet the needs of all learners in an inclusive setting. It is based on current brain and language acquisition research and best teaching strategies. This training influenced me greatly, and caused me to realize the importance of informing my practice through a combination of reading research, implementing inclusive strategies, and looking at my practice critically in order to best meet the needs of my students. Once I began using this approach, and I did immediately, I could hear angels singing. I am not kidding. My students were learning, having incredible success, and enjoying it! And for the first time, I truly enjoyed teaching.

CONSCIOUSNESS EMERGES

Once I felt fairly secure in my teaching, I began to more carefully observe the system in which I worked. What I saw was a world of low teacher expectations. My students could have said what Gaunty-Porter said of her school in Chicago, "I was very aware of the differences I had experienced at the two schools, namely, teacher expectations of students. It seemed to me that teachers in the school near the University of Chicago offered challenging assignments, whereas the teachers in the school near my house offered routine, game-like assignments. In other words, I felt that the teachers in this neighborhood school instructed us in playing lots of games, but I was not learning anything" (Gaunty-Porter, Chapter 3).

I heard conversations in the teachers' lounge that began with "These kids can't . . ." and "These parents don't care about . . ." I could not and did not believe what I heard. I knew what kind of success could be achieved by our students, but I was at a loss as to how to convince my colleagues of this reality. I had no political advocacy skills at that time and was not exactly one to speak my mind. I didn't think anyone would listen. I figured, "I'm only a third-year teacher. Who would listen to me?"

Having little confidence in any advice I could get from my lounge colleagues, I decided to seek knowledge from colleagues whose perspectives I respected. I joined a teacher research group, CARDC (Collaborative Action Researchers for Democratic Communities). I began reading research and educational journals. I became a Project GLAD trainer and a mentor teacher. And with the encouragement and support of a critical friend and teaching partner, I began my master's program. Through all these endeavors, many doors opened up for me. I had opportunities to present at conferences, write articles (SooHoo & Weston, 1994; Weston-Barajas, 1999), and most importantly, provide a meaningful and powerful education for my students. Looking back on these choices that I made, I believe I was unknowingly, implementing Freire's notion of praxis.

Collaborative action research provided an avenue for me to name and begin to transform my world. Reading educational journals, research, and studying in Chapman University's master's program gave me opportunities to read the word while I read my world. Becoming a GLAD trainer, presenting at conferences, and writing became the action of my praxis—my steps toward transforming my world. Reflection was an ongoing process in my praxis, which led me to continue the cycle of reading the word and world, critical reflection, and transformative action.

NAMING MY WORLD

I was very disturbed by the "teachers' lounge culture" and the perceptions about the community that existed at my school. I learned to deal with these issues in my master's coursework. My very first class, Democracy and Education, was unlike any other course I had ever taken. Students were encouraged to be critical—to think, act, and reflect. We were given the opportunity to be responsible for our own learning and to apply what we had learned to our own lives and educational settings. I had never been asked to do any of these things before. There was no "read the book and answer the questions" or "memorize this for the test" expectations. I was actually expected to apply what I was learning to my own teaching situation and to collaboratively work with my peers to bring about positive change, equity, and social justice in schools. I began to look at my school, my students, and my colleagues in a whole new way. I began to realize my incredible power as an educator. I have the power to name my world, inform my own practice, and provide an atmosphere where my students can do the same. Naming our world is the first step to social justice, and is best described in the words of Freire (1970): ". . . people develop their power to perceive critically the way they exist in the world with which and in which they find themselves; they come to see the world not as a static reality, but as a reality in process, in transformation."

All of my coursework at Chapman was built upon the premise that we must engage in a pedagogy that is critical, reflective, and caring. I shared my efforts with my elementary school students and my colleagues. I have learned there is great power in working together rather than working in isolation. I am not a special case. Any teacher can do these things; naming and transforming her own world and inform her own practice. It is my hope that others will join me in a process of praxis that results in a transformation of our world, and in turn provides the opportunity for our students to do the same. My experiences up to this point had definitely proved to be positive for my students and me. But knowledge comes from many sources, equally legitimate and credible. The most significant and unexpected influence on my career was yet to come.

BREAKING THE RULES: CROSSING THE BORDER

I had known Robert, our custodian, for five years. He was shy, quiet, thoughtful, hard-working, and possessed a strong ethic of caring. Robert cared a great deal about the students of Westside. He had wonderful rapport with the students, and contributed his own time after school as a basketball coach. Someone did it for him when he was young, and he wanted to do the same for the students of Westside.

Robert was a role model, resource, and support for our students. He was always willing to listen to them and to be a friend. He had been born and raised in the local community; he had lived there all of his life. His story of growing up paralleled the lives of many of my own students: low income, a broken home, and gang involvement. And like my students, Robert described his youth as full of love: love from his father, his brother, and love from his friends and their families. Robert had a knowledge and understanding of the community that was comprehensive and insightful.

After knowing Robert for five years, we began dating. Dating led to marriage. We have been married for three years and have been together for seven years. Our relationship and the dialogue we share informs my practice more than any class, book, or workshop ever could.

From Robert, I learned a cultural knowledge that I did not know existed. He told me about the need to feel accepted by the local community, which often resulted in gang involvement, despite the strong love and family orientation. Many families do not have very much time to spend together due to their work schedules. Robert explained that this is why many kids often turn to gangs; a sense of belonging is critical for all of us, and this includes children in urban settings. Robert also described the pressure that is placed on the young members of the community; many of the financial and caretaking responsibilities are shared by the children at a very young age in order for the parents to be able to work and provide for their families. These circumstances add to the need for belonging, acceptance, and love. Most importantly, I learned from this that being a teacher who embraces a pedagogy of care, love, and high expectations, all of which are based upon the students' cultural capital, can have a positive impact on my students.

I felt as if I was reading about Robert in many ways in the Cardinal chapter, particularly the discussions regarding manifestations of moral behavior:

> . . . the urban youth who engages in antisocial behavior is not morally bankrupt, but rather, that he needs to learn how to manifest his values into behavior consistent with the rules of "our" streets (the streets of larger society). (Cardinal, Chapter 2)

This was certainly true for Robert, and also for Westside students. These students have the same values and morals as those deemed acceptable by society, but these values manifest themselves in a different manner based on the community culture, the culture of their peer families. These students, like Robert, were not "morally bankrupt," but required an educational environment where urban children are revered for their values and shown by teachers how to "transition their behavior into more socially accepted norms" (Cardinal, Chapter 2).

What I have learned from my relationship with Robert has changed my teaching and how I deal with the community in many ways. Through this marriage I have learned some hard lessons about prejudice and "crossing the borderlands" (SooHoo, Chapter 7). When people hear I married someone from work, they immediately assume I must have married another teacher. When I explain it was the custodian, I often get a reaction of raised eyebrows and "Ooooooooh. . . ." The subject usually gets changed rather quickly, or jokes are made about how clean my room must be. It seems I have crossed a line that teachers are not supposed to cross. I guess teachers are not supposed to marry custodians.

My relationship to the community evokes a similar reaction by many of my coworkers. I have made many wonderful friends in the school community. Friendships with parents from my school are looked upon with troubled eyes by many of my colleagues. They make me feel like I am mingling with the marginalized, the unwanted. Teachers should not cross borders by befriending parents. Why is it this way? Why is it that teachers cannot build friendships or family in the community in which they work? Teachers at my school view the problems of my school and community as "out there," and they have conceptualized their role as one of "helping minority students," as "self-righteous missionaries with the answers for others" (Howard, 1999). They embrace the "dark side" of urban, and this impacts their approach to teaching and how they interact with the students and community in a negative manner. Expectations are low and missionary zeal is abundant. This approach to education creates students who are dependent and are unable to think critically and transform their world (Howard, 1999).

I have learned to ignore the sideways glances and raised eyebrows, and speak out against the prejudices and misconceptions that exist concerning my students and community. I have learned that I can best inform my practice through meaningful relationships with the community and that these relationships should not be avoided or feared, but be embraced and nurtured. A teacher's relationship to the community is like a relationship to a spouse in many ways. I listen fully and openly. I work hard at the relationship every day in order to make it successful. I strive to understand other points of view and compromise when needed. And I, as a teacher, work with the community in order to best meet the needs of our kids.

No, I am not suggesting that urban teachers marry someone in their community in order to learn about it. I am suggesting, and hoping, that teachers will not fear relationships with members of the urban community, but embrace them. I share my story to illustrate how I learned from someone in my community, and that these relationships are valuable and worth pursuing. Urban teachers need to cross borders beyond the schoolhouse doors. One thing I learned was to experience empathy. Howard (1999) explains the concept of empathy, which cannot authentically exist in the context of "missionary zeal" :

> Empathy means "to feel with." Empathy requires the suspension of assumptions, the letting go of ego, and the release of the privilege of non-engagement. In this sense, empathy is the antithesis of dominance. It requires all of our senses and focuses our attention on the perspective and worldview of another person. (p. 73)
>
> [W]e cannot fully know or experience the struggles of our students and colleagues of color, but we can work to create an empathetic environment in which their stories and experiences can be acknowledged and shared. (p. 75)

Engaging in meaningful relationships within the community in which I work has expanded my knowledge base in ways which I did not know were possible, in ways that are difficult to put into words. It is my hope by sharing my story that other educators will take the risk and become "border crossers" themselves. This is authentic learning.

URBAN EDUCATION . . . WHAT'S THAT?

A few years ago I was sitting next to a teacher I did not know in a district inservice. We introduced ourselves, and she asked where I worked. When I told her Westside School, a look of sympathy appeared on her face and she said, "I'm sorry."

Her response typifies the perceptions I have encountered concerning "urban education." Even though this teacher worked in the same district, she worked "in the hills," which is a wealthy and affluent area, literally on the "right side of the tracks." The elementary student population in the city itself is 43% Latino (X School District, 2000), who primarily live on one side of the tracks. Going to the "other" side of town is like going to another city. "Local border crossings can mean moving from one block to another" (Bryan, Chapter 6). This is certainly true in my district. When people think of urban, they think of schools more like mine, not the schools that are in the same city, in a "nicer part of town." People tend to associate negative things with urban education, such as violence, drugs, gangs, poverty, low test scores, run-down facilities, unqualified teachers, and underachieving students. This perception is fueled by the media, "Culturally and linguistically deprived, at risk, gang infested areas, poverty, violence, aging buildings, welfare, drugs, inadequate resources, and a shortage of licensed teachers: What do these words have in common? Answer: Media reports typically use these words and phrases to catalogue the urban communities of America" (Gaunty-Porter, Chapter 3). Although these problems certainly exist in some urban communities, these problems do not accurately define urban communities and urban education, and they certainly do not define the students.

These misperceptions are unfortunately found in our future teachers. As a new teacher, I was a prime example of someone who held these perceptions. Currently, I teach part time in a teacher education program. One of my goals is to prepare teachers to teach diverse populations. Sometimes we meet in my classroom at Westside School. I think it is important that the university students see my students and the educational setting first hand.

Last semester, one of my students said to me, "How can you work here? I would never work in a school like this." As I looked around the room, several of my students nodded their heads in agreement. I was mortified, yet I am glad it happened. I remembered I used to feel the same way; at one time I shared these beliefs. This experience made me realize that as an educator it is my responsibility to dispel the myths surrounding urban education. Freire (1998) extends this thinking:

> When inexperienced middle-class teachers take positions in peripheral areas of the city, class-specific tastes, values, language, discourse, syntax, semantics, everything about the students may seem contradictory to the point of being shocking and frightening. It is necessary, however, that teachers understand that the students' syntax; their manners, tastes, and ways of addressing teachers and colleagues; and the rules governing their fighting and playing among themselves are all part of their cultural identity, which never lacks an element of class. All that has to be accepted. Only as learners recognize themselves democratically and see that their right to say "I be" is respected will they become able to learn the dominant grammatical reasons why they should say "I am." (p. 49)

It is not enough to work for social justice and equity in my own classroom. If we are fortunate enough to have an impact on future teachers, we must take advantage of this opportunity to ensure that all teachers are not only prepared to teach in urban settings, but that they welcome the chance to do so. "As teacher educators and researchers, we must deconstruct this hegemony of inner city schools, deghettoize this bias, understand first hand what educational opportunities can be found for our student teachers. One needs to be 'there' to know 'there.' We must know our schools intimately in order to demystify misconceptions so that student teachers can realize the full potential of these settings" (SooHoo, Chapter 7).

Why do people have such negative perceptions about urban education? Most have never "crossed the border" themselves. Why is it that the violence in Columbine was seen as a horrific tragedy that made international headlines, whereas a drive-by shooting in East L.A. might make the local news four or five stories into the broadcast? Is one less tragic than the other? Is life less valuable in the urban setting? What has caused society to treat such tragedies so differently? Many at Westside School, as well as members of society, have climbed up what Argyris calls the "Ladder of Inference" (1990). This ladder serves as a model to understand how this "pattern of misunderstanding" comes to exist. On the first two rungs are observable data and culturally understood meanings. On the third and fourth rungs are meanings imposed by us and the theories we use to create those meanings. The misperceptions regarding urban education exist because many have moved up this ladder of inference and are operating on the third and fourth rungs with no sound data from the first and second rungs to ground their meanings and theories. Argyris explains: ". . . the evaluations or judgments people make automatically are not concrete or obvious, They are abstract and highly inferential. Individuals treat them as if they were concrete because they produce them so automatically that they do not even think that their judgments are highly inferential" (p. 89). It is movement up this ladder that prevents one from seeing urban settings positively.

Sapp illustrates in his chapter: "We share our stories so that we may enter into communion with each other in states of being, not seeming." The bottom rungs of the ladder represent states of being, and the upper rungs represent states of seeming. As a teacher educator, I see it as my job to bring my university students and colleagues back down to the first two rungs on the ladder, to the states of being. This is the first step in dispelling the myths and misperceptions surrounding urban education.

WHOSE KNOWLEDGE IS VALUED? WHOSE SHOULD BE?

My colleagues are very clear in this book about whose knowledge is being valued in urban educational settings, and it is not the indigenous knowledge of the communities in urban areas. It is the knowledge deemed valuable by those in power, namely white, male America (Apple, 1985, 1993; Giroux, 1995). Apple asks critical questions in this regard: "The curriculum begins from the critical question, 'From whose perspective are we seeing, or reading, or hearing?'" (p. 39). "Whose knowledge is taught? Why is it taught in this particular way to this particular group? How do we enable the histories and cultures of the majority of working people, of people of color, to be taught in responsible and responsive ways in schools?" (p. 41). Apple goes on to state: "The 'cultural capital' declared to be official knowledge, then, is compromised knowledge, knowledge that is filtered through a complicated set of political screens and decisions before it gets to be declared legitimate" (p. 68).

There is an obvious mismatch between the knowledge of value and the knowledge of the students in urban areas. As my fellow authors have made clear, this is one of the major problems with urban education. Society defines these students as "at risk," and they must be controlled and molded to fit into a knowledge base that has no meaning for them, such as the Stanford 9. These students do not have access to the knowledge capital.

What do we do? As educators, we must place emphasis on the students, using their knowledge base—the local knowledge—in order to provide a meaningful and relevant education resulting in success for students. "When we separate our children from their knowledge, we separate them from themselves in a way that has impacted our society most harmfully" (Osborn, Chapter 8). Freire (1998) addresses this issue as well:

> [O]ur relationship with the learners demands that we respect them and demands equally that we be aware of the concrete conditions of their world, the conditions that shape them. To try to know the reality that our students live is a task that the educational practice imposes on us: Without this, we have no access to the way they think, so only with great difficulty can we perceive what and how they know. (p. 58)

Giroux (1995) also describes the importance of emphasizing the local knowledge: ". . . the content of the curriculum needs to affirm and critically enrich the meaning, language, and knowledge that students actually use to negotiate and inform their lives" (p. 45).

We have seen examples of the power of this model in previous chapters, particularly in the SooHoo, Wilson, and Sapp chapters. The very nature of the research project described in the SooHoo chapter illustrates the value that must be placed on the local knowledge:

> As evidenced in this project, collaborative action research is a microcosm of democracy in the way in which it brings interested constituents together to work on projects to improve a community. Our purpose in establishing the collaborative action team was to bring forth all voices; all interested parties to engage in mutual inquiry as equal partners with equal status. In this way, our research would address the conventional hierarchical relationship of the researcher collecting data on subjects. By inviting subjects to participate as coresearchers, data is collected and interpreted with and by subjects. (SooHoo, Chapter 7)

The Newport Plan in the Wilson chapter also exemplifies an educational model that values the local knowledge of the students and community:

> Democratic formation involves much more than mere manipulation of teaching method and content. What is necessary is an emphasis upon the culture of educational experiences in which the entire environment, the *weltanschauung*, the democratic core becomes the means by which development is affected. Within this context, what if students could be freed from the existing restrictions, what if they had extensive time to engage in making major decisions about themselves and their own educational process? (Wilson, Chapter 4)

Sapp illustrates further problems in our textbooks regarding the lack of value placed on local knowledge: "The problem is that, in education and in our classrooms, the focus is always outward. These huge books contain the realities that we deem important and anything inside the teacher or the students is suspect" (Chapter 5).

THE CHALLENGE

Each of my colleagues present realities and ways of knowing that are very different from each other; they cannot be grouped together or labeled as the same due to the complexities surrounding their efforts.

There is a tendency to group all aspects of and experiences involving urban education into one category. This is a mistake. As the chapters in this book demonstrate, urban education is complex, diverse, and different for those who are involved in it. My colleagues and fellow authors are practitioners who have put these ideas to use; their espoused theories match their theories in use. This is critical, as outlined in the Bryan chapter:

> I need to know the meanings, shared and discrepant, that the participants make of these concepts because if we believe building leadership capacity for a whole community, such theories-in-use shape important decisions made in the educational environments in which we live, conduct inquiry, and work. (Chapter 6)

Wilson also addresses this issue: "The bald-faced functionalism and narrow positivistic implications of the nation at risk hypothesis is under siege by a dialectical counter attack formed from the notions of ethics, community, voice, and empowerment" (Chapter 4). The result is a transformative model of education that allows learners to transform the structure in which they live so they can become "beings for themselves" rather than "beings for others" (Freire, 1970, p. 55).

My fellow authors make a powerful and compelling argument for change in the power structure and valued ways of knowing in education. I have experienced the positive effects of transformative education and am dedicated to placing value in the knowledge base of students, using their realities and their worlds as a foundation from which to work. But working this way presents a challenge for educators. It is imperative that educators work to change the official knowledge that is currently valued in education (Bryan, Chapter 6; Osborn, Chapter 8). There are multiple ways of knowing, and all must be honored and utilized. One is no better than the other. The stories shared in this book demonstrate the power of learning outside of formal academic preparation. But there is the issue of the current valued knowledge base. If we do not provide access to this knowledge base, are we doing a terrible disservice to our students? Our task is two-fold: We must work to change the current power structure while ensuring access to it in order for our students to be successful. "One must use the language of power to deconstruct and transform existing power structures" (SooHoo, Chapter 7).

Another challenge we must tackle is perhaps more difficult. In reading the stories in this book and engaging in critical dialogue with my colleagues, I have come to the realization that the concept of multiple ways of knowing extends beyond the classroom and touches all of us. Every one of us who authored a chapter of this book has had different experiences with "urban education." Urban in Chicago is different from urban in southern California. We all have our own concepts, ideas, and thoughts regarding urban education; we all have multiple ways of knowing urban education. Like our students, we must value each other's knowledge bases and perspectives as professionals and use them as a platform from which to inform our collective work.

The work in this book is evidence of the complexity of urban education. In discussing our work, our "definition" of urban education was diverse, multifaceted, and ever-changing. We wondered if maybe there are varying degrees of urban, if maybe it was a question of different degrees of intensity. We did agree on one thing: Common misconceptions of urban were negative and impeded the success of the students who lived in these areas.

OUR PRAXIS

As authors, we came together with an objective; to deconstruct the myths surrounding urban schools through our experiences. In making use of all possible resources to achieve success in this effort, we have discovered the unexpected. We have discovered that urban education is much more complex than we had imagined. We have discovered that just as we must value multiple ways of knowing in the classroom, we must do so with our colleagues as well. I see the collaborative process of writing this book as evidence of our praxis; our process of reflection and action in order to transform our world and the world of our students. Regardless of our differences in experience and definitions, our common goal was to improve education in urban settings for students so they in turn can achieve success. We have challenged urban myths in an effort to change and contribute to the current knowledge base. We have grown in this collaborative process and dialogue. It is our hope that others can grow and continue the dialogue. Even if we are an "insider" in the world of urban education, ours is only a partial view. It is through sharing our stories and our praxis that we continue to learn and improve urban education for our students and aspiring teachers.

NOW WHAT?

So what is next? Writing this chapter and being a part of this project has been an incredible journey for me. The greatest lesson I have learned was the realization that, just like our students, educators have multiple ways of knowing and that this knowledge must be shared to advance our knowledge capital. Education is the most isolated profession (Sagor, 1992). We all work independently of each other when we prepare and teach our classes. All of the things that we know are best practice for students—collaboration, reflection, and sharing—are almost impossible for us to achieve with each other due to the isolating nature of teaching. We must fight this isolation and begin to work together and share our stories. We shouldn't fear collaboration, but embrace it. It is something I am going to fight even harder to do. We have opened a door—a door to sharing, collaboration, and dialogue—a door that I hope all educators will have the courage to walk through.

REFERENCES

Argyris, C. (1990). *Overcoming organizational defenses: Facilitating organizational learning.* Englewood Cliffs, NJ: Prentice Hall.

Apple, M. W. (1985). Making knowledge legitimate: Power, profit, and the textbook. In A. Molar (Ed.), *Current thought on curriculum: The 1985 yearbook of the Association for Supervision and Curriculum Development* (pp. 73–89). Alexandria, VA: ASCD.

Apple, M. W. (1993). *Official knowledge: Democratic education in a conservative age.* New York: Routledge.

Brechtel, M. (2001). *Project GLAD* [On-line]. www.projectglad.com.

Freire, P. (1970). *Pedagogy of the oppressed.* New York: Continuum.

Freire, P. (1998). *Teachers as cultural workers: Letters to those who dare to teach.* Boulder, CO: Westview Press.

Giroux, H.A. (1995). Teachers, public life, and curriculum reform. In A.C. Orenstein & L.S. Behar (Eds.), *Contemporary issues in curriculum reform* (pp. 41–49). Boston: Paramount.

Howard, G.R. (1999). *We can't teach what we don't know: White teachers, multiracial schools.* New York: Teachers College Press, Columbia University.

Krashen, S.D. (1994). Primary language instruction and the education of language minority students. In C.F. Leyba (Ed.), *Schooling and language minority students: A theoretical framework* (pp. 47–75). Los Angeles: California State University.

Sagor, R. (1992). *How to conduct collaborative action research.* Alexandria, VA: ASCD.

SooHoo, S., & Weston, S. (1994). Are mermaids real? *Counseling and Human Development Newsletter of the American Educational Research Association, 13*(1), 5–7.

Weston-Barajas, S. (1999). Teacher research: Praxis for the oppressed. *Democracy and Education, 13*(1), 19–22.

X School District (2000). *X School District* [On-line]. Available upon written request from the author.

10

Can We Talk . . . About Collaboration?

Chapman University Social Justice Consortium

Penny Bryan
Don Cardinal
Dolores Gaunty-Porter
Jan Osborn
Jeff Sapp
Suzanne SooHoo
Susie Weston-Barajas
Tom Wilson

Searching for an ending to our book, the book group decided to invest one more bankroll of energy by coauthoring a final talking chapter. We were inspired to use this literary form by Freire's and Faundez' work in *Learning to Question* (1989) in which they describe the process as "an interesting, intellectual experience, a rich and truly creative experience . . . (and) . . . in fact 'speaking' a book with one or two others instead of writing it alone represents, to some extent, at least a break with a certain individualistic tradition in the production of books. . . . By taking us out of the pleasant coziness of our study, it opens us up to each other in the adventure of thinking critically" (p. 2). In this discussion, we would investigate what we had learned through this experience, discuss the processes of collaboration and writing, and project how our work together might influence the other dimensions of our academic environment. What we discovered during the three years was that we had grossly varying ideas of what collaboration meant, what urban education meant, and even who each of us was in terms of urban education and scholarship. Many of the lures to writing a collaborative book slowly transitioned from romanticized euphoria of the perfect academic experience to academic realism. Less than half of us survived the journey. Meanwhile, we constantly questioned our responsibility in the group's dwindling size. In the end, when asked, nearly all of the survivors would do it all over again.

This project started with an open invitation extended to the School of Education faculty to submit a prospectus for a chapter in a book about urban education. From the main campus and 17 Academic Center campuses, consisting roughly of 40 full-time faculty members, 16 faculty members initially committed to the book project. Faculty authors met monthly to shape both the focus of the book and a collaborative writing community. Four cornerstones resulted from these early deliberations. We agreed we would (a) define "urban," (b) assume a social justice perspective, (c) personally situate ourselves within our chapters, and (d) offer something new to the education audience.

In an attempt to achieve the last objective, "new news," we invited one of our graduates to critique our work and write the last chapter of our book to include a practitioner's view of urban education, to have the last word, if you will. But, alas, that chapter was not enough. Challenging the norm of individualism in academe was seductive. This, plus the limited literature on collaborative scholars and our weakness to arrive at closure, prompted our desire to cast one more heroic effort to reshape the halls of academe. The benefits, the barriers, the sense making of the collaborative process, we reasoned, were best captured through a talking chapter. So on one warm sunny California evening, in a circle of plump, cushioned sofas in the School of Education Reading Center, we came together to nosh on a platter of Lebanese vegetables and talk. What follows is the good, the bad, and the ugly; the problems and promises of collaboration.

Suzanne SooHoo:
We decided to do a talking chapter about collaboration as our last chapter of our book. We hoped that it would be interesting as well as intellectually engaging. Co-constructed by eight of us, it would break the traditional notion of individualistic scholarship.

I don't know how we want to start tonight but one of the things that we suggested previously was that we would talk about the process of collaboration within our book group: what have we learned as a result of this experience together? What would we do differently? What was the good news and the bad news? Collaboration took a life of its own. Where has the experience brought us? Is this something we want to continue or avoid as inferred by Don's suggested book titles:

The Book That Took Two Millenniums to Complete
The Multi-Millennium Project: The Book
A Testament of Love But Never Again
Crickets Are Easier to Herd Than Authors
We Used to Know What This Book Was About

Can we start this evening with these questions? asks Suzanne.

What do we know now about urban education that we did not know before?
What do we know now about collaboration that we did not know before?

Penny Bryan:
When we added Susie Weston-Barajas to our group, we added the student and the practitioner's voice. Three of us faculty authors had her as a student in the masters program. I think our original thought was that we would get another perspective, that she would read all of our work and then kind of mirror back how that played against her experience as a former student and practitioner. I think what happened for me was that she just came in fully as another collaborator. What we have is not her synthesizing or summarizing our voices but presenting her own voice. She comes in as a full participant with a different perspective and to me that's a plus. We did not intend it that way, but how nice to think that somebody graduated from our program, came back, entered this inquiry process and fully participated in the way that she did. Instead of summarizing or reflecting other voices, she ended up expressing her own voice and her own perspective. I really like what happened better than what we planned, somehow what evolved feels more democratic.

Suzanne SooHoo:
How does that shoe fit Susie?

Susie Weston:
I have been real frustrated because when this project started, I received so many different ideas about what to do; telling my own story, being a critical friend to all of you, critiquing the chapters, looking at the book from a practitioner's point of view and trying to apply it. That was just way too much. I couldn't focus. I think that showed in my first draft. I'm up and down and back and forth and I'm not quite sure where to land.

Jeff Sapp:
You know, I felt that as well as we began to each draft our own chapters. I was all over the place. And we've had several years to get our focus.

(group laughter)

Susie Weston:
This is not helping me.

Suzanne SooHoo:
These are our pimples and warts.

Jeff Sapp:
Well, but do you get my point? I think your level of frustration is completely understandable. This is my third year at this institution and I started working on my chapter my first month here. And the rest of you all had actually started *before* I came here.

Penny Bryan:
Three years to produce this book. Dare we admit this?

Jeff Sapp:
So I think it's only an absolutely natural response that one would be a little upset because we had several years of a running start, to do what you have actually accomplished in a much shorter time. The affirmation from me is that I'm in awe of you that you did it this quickly and this well when it took me much longer to do it.

Susie Weston:
But I do still feel I need a little direction. I didn't know what was expected and I don't know that I know that now.

Tom Wilson:
We didn't either.

Don Cardinal:
It's very true that we didn't know exactly where we were going and we don't know now. Look what Penny just got through saying, "Well, we said we really wanted you for a specific reason, but I really like what you did. I like it even better." That's what has been very interesting about this group. The idea that there is no truth. That we're just "seeks" and what you did was "seeking." You joined our seeking. So, I agree with frustrating, but not with it being a bad thing.

Jeff Sapp:
How does that reflect on many of the things that we work from in regards to banking education and problem-posing education when we

have the tendency to say, "You just tell me what you want because it's so much easier for me to frame than this 'not knowing.'"? This is much more difficult, the problem posing. It connects to a foundational point for me regarding Paulo Freire's work even after finishing graduate school and being in higher education. We're still often uncomfortable with the problem posing as living in the question, as Rilke, the philosopher, puts it.

Suzanne SooHoo:
And Susie did all this without the benefits of high context; a series of collaborative meetings in which each one of us revealed our vulnerable spots like "I'm having trouble with this" or "Was what I wrote good enough?" "Should I add this?"

We were crossing traditional academic lines without any roadmaps. Remember how we felt when Penny said, "This is the only book I know in which such an insertion of the personal self is made in the chapters. This is new news."

We conscientiously constructed that part as a way to offer something unique and different. In so doing, we crossed a lot of ambiguous borders. My point is, we did this, in many different meetings and Susie came in without the benefit of hearing that collective "process of seeking." No wonder she is trying to figure out where things go. The question for me is, "With more meeting time, would Susie's chapter have been different?"

Something ironic occurred last week on e-mail. I had written to Susie asking her if she felt comfortable enough as a member of the group to be more critical of us. I felt that her critique would offer a valuable dimension and may help in lengthening her chapter. She wrote back saying she was real frustrated and could not write anymore. She felt our collaboration was real loose and she had not been given enough direction. I recall looking at the e-mail message and thinking to myself, "I asked for critical, so here it is!" What a gift!

Susie Weston:
I decided that I was just going to lay it all out on the line.

Suzanne SooHoo:
You identified a hole in our collaborative community.

Don Cardinal:
We go forward as if we understand this word "collaboration." It certainly has been redefined, redefined, and redefined and now completely undefined for me even at the end of this process. We seem to have multiple definitions.

Does "collaboration" means if I write something, and you and I are collaborating, then you owe me a read? And if you don't do it, you're not collaborative? And if you do it, you're collaborative? Furthermore, if you don't give me very much input or it's BS, then you're not being collaborative? You're almost lying to me?

In my new understanding of collaboration, derived from this group, it is just as collaborative if Suzanne calls me at home and says, "You seem stuck. What can I do, unrelated to your chapter?" That's a form of collaboration, although it had nothing to do with the book itself.

Collaboration is a feeling I get when I'm in a room with everyone in this group. I remember two meetings where I would think, "I really want to take these chapters home and sleep with them for a while." At those meetings, *that* was collaboration. Now nobody read my chapter during those meetings. It wasn't about my writing. It wasn't about anyone's writing necessarily but the collaboration was there. Hard to define.

Unfortunately Susie missed out on some of that part and she came in at a time where we said, "We need a product from you." I'm a product kinda guy. When someone says "product" to me, I say, "Big deal! I can do products, I wanted to play with the process." That was the fun part of doing this. I've really enjoyed the process part of this group. The product part really has had little impact on me, other than the actual writing of the chapter. The collaboration part is what I really wanted from this group, and, at times, I felt cheated in the process, and, at other times, I felt gifted.

Tom Wilson:
Maybe the notion of collaboration as developmental would make a difference if we think of it as different stages of thinking. And perhaps it is helpful if we think of systems theory; whereby the integral parts communicate. We could be sitting in this room yet not communicating and thus not a system. However as the communication develops and the more we fully understand each other, the more integrated we become. For example, saying, "If I ask for a feedback, you better give me critical feedback" is a higher level of communication than if I ask for feedback and you're just polite to me. The integration and authenticity just aren't there. I think collaboration may be thought about in developmental terms whereby we increase the ability to be authentic and integrative in communication with each other.

Penny Bryan:
I think authentic communication concerns things that matter or things that count in terms of meaning and significance to the commu-

nicants, rather than frequency. Collaboration is less about frequency of time and more about the quality. What you are saying is that a couple of times at our meetings, when there was depth to the conversation, the quality was there. It was worthwhile and *that* seems to be getting closer at what collaboration really is. What I remember was the writing process. I noted two things. I remember the first time that I went public with my writing to the group. I loved the conversations and I loved the solitary writing. But the first time I went public and actually gave my chapter to someone in this group, I was apprehensive. I have shared my writing with other colleagues, other ethnographers, and other qualitative researchers, but to present my work to my colleagues with whom I teach and work was a *big* step. I also remember Don saying, "This is a different kind of writing for me." It was a big step in terms of situating ourselves and in going public with private thoughts.

Don Cardinal:
I would not have written my chapter if it weren't for the group. I don't write that way. It would never come to mind to write personally, in first person. People prompted me on that. Suzanne particularly has prompted me to write on something "nonnumeric, nonstatistical."

(laughter)

Dolores Gaunty-Porter:
When I think of collaboration, I think about cooperative learning. And the focus of cooperative learning is that we have this project, we have this goal, we've got something we've got to work on. And for us it's always been the book and we never deviated from that. It has never been, "Well maybe we should make a video instead or maybe we should develop some teacher materials or something. We've never said that. It's always been the book. No matter how loosely connected we may have felt or appeared to be, its always been the book because we have always had that as our goal. These chapters have always been about urban ed. Its never been "let's change that." So we've always had that. To me collaboration has been the entire process, even when we were tired, even when we did not feel nor look like we're really working toward this goal. Collaboration has always been there, so I look at it as being a process.

I keep taking it back to the classroom because I've worked with students to establish cooperative learning groups. Sometimes students say and do things where you just say, "Now wait a minute, are you helping with this goal or not? Here you are rocking back on your chair. You didn't bring the assignment. You were supposed to bring a newspaper article today. Are you with it here?" And so, sometimes people have to be brought back in to the group in order to keep them focused. For us, like I said, we've never veered from the fact that we were working on this book about urban ed. It's never been a curriculum piece for teachers or a series of poems or something. I mean, we've never veered from that. So to me, we've always kept that focus, that goal. It's just that my concept of collaboration has been the entire process.

Jeff Sapp:
I would disagree with some of that. I disagree because originally wasn't there one of our colleagues who was going to do a series of lesson plans?

Dolores Gaunty-Porter:
But the point is, they're not here.

Jeff Sapp:
When we first started writing, three years ago, I remember Jan saying, "Is this poetry piece okay,?" Now interestingly enough, at the end, there's less of that writing diversity. The chapters do look different than most academic pieces that we see, but some of that was lost along the way. Initially, there was more variety.

Suzanne SooHoo:
The original prospectus said that we would write essays, literature reviews, case studies, poetry, whatever variety of styles that we felt would best amplify our voices. This is curious that the final contributors all chose similar styles of writing.

Dolores Gaunty-Porter:
That's what happens to a group of people, right?, even gang bangers? They all start looking and acting alike. Were the people who are no longer part of the project ever told, "Look, you cannot do this," or was it their choice to leave? Let's say you expect me to reshape this and I don't want to do that. At any point I could have said, "I don't want to do that."

Tom Wilson:
That didn't come through in any of the information we got back from our survey. The people who did not participate from the Academic Centers dropped out primarily because they did not think they were getting the kind of support they needed to do it.

Penny Bryan:
That may have been so, but I also remember Suzanne saying, "What's new here?" The chapters had to say something new. We

came up with cornerstones, like social justice. I think that some people didn't fit or didn't think their work fit within the social justice piece. They couldn't find themselves there. I don't think it was because they didn't feel support.

Tom Wilson:
Well, Don said here at the Orange campus, we didn't have support either and we did it.

Dolores Gaunty-Porter:
Most people sitting here could have said at some point, "You know what, I'm ready to pull out."

Jeff Sapp:
I did at one point say that. I felt pressure about tenure. My chapter was done and ready to go. We weren't getting anywhere. I wanted to know whether it was okay if I pull out.

Suzanne SooHoo:
We talked about this disjuncture at a few of our meetings. Do you remember? We asked ourselves, "Don't we want a product? Don't we want to get it done?" Then why weren't we delivering our parts?

Jeff Sapp:
There was a saturation point for a lot of this.

Don Cardinal:
Can I throw in another factor? Allow me to use a quantitative study design. I wonder if the people who finished the chapters for this book are people who had more experience in writing?. I wonder if this characteristic is prerequisite to being a successful contributor in this group?

Tom Wilson:
But there is a support factor here at Orange. Susie, correct me if this is an error, but if you had to write a chapter in some way divorced from all of us, it would have been extremely difficult. It was probably your first book chapter, is that correct?

Susie Weston:
(nods affirmatively)

Suzanne SooHoo:
It's not her first publication however.

Tom Wilson:
No it's not, but I'm saying the people in the Academic Centers felt, if they had the support of colleagues there, they could have done it

Suzanne SooHoo:
Do you mean physical or electronic support?

Tom Wilson:
Physical support; just the notion that one could bump into somebody at the water cooler and could talk about the writing.

Suzanne SooHoo:
If it were *that easy*, this book would have been completed two years ago.

(laughter)

Don Cardinal:
Remember life is a multivariate model and I was only proposing one or two variables to try to explain it. That could be another variable that explains some of it. I'm just saying a piece of it; some indicators might simply be the experience that people had before. Maybe there was a prerequisite technical skill that a group didn't have and that we assumed they had.

Tom Wilson:
Okay, that's true.

Don Cardinal:
As colleagues we tried to not embarrass them. Let me personalize that—I tried to not embarrass people who I know have never done that. I didn't say, "Do you want some help doing this?" "Do you want some clues on how to make this happen?" or "Hey, have you ever done this before?" I just assumed and let that happen. And I think others did also. And in doing that, we really ignored something that very possibly might have been a key support factor.

I wish we had the meeting at Jeff's house on video. I wish we had the transcript of that one because there was a lot to think about. For example, remember when some members of our earlier group, the larger group, talked about the writing process? They talked at length about the struggle they went through to produce writing. When we asked, "So do you have a draft that we could look at?" The response was, "Oh no I haven't written a word yet." So those ideas were not even down yet. Remember that over a year had passed since we were charged with writing the chapters.

I remember another exchange at the same meeting. Another person was asked the same question. The response was, "Oh yes, I've been writing and writing and writing." and then when we finally saw a draft, it's just a matter of a page, maybe a page and a half. So there were different concepts of what it meant to get 20 pages out. Everybody has a different writing style and the people who dropped out possibly had a misestimate of the hours it takes in front of a computer or what that writing process is. I don't think we're looking for *the* answer, it's just one of the possibilities.

Tom Wilson:
Another variable other than collaboration, is the understanding of the word "critical." The meaning of critical was of great variance. Just listening to what potential authors said they were writing in spite of all rhetorical frontloading of the critical nature of the book was quite disturbing. That's the thing that stands out the most significantly for me.

Penny Bryan:
Right—We didn't start from scratch. Suzanne shared a charge from the series editor. This book is part of a series. The series is on urban education. We didn't start from nothingness and say, "What does the School of Education faculty want to write a book on?" Suzanne came and said, "Here's the charge. This is part of a series. Is urban education a significant topic to this group?"

Critical theory and urban education were the parameters. People had different ideas of what that meant. I think as we went along, we realized that we needed some dialogue around defining what those ideas meant. I think some people interpreted that as "Can I do more of a literature search of what exists?" or "Can I do lesson plans or something very practical?" We started out saying we would look at a whole range of responses. Chapters could be practically focused or more theoretically focused.

Don Cardinal:
And you know, Suzanne, something we have to take out of the closet, something we didn't talk much about afterwards. We made some decisions as a group, in that room right over there, that certain chapters were way off target. They really didn't meet the cornerstone criteria.

Suzanne SooHoo:
That's why there would be a renewal of the cornerstones at every meeting. We asked each author to carefully screen his/her articles for the inclusion of the cornerstones. And then there was the public read; the read-aloud also caused some folks to self-select out.

Jeff Sapp:
I think I'm going to concur with you and look back at when some of our colleagues were reading their chapters. It was evident to them

that they had missed something and as they continued to read, they grew more and more uncomfortable.

Penny Bryan:
I think what it points out is that collaboration is easier, more "feel good," when it can be affirming. When somebody does something and you really get excited about something that somebody does, you affirm it and the energy builds. Collaboration is tougher when you have to face conflict or when you have to make a judgment that is in some way critical.

Don Cardinal:
Taking that one step further, sometimes I think when people talk "collaboration," there is an assumption of niceness. I think a lot of the niceness is bullshit because it is false at times. It's so much easier to tell people, "Oh this looks so good!" and I'd think, "god, it's so dishonest and it's so not right!" We're guilty of this. By trying to be nice, in a way, we gave a false sense of value of each other's work.

Tom Wilson:
Chris Argyris calls that "cover-up." And it's a cover-up, but everybody knows it's a cover-up so they cover up the cover-up. Everybody knows what's going on. We're socialized to respond that way.

Penny Bryan:
We're socialized to be nice.

Don Cardinal:
You are.

(laughter)

Suzanne SooHoo:
I do "nice" on certain days.

Tom Wilson:
The way to deal with that is to deal with it in a more direct way.

Penny Bryan:
Many people in our culture are socialized that way. So to face the hard issues or to face the critical issues is tougher. And so collaboration works really well when it's easier. It's easier when you can be affirming. When I read something that I really like, that's wonderful.

It's when facing the tough issues, however, that collaboration can be significant. For example, in our collaboration, we didn't really spell out the role of the editor. What was Suzanne's role? In a traditional, individual piece, the editor would say, "This is thin. This doesn't have this. This doesn't have that." Suzanne was put in a tough decision-making role because here was this collaboration, where everybody was welcome to submit, and then the incoming products fell short in terms of quality.

Tom Wilson:
How did we put her in that position?

Penny Bryan:
I think it was by default.

Suzanne SooHoo:
How would you describe my role?

Don Cardinal:
The only committed person to the process; that's the way I'd put it. I felt that any time anybody could have dropped out and Suzanne was the only one I knew wouldn't drop out. If I were betting, she's the only one I would put the bankroll on. That she was going to see it to the end. If she had dropped out, the book would have been gone. She was also the "go to" person, the getting-things-done person. Suzanne has been it all the way through.

Jeff Sapp:
Actually, I don't know that that's true because I think there was a time when Tom said, "I can't put my name in with these people if this is what the chapters look like. They're not a professional image."

Tom Wilson:
In that situation, absolutely! In terms of seeing the process through, I never thought about dropping out unless other possible chapters did not measure up. I couldn't abide with chapters that didn't meet the markers.

Dolores Gaunty-Porter:
Well let's take what Penny said. You were saying that Suzanne was put in the position and we never really talked about it. I don't remember a time when we said, "Look, let me tell you why I'm here and my position in all of this." We just assumed that because you sign up, you were going to study. And then, some people didn't. But we never sat back and just really said, "Okay, I Dolores am committed to this process." I never said that. I didn't and I don't remember anyone else saying that. And I understand that sometimes people are going to say things to me that I might not like. And it may not be comfortable, but I am committed to this process. I am committed to trying to support other people in anyway that I can. I am committed

to letting people say whatever they think they need to say to me that will help me and help them get their job done because our goal is this book and we've never said any of that.

In cooperative learning, you do that. Everyone knows what their role is. We also talk about what kind of language you're going to use. What does it mean to disagree with the idea and not disagree with the person? I'm such a cooperative learning kind a person. And that covers everything that we're talking about.

So you're going to collect the crayolas, okay you're going to be the editor. All right, so your role is going to be what? Do you want to take that on? Do you agree to that? Because if you don't agree to collect the crayolas and pass out the scissors, we're going to have some trouble here.

Penny Bryan:
I think that "collaboration" in terms of the way I was thinking of it leaves that a little fuzzier. Collaboration to me means sharing roles. There isn't a specific role per person.

Suzanne SooHoo:
My role has been like a jazz band manager. It's like here's this jazz band. All of you bring your instruments. You come and we start to create music. And then I pick up any instruments that are left afterwards and make sure everyone gets their instruments back and that kind of stuff. That's how I saw myself.

Tom Wilson:
But you're still playing first tuba in this whole thing.

Suzanne SooHoo:
I felt comfortable facilitating the writing process. I felt like I encouraged us to move through different stages of writing. I consulted with the other literacy folks within this group and asked, "What do you think we should do next? Should we do some peer editing, or author's chair?" But I fell short in facilitating any critical questions about urban education. I deferred my role of facilitating those conversations to those of you with more historical and foundational knowledge.

Penny Bryan:
But what about the quality of a piece in terms of the theoretical grounding; in terms of saying something new, in terms of hitting the cornerstones? A traditional editor would come back and say, "Great example, a little thin on theory. Where did you ground this? or too much theory. Can you make it more concrete?" Now did you feel like you did those kinds of things?

Suzanne SooHoo:
Most often, when those situations came up, I brought them back to the group.

Penny Bryan:
So that doing a collaborative book changes the role of the editor, and I think maybe that's a small piece that is new in our work together, too.

Suzanne SooHoo:
There have been interesting roles that have emerged in our work together. For instance, there are those people who felt context was important in this collaborative project and opened their homes for our meetings, providing a retreat from the workplace. That's a sign of collaboration isn't it?

Jeff Sapp:
I think we took on different roles and I can tell you that when I sent that e-mail and said I might pull out, I was being much more deliberate. I was lighting a fire under our butts. I was trying to drive some energy at that point. It was deliberate.

Don Cardinal:
That's how I took it. I thought you really would have dropped out if people didn't move.

Penny Bryan:
As committed as I was to the process, I would have supported Jeff's move because I understood the tensions and the pressures of seeking tenure. He was saying, "Folks I need to pull back. This isn't working for me. I've got to take this and do this." I really was prepared, if he had done that, to support him in pulling out.

Jeff Sapp:
Which actually brings up a different topic that I very much self-identify as a writer. bell hooks talks about this in *Remember Rapture*; the difference between being a writer in the academy and writing to produce for promotion. One is product driven and the other is process driven. Part of the process for me that was stressful was that I publicly, for the first time in my life, had to be more product driven.

Suzanne SooHoo:
This is the part I probably worry throughout the entire project. It started all the way back when Jan started with her question, "Do I belong here?" Throughout the project, there was this tension between individual autonomy and group interest. How do we respect both the

integrity of the individual and the group? How do we not let the group take over the individual and yet not let individual autonomy and self interest drive the collected efforts of the book? Maybe we didn't need collaboration to produce this book. Did we?

Jan Osborn:
We didn't. I think that again we're back to the very beginning here with the questions, "What is collaborative and what isn't?" It isn't that I don't think that some of the conversations have not been excellent. They have been great. I don't think what we did was collaboration in terms of writing as much as it was collaborative in terms of getting together and talking about some of the issues of education.

Dolores Gaunty-Porter:
We wrote about "urban." And when we got together, we talked about "urban." I believe that you write from what you hear and experience. So our conversations added to our chapters. However, I don't think we necessarily left those meetings with the thought that "I'm going to change my chapter."

Penny Bryan:
I did. I can think of a part that was right near the end which came from Jan and that was the difference between urban and inner city. I had been trying to get suburban leaders to stop thinking of "us and them" and to say that it's a "we." What you think is homogenous suburban really has a lot of urban edge to it. And then, at the very end of our conversations, I got from Jan, there are still some distinctions between inner-city and urban. So that was a real learning for me that I didn't get on my own. I got it out of our dialogue.

We continually asked ourselves, "What's new about this book? What's different?" Well, one of the things that was different was the self-situating. I wonder if the collaboration had something to do with the degree to which the self is in each piece? I wouldn't have done that without the group. I've never done that before. And without the collaboration, I wouldn't have.

Suzanne SooHoo:
How do we define our collaborative group? I don't know if we are a group or if we are one plus one plus one plus one. When I was writing Chapter 1 with Tom, I wondered, "Is this my chapter or our chapter? Whose is it?" I wrote that we were so hungry to come together as a group of scholars, to break out of the administrivia, and not to work the scholarly life in isolation. I remember us saying it is so nice to get together and not talk about program coordination or School of Ed strategies. We were fighting for space and time to be scholars. We

wanted to institutionalize academic dialogue, time to come together, to be scholars, to be academics. Did I represent *our* feelings or *my* feelings.

Jeff Sapp:
You've reminded me of a distinction about the collaborative process in Buber's work. Often the way the institution runs, we interact as "I-It." In this situation, having so much more "I-Thou" made it feel collaborative. I can still be collaborative in an "I-It" situation. For instance, we're doing program. This was much more what Dewey calls the difference between "seeming and being." I don't know that I got much feedback from anyone on my chapter except for Suzanne. A lot of the conversations and house meetings and things like that that were fodder, is that the right word?—like compost. It was really helping me. Their soil made my writing more rich, more fertile.

I can remember conversations about my chapter being situated in myself as a gay individual and that lens that I look at the world through, a gay lens. Those conversations I've had about my gay lens have definitely shaped my chapter. Even at the very end when I said, "Here's my final draft so don't mess with me." Then I said something about urban and that I felt like a fish out of water not being in the urban environment because for me, the safer place as a gay male, is in Los Angeles. It is not safe for me to be in what I consider a less urban environment in Orange County. It's more dangerous here. Urban is safe to me as a gay male. And so, those conversations really helped shaped a lot of things for me from a critical theory point of view in my own personal life and they felt collaborative. That's what I think a lot of the Academic Center people didn't have—those conversations that we had because of our close proximity to each other.

Penny Bryan:
I will just throw something in here. A close friend of mine, an early contributor from the Academic Centers, was the last to drop out. She said all along, from the very beginning, "I never cared as much about the product as I did being part of the process. I wanted to be down here at the Orange campus. I wanted to be part of the conversations." She said it came down to telling herself, "I essentially have to really rewrite this. It's true that there is nothing new here in my chapter." That was the critical question for her, "What's new in this? What do I have to say?" She said, "I decided that the value for me was not in the product. I really wanted to be part of that group and part of the conversations."

Suzanne SooHoo:
There have been some wonderful conversations. I still remember when Dolores had this conversation with another colleague. It was in Jeff's kitchen and they were discussing "Is white right?" And I thought these conversations were so different from the two-day marathon program coordination meetings that we have once a month in our school.

Jan Osborn:
The conversation was good sometimes; beneficial and helpful. Other times it was extremely frustrating, especially towards the end. I guess I had a different concept of what a collaborative book would be. I thought much more of our time would be spent writing together. That's where I'm coming from.

Or looking at each other's manuscripts and talking those through. That's maybe how *I* was framing a collaborative book. I had hoped that we would actually *write together* and work on our writing together. So that's what I meant when I said it wasn't a collaborative book. I just wrote a collaborative article with a colleague. We got together; we wrote together; we wrote paragraphs together; we crafted sentences together; and we submitted. So, that's what I was thinking. Maybe that can't happen in a collaborative book with eight people.

Don Cardinal:
I think it can but I would be very intimidated to do that with you.

Tom Wilson:
Maybe it's in the process collaboration, yet a weaker form of collaboration wherein we really didn't sit down and say, "Okay, I read this paper now. What are the ideas that you're getting at?" I only got one feedback on my original piece and that was from Suzanne.

Suzanne SooHoo:
We did do some group reads and author's chairs.

Tom Wilson:
We did some group reads at Jeff's house, yet I never received direct content response except from Suzanne.

Don Cardinal:
I had the first one and I've got to tell you, I can't tell you which one of you *didn't* respond. To the best of my knowledge every one of you responded to mine, and so my perception of this, listening to people talk, is a pretty interesting dichotomy. Now of course I needed nudging. I needed somebody to say this isn't totally off the wall and it's okay that you do this. I won't think badly of you for doing this. I

needed that or I probably wouldn't have written the chapter as honestly, as personally, as I wrote it.

Penny Bryan:
I thought your chapter was so exciting, though.

Jeff Sapp:
I want to go back to a comment that Don said about how when you looked at Jan and said, "I would have been really intimidated to write with you," because it brings up one of the major things for me in watching our process. One of our cornerstones was to situate ourselves in our chapters, which I am so comfortable with. It was really kind of like this sociological study to watch people struggle with that when we presented to the group. Penny said, "As soon as I got past that hurdle, then I was better." The element of fear was so unbelievably tangible because our colleagues were going to read this. It was such as interesting aspect for me to just sit back and watch, and I think its demonstrative that schooling and education tends to be a culture of fear.

Penny Bryan:
Having done a lot of staff development, I readily go into another school or another place and present, but the most nervous that I have ever been was when I first had to present to my own faculty. I can still remember it, though it was years and years ago. There is something about sharing with your own colleagues, those that you work with, day to day. That's *different* for me.

Don Cardinal:
And for me it's 180 degrees the other way. I can trust you guys and no one in this room is going to hurt me. You've already promised me you won't hurt me. I can lay out anything in the chapter. I had very little nervousness. I was more nervous about how my chapter will play with my peers, outside of us. I got encouragement from all of you. I have to tune out the fact that this will be in book—in a book—and it will be read by people who I don't know and that don't know me and are only going to know me from that chapter.

Dolores Gaunty-Porter:
I have a hard time with that too.

Don Cardinal:
There is no context for them. From most of you, your comments were "God, you went through this and now look at you!" Those from the outside might say, "Oh, you did *this*?" You've just defined yourself and it can be interpreted in some many different ways.

Jeff Sapp:
There was fear at multiple levels and I think that was an intriguing part for me to watch.

Tom Wilson:
I don't feel that. I mean I personally just kind of put my writing out there and people do what they want with it. I don't believe I have fear about doing so.

Jeff Sapp:
I get that about you.

Tom Wilson:
I guess the only time in my life I was really nervous was the first time I did anything for AERA. I almost lost my voice, 200 people in the room or something like that. I knew what I was talking about. I had this rather solid paper, I thought, yet I momentarily froze. It was weird.

Penny Bryan:
Susie, this was very different than your master's thesis that was about ideas. It was pretty risky in doing your master's thesis. This was your story. Was that high risk or low risk for you? How did that seem to you?

Susie Weston:
I was only nervous about one person and that was Don. I think it's because he is Mr. Quantitative and I'm not.

Suzanne prompted me to tell my story. We were sitting in her car on the way home from this conference and she says, "Okay, tell me about this and tell me about that." I'm thinking, "Oh God, I don't know how this is going to fly." I just kept thinking about what Don would think. But then reading his chapter, it made it all okay because he put himself on the line. Then it was like, "Okay, I can do this!" But that was the only time I was fearful.

Jeff Sapp:
Vulnerability is an important aspect of collaboration. I don't think that we're a culture that does vulnerability well. Consequently, I think that it was really significant that we situated ourselves in our chapters. My first semester here, Don was on sabbatical. And then my second semester you were back and one of the *very first* things I got, was your chapter. Even before we started school, I read your chapter. My response to it was, "What a lovely way to introduce yourself to me!" I think this is what vulnerability does. I really like that. When I am vulnerable as a teacher or a colleague, it opens up spaces

for the rest of us to be vulnerable as well. I think that's an element of community and collaboration.

Suzanne SooHoo:
That's how I deal with community in my class. The only way that I can get into those gnarly issues of race, class, and gender is to first put myself out on the first night of class. I usually ask students, after going through the syllabus, "How do you think this class will be different from other sections because it's being taught by an Asian woman?" The students are often stunned by the question because they never thought race and gender made much difference and because the question made me vulnerable to their ignorance.

The idea of reading my personal narrative aloud to the group is aimed at bonding through vulnerability. Susie just now self-disclosed that she was most fearful of Don. But when he gave the gift of vulnerability to the group, she responded with her gift in return. I try to make this happen in my class as well.

Jeff Sapp:
And I would also add, your gift of vulnerability is to every reader who's going to read this. My anticipation is that instead of anyone reacting negatively to it, it's going to be overwhelmingly positive for our colleagues across the nation.

Penny Bryan:
It already has.

Don Cardinal:
You mailed it to somebody or what?

(laughter)

Suzanne SooHoo:
It's already been peer reviewed by AERA Division G?

(laughter)

Don Cardinal:
It's posted on a website. No biggie!

(laughter)

Penny Bryan:
At one session, Don, you talked about forgiveness. I have used that in my classes. It made a tremendous difference to me. I just learned that lesson from you. You can screw up, forgive people. "Look where I've been," you said to all of us.

That idea of forgiveness has just been very prominent in my teaching ever since you said it. Now if we hadn't had these discussions, if we hadn't had the collaboration, I wouldn't have gotten what Suzanne calls "that gift." That gift would not have come out because it came out in the dialogue.

Also, I'm having one of those "Duh!" moments. We could have written together in the way that Jan described. I would have liked that too. I don't know how in the world we would have figured the time to do that.

Suzanne SooHoo:
We are doing that right now. We're writing together in a sense by recording this talking chapter.

Jeff Sapp:
Next time.

Suzanne SooHoo:
Next time? I just want to make sure that I heard you said, "Next time." This is on tape and so when we approach you about next time, you can't say, "I never said next time."

Jeff Sapp:
Yeah, yeah. But this tape will never work out. When we videotape, it never works out.

(laughter)

But the next time, if you and I got together and wrote the transitions between our chapters collaboratively, if there would be a page or two between chapters, wouldn't that be cool? Not that I want to add that at this time.

Penny Bryan:
Well, it won't be *this book.*

Don Cardinal:
A follow-up article might be real nice.

Jeff Sapp:
I also want to mention another vulnerability aspect. One of the places that I can really remember reading about that was in bell hook's *Teaching to Transgress*. She does a talking chapter. It's there that I found the quote about the professors taking the first step in situating themselves through personal narrative in the classroom and how that opens that up for students.

There's no one way to situate yourself. There's lots of ways. When we take a concept like vulnerability or collaboration, we recognize there are a lot of layers to a onion, so it doesn't just mean one thing. It means this and that, this and that, and this and that. It's kind of hard to nail down sometimes. Sometimes that alone makes us anxious.

Don Cardinal:
There's that one part in my chapter where I say, "I can't say anymore about this because I don't know who's reading it and I don't think they're going to understand." There is a high chance of misinterpretation. And I wonder when one self-discloses, does one think, "Are you going to stick around my life for a really long time and listen to me say this in many different moods and be sure you really get who I am? If you're not, I'm not going to bother saying it to you."

I used to work in a psychiatric hospital for three years in the intensive treatment unit, which is the locked unit. Students would come in and out on a regular basis, six months in, a year out, six months in. You'd ask them, "So tell me, why did you just slash your wrist?" And they'd say, "How long are you going to be around? a year? After I tell you, will you be here when I get real sad? Will you be here tomorrow? Will you be here when I get out? Can I call you when I get out?"

Not every person did that but many people did. It really taught me that you don't have the right to pretend to many people that you are their buddy, that you will listen to them.

Suzanne SooHoo:
Would you like us to send accompanying videotapes so people will have more contexts of you in the chapter?

Jeff Sapp:
For $9.99 extra.

(laughter)

Suzanne SooHoo:
And with three payments of $29.95 you can purchase the videotape to get a higher context.

(laughter)

Jeff Sapp:
And a Chapman University mug!

(laughter)

Suzanne SooHoo:
If you order right now you . . .

Dolores Gaunty-Porter:
You can even get a sweatshirt!
(laughter)

Tom Wilson:
And a web page to get links to all this stuff.

(laughter)

Suzanne SooHoo:
Getting back to Jan's point about collaborative writing; if our work wasn't a collaborative book, what *did* we do?

Tom Wilson:
I think it's a collaborative book. Maybe we're just deconstructing the word "collaboration" a bit. What does that mean? What do we believe it to mean?

Penny Bryan:
Tom, you situated the book in the School of Education. You said that by looking at points of conflict and tension in the book process, we can examine points where a larger system like the School of Education is in terms of changing its system and culture. I don't know that we ever had that conversation. Maybe I missed it, or is it something that Tom sees from his perspective? Has the group talked about that? Is the group taking the results of the survey and using them for future action?

Tom Wilson:
The book doesn't die when it's published. From the book we continue to look at the relationship of the Academic Centers and ourselves.

Penny Bryan:
I guess it's a way of moving the conversation and asking does the project end with our final chapter?

Tom Wilson:
I like to see us move beyond just the completion of the book.

Don Cardinal:
There's no end to this, is there?

Suzanne SooHoo:
Going into the next millennium. . . .

Jeff Sapp:
There's a great children's book by Margaret Mahey called *The Haunting of Miss Cardamon* where the very last sentence is "and so it all began."

Penny Bryan:
And there are other changes in the larger system that are happening concurrently and who knows how our project will influence that work.

Suzanne SooHoo:
One of the things that we named at our general meeting yesterday was our desire for an emphasis, in our future, on scholarship and research, whatever way that plays out, maybe in an Ed.D program. That was one of the things that came out of the easel board brainstorming process. What you made me think of is, could our experience in this collaborative writing project play a part in informing the future School of Ed? Should our new provost read this book?

Penny asked this question three years ago. She asked, how will this work together fit into the greater order of institutional change and changing the culture of the School of Ed? How might this change the way we work with schools? At the time, we weren't ready to answer those questions.

Penny Bryan:
It's a way of framing and saying, "Okay we got the book, we got the process, how do we leave it? Is there a next step?" Once we have closure on the product, then what do we do with the process? Do we have something worthwhile upon which to build? How did we do that? I wasn't at the meeting yesterday, so I don't know where you took it. Did you find a place for it out of the conversation at the faculty meeting yesterday?

Jeff Sapp:
Well, certainly one of the main themes of yesterday's faculty meeting is that we all want more time for scholarly creative activity. It came up at all three table groups.

Don Cardinal:
As well did process, that we have some moral, democratic rules of how we interact, the way we spend our time, where we allocate ourselves, some agreed-upon boundaries to how we conduct ourselves.

Penny Bryan:
"Agreed-upon boundaries" says to me these boundaries can't be encroached upon.

Tom Wilson:
Principles might be a better word than boundaries.

Suzanne SooHoo:
I agree, principles of working together that may be more explicit than we ever had before. I used a word yesterday that triggered something, I suggested we "reclaim" working democratically. Because from my own perspective, we have distanced ourselves from working democracy for about a year and half because, I guess, of preparation for accreditation.

I was sharing with Don earlier today that I can't wait until things get cozy again; when the feeling of groupness returns again. I think that preparing for accreditation dissipated a lot of the energy needed to work collaboratively and democratically.

Jeff Sapp:
Maybe "reclaim" is not the right word because democracy is a process. It's like when you have kids and you're teaching different grades of history and people say we've done the civil rights, why do we keep talking about this? "Reclaiming" is not the word I would choose. It's just that continual process. I mean, we say we are a democratic school and a democratic environment. You don't ever get to a point where you are or that you can say, "Wow, okay and now we're done with that." It is always going to be that process and I think we always have the right to say, "This doesn't feel democratic to me right now."

Don Cardinal:
You know when you say, "Where do we go from here?" how do we not go from here? I mean, if this process has impacted us, if it's brought some things up to the surface, made us rethink what collaboration is, how does it stop here? Everything that we do from here on is going to be influenced by this work. I don't mean to get too touchy-feely, but it's really hard once you transformed, to not have those pieces. That process influences all else that you do. And how much of what went on yesterday at the School of Ed meeting, in the sense of us demanding that we slow down, that we have some quality time, that we do some reflection on our own scholarship, how much of that has to do with this very group?

Don Cardinal:
I'd like to point out something else, something that happened at yesterday's meeting. Imagine a play, where everything is dark and the spotlight is on a single person. There is a pregnant pause and you just know this person is going to say something important.

Jeff Sapp:
This person, a colleague from Liberal Studies who attended our School of Education meeting, said, "I've been around a long time and I'm in a lot of different departments and meetings but I've never seen any group be able to do what you all do here. It's unprecedented on this campus." She said our faculty is why she makes time just to remotely be associated with us because she wants to be involved with us, even just a little bit.

Don Cardinal:
And then she started to label our relationship among each other as unique and she asked, "Do you understand what you have here?" And of course I'm in tears thinking, "God, maybe we need to acknowledge that the collaboration and democracy, which we ragged on ourselves so much for never having reached our promise. Maybe to a degree, we are there and we just don't see it."

Suzanne SooHoo:
It's like the fish trying to read the water that we're swimming in, right? She comes from another department, from outside of the fish bowl, and asks, "Do you know how special this is?"

I remember last year, a new faculty member said the same thing to us. He said we are the only group he had ever met that spends all this time asking ourselves, "How are we doing? Are we processing this democratically? Are we treating each other right?" He said there was no organization that he'd ever worked with that talked about collaboration as much as we all do.

Penny Bryan:
I think that this supports what we've said before. There was a group of people who were hungry to come together, to have that kind of constructivist conversation, to talk about ideas. That is what brought the group together in the first place. What I heard in the larger group yesterday was a reiteration of that. We may have been the forum for that need during an interim period when that notion of dialogue and inquiry was not evident in the larger group. So, those who were really the most hungry for that, this group, did serve as forum to come together and do that. Also, what I am realizing tonight is that there are levels of collaboration. We may have done what we did and produced this product, but there are other levels to collaboration that we didn't experience.

Jeff Sapp:
I also want to underscore our fishbowl metaphor. Our Liberal Studies colleague wanted to immerse herself in the situation to know the sit-

uation. It's that whole qualitative heuristic phenomena. Her comments were incredibly poignant for us because they gave us another perspective. Robert Frost says we need to have whole vision and see not only just from the eye of the mind, which is what schooling tells us to do, but to have full sight and add the eye of the heart as well, to have the whole vision. That was what I was looking at in being a part of this group, a chance for me to have whole vision.

Penny Bryan:
There are lots of tensions in any whole; there's the tension of your heart and your mind, of I and Thou, as Martin Buber describes between each individual self and the coming together as a group. There's also Miles Horton's two-eye theory where one eye is on the present and the other is on future possibilities, which is also Freirian. We opened ourselves to all of those tensions and they came out in a book effort like ours.

Tom Wilson:
It's also Deweyan in terms of an aesthetic, in terms of an experience that has quality in and of itself beyond any explicit purpose of that activity. That alone speaks for collaboration. We do it because it feels "good," it is beautiful in its own right whether it has an ulterior purpose or not. Hopefully the current collaboration will lead to further good. We are touched emotionally and aesthetically by our immediate experience—we have profited. Future benefit may accrue, but if not, we have not failed. It's like viewing a painting. We look at a Cezanne and say, "My god, how beautiful, how exquisite!" I saw a colleague of ours from the University of California, Irvine, cry in front of a Monet at an exhibit of Impressionism because it was so beautiful in and of itself. Now if he then tells his children about the Monet, the aesthetic experience moves to an instrumental purpose, yet if it does not, no diminishment of the Monet moment occurs.

Suzanne SooHoo:
That was beautiful, Tom. Should we stop here or can I move us into one more piece before we leave? Who benefited from our work?

Dolores Gaunty-Porter:
How did we benefit? How did the university benefit? How do the future readers benefit?

Jeff Sapp:
I benefited. I benefited from the dialogue and the whole process. You have to remember that this was the beginning of my experience with you all. Consequently, one of my first journal entries came from our very first meeting.

I thought Tom was an imbecile. I was just mortified because Tom stopped the process and said, "Who does this benefit and who are we?" and I was horrified. Now I know Tom as this moral thermometer. He has this way of stopping the train and saying, "What is that about?" I didn't know that the first time we met. All I had known was we were going along fast and Tom stopped the train and I didn't like it. So one of the ways that I benefited was getting to know everyone much better.

Susie Weston:
I couldn't stand Tom when I first met him and now I love him. It just that kind of thing that happens when you meet somebody who is very different from anyone you've ever met before, and who deals with people in such a different way. It's a shock to your system, and immediately you feel uncomfortable, so you don't like it. But then you learn to love it. You learn to love that uncomfortable feeling cause you know it's going to lead somewhere great.

Dolores Gaunty-Porter:
Before you go on, something that Jeff said was very interesting. He said something about situating ourselves from the inside as insiders looking out, which is quite different from your premise of us as outsiders looking inside at urban schools. I don't feel like an outsider.

Suzanne SooHoo:
When I wrote that part, I was thinking of teachers like Susie from the teachers research group (CARDC). The idea of establishing creditability with an urban classroom teacher, to me, takes working side by side, next to her, listening to her, having a long relationship and then maybe, I can say a little bit about urban education, but certainly not to the extent that Susie can tell us. So I was thinking of people like Susie reading this thinking, "Who the heck do you think you are writing about urban education? You haven't been in *my* classroom!"

I think that we could be criticized by some folks, who may think that those of us in academe lack credibility because we are sheltered in our ivory tower, but I also argued that the best we can do is interrogate ourselves and then work closely with urban practitioners.

Dolores Gaunty-Porter:
I don't have to say anything, but walk into the room and I have creditability, generally speaking, in the urban community. Then, when I open my mouth, I would have to talk like I was from Mars to lose my creditability because right away, I am expected, because of my outer appearance as a browned-skin African American, to understand *urban*. That is just expected.

I'm saying that when I just walk into most settings, I don't even have to say anything and people say, "Okay you're going to know something about urban." Then, I keep talking and they say, "Oh, okay, maybe she does know something." I don't think everybody is going to automatically read this and say, "Who are you (speaking of our group) and do you really have a right?" I don't feel like an outsider. Do you feel like an outsider?

Penny Bryan:
I don't feel like we have the answers, Dolores. I feel like we're posing questions, sharing some thoughts and ideas, and having the conversations. I don't feel like we have the answers.

Don Cardinal:
I agree. I don't think any of our chapters said "here is the answer."

Jeff Sapp:
We've had that conversation somewhere before that we are posing questions.

Dolores Gaunty-Porter:
We have. But that's not my point. My point is this, that the person that reads this book and who wants to know who we are, might question, "Who are they?" "How much do they know?" Therefore, I want our work to be so solid that we don't have people asking that. Then maybe we can dispel some questioning.

Penny Bryan:
So who has the corner on knowledge?

Dolores Gaunty-Porter:
There's a certain amount of knowledge that you have from experience that just comes along with life.

Penny Bryan:
That's *your* knowledge and *your* experience. I wouldn't presume to answer the experience in an urban classroom.

Dolores Gaunty-Porter:
But there is a language that you have because you have lived and walked an environment. There is a language that goes along with your household.

Suzanne SooHoo:
But how would your sense of urban resonate with a poor, non-English family? How would you know *that* experience?

Dolores Gaunty-Porter:
Okay. Now, this can be a bit complicated but let me see if I can explain this. It's been my experience that when an African-American person makes comments to other African-American people that in any way suggests that he or she can't relate to urban, whether its people, places, and things related to urban, then African-American people think that that person is just trying to pretend there is distance between him or herself and the urban community. For that reason I say that I don't have to say anything, but walk into the room, and many African-American people just assume that I have credibility, generally speaking, in the urban community. I've also found this to be true in the way white people approach me—this sense of assurance that I know urban. Then, I keep talking and they say, "Oh, okay, maybe she does know something."

Suzanne SooHoo:
But we're academics seeking, not answering. And these are essays. They're not research driven. In other words, the research wasn't conducted so that we could be conclusive. We're not Jackie Irvine or William Ayres. We are not those urban educators. We are problem posing, problematizing the social construct of "urban."

Jeff Sapp:
I feel that this point is in reference to the metaphor in Chapter 1: Can a fish critique their own glass walls from outside the fishbowl and inside the fishbowl? I can feel inside the fishbowl. But my inside the fishbowl is very narrow. I spent 35 years in Appalachia. I spent seven years in Los Angeles and my seven years in Los Angeles was particularly through a gay, urban lens. And so I know *some things* about what it means to be urban. It is just *this* much though, but I want to add that to the conversation.

Don Cardinal:
Dolores is saying there's a piece of her "inside" and that piece is valuable enough to make her an insider.

Tom Wilson:
But the chapters have to stand *on their own*. It seems to me, if we go back to theoretical position in terms of the nature of belief systems, of openmindedness, we need to consider the critical move of separating authority from what authority says. Does a chapter say something reasonable regardless of who wrote it? Can we separate out who wrote it from what is within that chapter? To not mix up the authority of the author with the authority of the context ought to be a significant and critical consideration.

Don Cardinal:
When I was at Cal State Fullerton 12 years before I was here, I was still far away from the drug time in my life and hadn't had any problems with the law. I was dressed up and I was going to a presentation I was supposed to give at Cal State. It was on a Saturday. I drove across the parking lot and I got pulled over by the campus police. They ran my license and said you have an outstanding ticket. To make a long story short they took me to jail. They handcuffed me, put me in the back seat. They took me to the county jail. They striped my clothes off. They sprayed me with a de-licer. They looked up my ass for drugs or weapons. I got the county jail clothes on. I got put in with the newbees, which is a pretty dangerous group. You gotta be careful. I immediately switched. It was almost scary to me.

Dolores Gaunty-Porter:
I know, I know all about it.

Don Cardinal:
I went immediately to tough guy. I figured out exactly who the guys were I was going to have to stand up against. I knew who was going to fall right behind me and be my little ducklings. I certainly had my eye on the people who looked like they were in a bad mood or drugged and who might get aggressive. I knew exactly what to do with my food when I was there. Who to give my food to, who not to let touch my food. It was all there and it was amazing how quickly you can go back to that after so many years. I think there's that piece that is "in."

Dolores Gaunty-Porter:
I never did drugs, I've never been high. I have been around drugs. I saw people rolling and smoking. I just didn't do any of that. So, that's where I am.

It's just very comfortable for me. No one knows all of anything, and certainly not urban. But, I am certainly not on the outside. I can step in and keep my mouth closed and do very well.

Tom Wilson:
Paulo Freire says one foot in and one foot out. That's the way he uses it. Dewey said essentially the same.

Penny Bryan:
I think just the opposite of Dolores. I am never fully "in" or comfortable. Maybe because I am Jewish, I always feel a little bit on the outside even though I know something of both worlds. I never feel full membership. I always feel like I am building bridges. When I sit

wholly in one group, I think, well that's not completely me. I'm never fully inside.

Dolores Gaunty-Porter:
Well see, that's where I am. I am never fully outside.

Penny Bryan:
I always feel on the edge and I've come to think that's just the way I am.

Don Cardinal:
Before we leave tonight, I'd like to mention that there are two things that we've really missed and we can't discuss them now. We did not really talk about the way we complained for three years about not getting a place for us to meet when our times were taken away from us. That is a real important component in our upbringing and maybe what part of our anger was and part of what we wanted to claim yesterday. That was built-up tension. I think that is what some people meant by lack of support. We need to define support and I think a lot of that was it.

And one last point, I did not really say what I felt I needed to say regarding Susie's entrance. We wanted Susie to come in for a specific, almost surgical purpose, and it's grown to be more than that. For me, it's been a very legitimizing experience and I'm not exactly sure why. Her participation legitimized the book and it's not just because of where she teaches. I guess, simply because I always like when I get a view from someone who sits in a seat other than mine. I think, in many respects Susie's work has done that. It turned out to be an additional chapter, not a reflection piece of all the other chapters, although you did bring in part of that. Whatever we do with it, whatever our comments are regarding it, I think that that itself has some real value to the overall book. It balanced of the book for some reason for me.

Suzanne SooHoo:
How do you feel about your chapter, Susie?

Susie Weston:
I am really sad that we are not going to get together again and that disappoints me to no end. (Editor's note: the group did get together again.) Because I really feel like I came in so late. I didn't realize how late until Jeff said he came in late, too.

(laughter)

The situation was like this: "Here you go. You have to read everyone's chapter and you have to do A, B, C, D and E." I thought to myself, "Holy smokes, how am I going to do all of that." You all said you brought me in for a specific purpose, but that purpose was never made clear to me.

Don Cardinal:
It wasn't clear to us either.

(laughter)

Susie Weston:
I still don't know where I am going to land. I wish we were going to keep getting together so I could take more in. I am nowhere near completion.

Suzanne SooHoo:
Susie's progress makes me think of a related concern. I think one of the reasons she hasn't spoken much tonight may be related to her late entry into our group.

Susie Weston:
That makes sense to me. I am a newcomer and have only begun to understand and feel comfortable with the group's dynamics.

Don Cardinal:
You were supposed to be our conclusion.

Penny Bryan:
Because we couldn't come to closure, we figured we'd invite you in. Your chapter was supposed to be the end of book and end of story. Instead we socialized you and we're still not at the end.

Don Cardinal:
We really thought we were done. We were done except for this one piece. It was unfair but we were using you for a conclusion.

Susie Weston:
I feel so used, I've got to go.

(laughter)

Suzanne SooHoo:
But just think, out of all students, you were the chosen one to get "used."

(laughter)

Susie Weston:
I'll have to think about that.

Dolores Gaunty-Porter:
Who would we like our audience to be? Anybody?

Penny Bryan:
Will anybody read our book?

Dolores Gaunty-Porter:
Who would we like our audience to be or do we care?

Tom Wilson:
Anybody who buys the book.

Don Cardinal:
Anybody but my mom.

Penny Bryan:
And my family.

Suzanne SooHoo:
Just to be clear of what happens next. A transcription of this evening's meeting gets developed and everyone gets a chance to look at it and ask, "Did I say that? Would I ever want this in print? What next?"

* * *

And so it all began . . .

REFERENCES

Freire, P., & Faundez, A. (1989). *A pedagogy of liberation.* New York: Continuum.

Author Index

A

Alba, R. D., 61, *81*
Alcoff, L. M., 58, *81*
Anderson, G., 150, 157, 158, *160*
Anzaldua, G., 167, *181*
Apple, M. W., 90, 91, *111*, 208, *212*
Argyris, C., 12, 19, 91, 96(*n*1), 143, 144, 147, 151, *160*, 207, *212*, 227
Arnold, M. L., 151, *160*
Authos, A., 12, *26*
Ayers, W., 10, 89, 189, *194*
Ayto, J., 58, *81*

B

Baker, L., 61, *81*
Banks, C. A. M., 72, 76, *81*
Banks, J. A., 72, 76, *81*
Barzun, J., 187, *194*
Bateson, M. C., 2, *4*
Beane, J., 91, *111*
Beck, L., 147, *160*
Bennet, C., 76, 77, *81*
Bishop, R., 168, 169, *181*
Blair, C. J., 59, *81*
Blase, J., 145, *160*
Blum, L., 108, 110, *111*
Bohlin, K. E., 147, *161*
Borko, H., 16, *27*

Boyd, D., 151, *160*
Brand, D., 62, *81*
Brantlinger, E. A., 60, *81*
Brechtel, M., 200, *212*
Brice Heath, S., 167, *181*
Brown, G., 90, 100, *111*
Buber, M., 126, 128, *132*, 243
Buras, K., 91, *111*
Byrk, A., 105, *112*

C

Cambron-McCabe, N., 146, *162*
Campbell, A., 96, *111*
Canada, J., 142, *160*
Capra, F., 157, *160*
Carini, P., 106, *111*
Carlson, R., 149, *160*
Carter, T. P., 59, *81*
Chatfield, M. L., 59, *81*
Conway, T., 96, *111*
Cooper, J. E., 139, 149, *161*
Counts, G., 110, *111*

D

DeBaryshe, B. D., 61, *81*
Delgado, R., 62, *81*
D'Emilio, J., 120, *133*
Denzin, N. K., 118, *132*
Dennis, J., 96, *111*

AUTHOR INDEX

Denton, N. A., 66, *82*
Dewey, J., 19, 21, 23, 24, 88, 92, 96, 107, *111,* 117, 124, 125, 126, 128, 131, *133,* 186, 187, *194,* 243-244
Diallo, Y., 191, *194*
Diaz-Rico, L. T., 191, *194*
Donnellan, A. M., 37, *55*
Dudley-Marling, C., 12, *27*
Dutton, J., 146, *162*

E

Easton, D., 96, 106, *111*
Eaton, W., 106, *113*
Ekstrom, R., 106, *111*
Ellison, R., 62, *81*
Elmore, R., 90, *111*
Erbaugh, S., 39, *55*
Evans, R., 145, *160*

F

Fairbanks, C., 106, 108, *111*, 189, *194*
Faucher, T., 106, *113*
Faundez, A., 215, *251*
Fine, M., 76, *81,* 108
Flaxman, E., 60, *81*
Ford, P., 10, 189, *194*
Fowles, J., 110, *111*
Freire, P., 1-2, 4, 9, 14, 16, 20, 25, 26, 88, 89, 90, 96(*n*1), 107- 109, *111, 112,* 124, 126, 127, 129, 131, *133,* 141, 144, 151, *160,* 166-167, 171, 178, *181,* 192-193,202, 206, 208, 210, 212, 215, 219, 248, *251*
French, J., 96, *111*
Fry, R., 109, *111*
Furman, G., 146, *160*

G

Gardner, H., 139, 149, *161*
Gardner, M. E., 139, 149, *161*
Garrod, A., 91, *112*
Gay, G., 76, *81*
George, L., 179, *181*
Gibb, J., 97, 100, *112*
Gibboney, R., 107, *112*
Gilbert, A., 93, *112*
Gilliagan, C., 147, *160*
Giroux, H., 10, 146, *160,* 167, *181,* 208, *212*

Goertz, M., 106, *111*
Goodlad, J., 11,12, *27*
Goodman, J., 91, *112*
Goulet, T., 192, *194*
Gove, P., 12, *27*
Greenberg, S., 63, *81*
Greene, M., 117, 124, 125, 126, 128, 131, *133,* 144, *160*

H

Hamilotn, C., 10, 165, *181*
Harris, M., 126, *133*
Heron, J., 1, *4*
Herr, K., 157, *160*
Heslep, R., 139, *160*
Hess, R., 96, *112*
Higgins, A., 91, *113*
Hill Collins, P., 1-2, *4,* 15, 179, 180, *181*
Hilliard, A. G., 76, *81*
Hixson, J., 72, 76, 78, *81*
Hongo, G., 193, *194*
hooks, b., xi, 15, 122, 123, 124, 126, 128, 130, 131, *133,* 141, *160,* 171, 188, *194,* 230, 238
Horton, M., 109, *112,* 243
Howard, G. R., 10, 204, 205, *212*

I

Ilmer, S., 39, *55*
Inger, M., 60, *81*

J

Jacoby, R., 110, *112*
Jennings, K., 121, *133*
Jenson, E., 125, 128, *133*
Johnson, B., 8, 27
Johnson, D., 144, *160*
Johnson, F., 144, *160*
Jones, F., 150, 157, 158, *160*
Jones, J., 100, *113*
Jourard, S., 100, 103, *112*

K

Kanpol, B., xi, 10, 15, *27*
Keeley, M., 21, 22, *27*
Keen, S., 117, 122, *133*
Kenney, R., 91, *112*
Klein, N., 141, *160*

Kleiner, A., 146, *162*
Knapp, M. S., 60, *82*
Kochan, F., 4, 7, *4*
Kohlberg, L., 91, *113*, 147, *161*
Kotlowitz, A., 189, *194*
Kozol, J., 10, 60, 82, 142, *161*, 186, *194*
Krashen, S. D., 198, *212*
Kretovics, J., 11, *27*
Kurtz, 39, *55*

L

Lambert, L., 139, 149, 157, *161*
Lambert, M. D., 139, 149, *161*
Lane, R., 96, 108, *112*
Lather, P., 1, 15, *4*
Lawrence, T. A., 130, *133*
Lee, V., 106, *112*
Levin, M., 94, *112*
Levine, D., 91, 108, *112*
Lipset, S. M., 63, *82*
Lipton, M., 26, *28*
Lowe, R., 91, 108, *112*
Lucas, T., 146, *162*

M

Maeroff, G., 10, *27*
Malarkey, T., 91, *112*
Margulies, N., 97, *112*
Martin, J. R., 147, *161*
Martinez, R., 181, *182*
Maslow, A., 49, 95, *112*
Massey, D. S., 66, *82*
McConnell-Celi, S., 118, 121, *133*
McLemore, D.S., 62, *82*
McQueen, M., 57, *82*
Means, B., 60, *82*
Meier, D., 91, *112*
Miller, J., 93, *112*
Mishler, E., 138, *161*
Mita, M., 168, *182*
Moje, E. B., 190, *194*
Moore, D. W., 190, *194*
Morgan, G., 10, *27*
Mosher, R., 91, *112*
Moustakas, C., 118, *133*
Mullen, C., 4, *4*
Murphy, S., 12, *27*

Myss, C., 127, *133*

N

National Council for Accreditation of Teacher Education, 76, *82*
Nee, V., 61, *87*
Nihlen, S., 157, *160*
Noddings, N., 96(*n*1), 130, *133*, 147, *161*
Norton, D., 93, *112*
Nussel, E., 11, *27*

O

Oakes, J., 26, 60, *82*
Obgu, J. U., 60, 62, *82*
Onion, C. T., 9, 10, 12, *28*
Orfield, M., 142, *161*
Otto, H., 102, *112*
Ourlian, R., 141, *161*

P

Pallas, A., 106, 107, *112*
Palmer, P. J., 15, 89, 119, 124, 126, 127, 128, 129, 130, 132, *133*
Park, P., 167, *182*
Passmore, W., 109, *111*
Pedersen, E., 106, *113*
Peterson, B., 91, 108, *112*
Pfieffer, W., 100, *113*
Pounder, D., 12, 15, *28*
Power, C., 91, *113*
Puente, M., 58, *82*

Q

Qoyawayma, P., 175, *182*

R

Raia, A., 97, *112*
Rawls, J., 21, 22, *28*
Readence, J. E., 190, *194*
Regosin, R., 17, *28*
Rippey, R., 17, *28*
Rock, D., 106, *111*
Rokeach, M., 96(*n*1), 101, *113*
Romo, H.D., 62, *82*
Rosaldo, R., 167, *182*
Rumbaut, R. G., 61, *82*
Ryan, K., 147, *161*

S

Sagor, R., 212, *212*
Sarason, S., 90, 94, *113*
Sartre, J.-P., 131, *133*
Scheurich, J., 167, *182*
Scholes, R., 191, *194*
Schon, D., 139, *160*
Senge, P., 139, 146, *161*
Serpell, R., 61, *81*
Sharpe, D., 58, *82*
Slack, P. J. F., 139, 149, *161*
Smith F., 192, *194*
Smith, B., 146, *162*
Smith, J., 16, 90, 105, *112*, *113*, 192
Smith, L., 16, 166, 167, 168, 169, *182*
Snyder, J., 39, *55*
Sobol, T., 76, *82*
Sonnenschein, S., 61, *81*
SooHoo, S., 180, 201, *213*
Spiegel, D. L., 61, *82*
Stanfield, J. H., 168, 169, 180, *182*
Star Power, 100, *113*
Stone, J., 61, *82*

T

Talmadge, H., 20, 25, *28*
Tenorio, R., 91, 108, *112*
Thompson, A., 108, *113*, 147, 148, 151, *161*
Tiernery, W., 76, *82*
Tye, B., 14, 90, 94, *113*, 156, 157, *161*

U

U.S. Department of Educational National Center for Educational Statistics, 61, *85*

V

van Dijk, T. A., 58, *83*
Vickers, R., 96, *111*
Villenas, S., 167, *182*

W

Wagner, J., 143, 144, 145, *161*
Walker, D., 139, 149, *161*
Weber, M., 145, *161*
Weed, K. Z., 191, *194*
Wellman, D., 179, *182*
West, C., xi, 2, *4*, 87, 110, *113*
Westbrook, R., 23, 24, *28*
Weston, S., 201, *213*
Weston-Barajas, S., 201, *213*
Wheatley, M., 144, *161*
Whitmore, R., 95, *113*
Wigginton, E., 129, *133*, 167, *182*
Willis, M., 106, *113*
Willower, D., 147, *161*
Wilson, T., 17, 91, 94, 95, 96(*n*1), 105, 106, 107, *113*, 144, *162*
Witherall, C., 147, *162*
Wolpe, D. L., 138, *162*
Wood, G., 91, *113*
Wood, N., 94, *194*

X

X School District, 205, *213*

Y

Young, J. P., 19, *194*

Z

Zeichner, K. M., 72, 76, *83*
Zukav, G., 127, *133*

Subject Index

A

aesthetics, 23-24
addiction, 38
adolescent literacy, 190
antisocial, 36, 37, 39, 54
  behavior, 37, 38, 39, 47, 54
Asian, 166, 173-174, 176-179, 236
at-risk youth, 51
Auston, A., 12

B

Baldwin, J., 188
Blacks
  middle-class family, 59-63
  visible and invisible middle-class, 63
bilingualism, 191

C

care, 147-148, 151
center for equity and social justice, 9
collaboration, 10-13, 25
  and social justice, 25
  etymology of the word, 12-13
  negative sense, 12
Collaborative Action Researchers for Democratic Communities, 201, 245
collective subjectivity, 39
community, 137, 139, 146, 152-157, 159
community experts, 171
community of learners, 146, 152-157
colonization, 167-168, 171
constructivist, 139, 155
co-researchers, 180
critical theory, 137, 143, 146, 167, 226
cultural collaborators, 180
cultural fusion, 179
cultural knowledge capital, 203, 208, 210, 212

D

democracy, 24, 144, 145, 149, 151, 155, 159, 171, 241, 245
disability, 44, 52
duality of behavior, 39, 40
drugs, 37, 38, 47, 50, 51

E

education colonialism, 191
educational leadership, 137, 139
  capacity, 144, 148, 155
English language learners, 196, 198, 199

F

forgiveness, 237

254 SUBJECT INDEX

G

Gadotti, M., 91
gang/gangster, 36, 41, 43-44, 47-49, 54
gay lens, 232
ghetto, 10
greater society, 36-40, 43, 45, 54
Guillory, J., 191

H

homophobia, 121

I

Indigenous peoples, 168
individualism, ethics, democracy
   moral responsibility, 93
   relations among, 92
inner city, 40, 46, 47, 48, 165, 179
insiders/outsiders, 16, 166, 169, 171, 245-249
intellectual metiza, 167
internship, 197

J

johari window, 100

L

language, 137, 139, 149, 156-157
Latino, 168, 169, 174-175, 177-180
Lewin, K., 96
liberation, 45, 52
local knowledge 208, 209

M

Magsaysay, J., 138, 152-157
media influences
   images of Black people, 59
   and urban communities, 57, 71
missionary zeal, 204, 205
modes of inquiry, 14
moral, 138, 143, 148, 150, 155, 157
   bankruptcy, 36, 37, 54
   guide, 39
   singularity, 38-39
   tenets, 36, 38, 39, 40, 44, 54

N

narrative inquiry, research, 137, 138, 150, 151, 153, 158
story, 137, 151
storytelling 138, 151
Newport Plan, 95-110
   characterized by, 96
   operational design, 97
   organization, development in, 97-98
   educational community, 98
   activity schedule, 101
   democratic emergence in, 98-100
   orientation activities, 100-103
   terminal values in, 101-102
   tutorials, 103
   tutorial rotation, 104
   yearly schedule, 97
   results and significance, 105-110
   caveats, 109-110
   current relevance, 106-107
   shortcomings, 107-108
narrative inquiry, research, 137, 138, 150, 151, 153, 158
   personal, 124
   story, 137, 151
   storytelling, 138, 151

O

oppression, 41, 42, 46, 47
organizational justice, 21
otherness, 180

P

participatory consciousness, 169
Paulo Freire Democratic Project, 9
phronesis, 139
Pio Pico, 138, 152-157, 170
postmodern, 141, 142, 144, 146, 148, 157
practitioner's voice, 16, 217
praxis, 201, 211
problem posing, 219

R

research design, 179
research question, 170
research teams, 169, 170
researcher of color, 180
regret and social justice, 22
rules for social interactions, 39

S

self-awareness, 130
similarity within differences, 179
social conscience, 38
social justice, 25-26, 44, 141, 143, 156, 159, 202, 207
Speer, A., 21
standards/standardization, 145
starpower, 106
stereotyping, 36, 38
student and teacher authority relationship, 95
subjective self as source of knowledge, 15
suburban, 44

T

Tatum, A., 188
Taylor, R., 91, 108
teacher education, 39, 52, 200, 201, 202
teacher research, 166-167, 179, 181
transactional evaluation, 16-20
    process of, 16-18
    results of, 18-20
transformation, 132
transformative model of education, 201, 202, 210
tracking 197

U

unityping, 35-36, 38, 40, 45, 47, 54, 199
urban, 35-36, 39-40, 42, 44, 45-46, 54, 137, 139, 141-143
    child, 36, 39
    communities
        education, 39, 196, 199, 204, 205, 206, 207, 210, 211
        life, 40, 43
        school in, 59, 60, 63-65
        teaching in, 63
    meaning of, 9
    misconception of, 26
    thoughts on, 9-10
    youth, 37-39
voice, 189-190
vulnerability, 236

W

white ideology, 179

Printed in the United States
17855LVS00005B/211-225